Financial
in the *Age* of

Survival
New Money

by Gordon Williams

SIMON AND SCHUSTER
New York

Copyright © 1981 by Gordon Williams
All rights reserved
including the right of reproduction
in whole or in part in any form
Published by Simon and Schuster
A Division of Gulf & Western Corporation
Simon & Schuster Building
Rockefeller Center
1230 Avenue of the Americas
New York, New York 10020

SIMON AND SCHUSTER and colophon are trademarks of
Simon & Schuster
Designed by Irving Perkins Associates
Manufactured in the United States of America
10 9 8 7 6 5 4 3 2 1

Library of Congress Cataloging in Publication Data
Williams, Gordon, date.
    Financial survival in the age of new money.

    1. Finance, Personal.   2. Investments—United
States.   3. Money—United States.   4. Inflation
(Finance)—United States.   I. Title.
HG179.W534   332.024   81-9072
                                 AACR2
ISBN 0-671-25474-X

To my dad

ACKNOWLEDGMENTS

This book has incurred debts of gratitude that extend back for years to the teachers, colleagues, and advisers who were sources of inspiration as well as criticism—all those who, when I needed help, were kind enough to take seriously my most naive questions.

William McChesney Martin, Jr., who was Federal Reserve chairman when I was a Washington correspondent, took many hours out of a hectic schedule to teach me about money—as did such Fed governors of the past as Bob Holland, Andy Brimmer, Sherman Maisel, and Dewey Daane. I have tracked the incumbent chairman, Paul Volcker, from job to job—reporting on his doings at the Treasury, Chase Manhattan Bank, the Treasury again, the Federal Reserve Bank of New York, and finally at the Fed in Washington.

I value the time given me by men who were very busy running some very big banks: Walter Wriston of Citibank, David Rockefeller of the Chase, Gabe Hauge and John McGillicuddy, both of Manufacturers Hanover.

I count Henry Kaufman of Salomon Brothers and Al Wojnilower of First Boston Corporation—each of them very wise about the workings of money—as both teachers and long-time friends. And there is Sidney Homer, now retired from Salomon Brothers, whose knowledge of money knows no bounds.

There is the brave band that read my manuscript and offered advice and counsel: Dave Jones, the very astute economist for Aubrey Lanston and Company in New York; my *Business Week* colleagues Sally Powell, Bruce Nussbaum, Karen Pennar, and Robin Grossman; and some former colleagues who have strayed—Jill Bettner (to *The Wall Street Journal*), and Karen Arenson (to *The New York Times*). Any errors or follies that remain are my fault, not theirs.

There's Trish Lynn, who not only typed my manuscript but tidied up my spelling, punctuation, and grammar.

And finally, my thanks, gratitude, and apologies to my wife, Irene, and my kids, Debbie, Nancy, and Steve. Through it all they were tolerant.

Contents

4. The Printing of the Green 70

We Americans use ten times as much cash per capita as we did in 1940. So the government's printing presses and stamping machines run around the clock to satisfy our demand for cash. But the counterfeiters of our money have lost their Old World pride of craft.

5. How the Fed Manages—and Mismanages —Your Money 85

Only God can make a tree and only the Federal Reserve can make money —creating it out of thin air. There's the Fed boardroom in Washington where the key decisions about your economic future are made (in secret) and the trading room in New York (closed to the public) where $750 billion in government securities changes hands each year.

6. Why You Can't Make Money Grow Like Magic and Your Banker Can 116

Give the U.S. banking system a dollar, and through a process called multiple expansion, it will turn it into many dollars. It all begins when you ask your banker for a loan.

7. Why the Government Is Dangerous to Your Financial Health 124

Inflation didn't just happen. It took the White House, Congress, the Federal Reserve—and you and me—to make it happen. In our economy, we all want everything we see, and our government has done its best (or worst) to give it to us. Why Ronald Reagan probably can't turn things around.

8. The New Banking: or Why Your Banker Sells Money Like Kellogg Sells Cornflakes 143

There was a new banking before there was a new money—the once-prudent banker is now prowling the globe in search of money and borrowers. The goldsmiths of old London paved the way for today's banking. And there's a newer banking still developing as old, repressive laws come tumbling down.

9. If It Walks Like a Bank and Talks Like a Bank, It May Be Sears, Roebuck 173

Locked in mortal combat with the banks for your money are the giant savings banks and savings and loan associations. But these old-line thrift institutions are fast changing. And then there are the "near-banks"— including Sears—that are giant financial institutions in their own right.

10. Why Stocks Are No Longer the Only Game in Town   185

The stock market still has its moments, and trading volume is bigger than ever. But when you buy stock, you're a hostage to fortune. Lately fortune hasn't been very kindly, so the stock market isn't what it used to be—and it may never be again.

11. What to Do When Stocks Don't Suit—and Why It'll Probably Cost You a Bundle   203

The age of new money sends more of us into the byways and back alleys of investing. There are the huge markets in bonds and real estate, and the flashy markets in commodities and options. And then there are all the rest —from postage stamps to Mickey Mouse watches. Which markets should you try and which should you shun?

12. Gold, Which Needs No Further Introduction   237

For some, gold is a safe port in economic storms. For others, it's a red-hot speculation. Those who forget the past push for a new gold standard. Beneath the streets of New York is the world's richest hoard of wealth— nearly $200 billion in gold bars (and why not a penny of it belongs to us).

13. Eurodollars, Petrodollars, and the Gnomes of Zurich   253

Eurodollars and petrodollars aren't as dark and mysterious as they sound, and the Gnome of Zurich is a mythical beast. But the world economy is a frail craft in a stormy sea of Eurodollars, and OPEC's wealth may be a more powerful weapon than its oil.

14. Electronic Money: Tomorrow Is Already Here   282

All the pieces won't be in place until the twenty-first century, but enough of them are here now to give you a taste of what it'll be like when blips in a computer network replace most of our money. Buried in your TV set is the bank branch of tomorrow. Why your banker wants to practice truncation on you, and why you may not like it.

Billions of dollars are smuggled across borders each year, and Switzerland isn't the only place with secret bank accounts. There's the "Florida connection," and the "architect" who wrote the book on washing dirty money. And then there are Enstam and Oldham, who told their story to the wrong people.

If you aren't rich, the tax man is going to get you. If you are rich, you can hire the likes of Mr. X, who'll show you (for a price) how to keep the tax man away. Why most tax havens and tax-exempt foundations have lost their allure.

It won't be easy, because getting by today takes luck and pluck and a lot of hard work and common sense. But there are rules for survival, and by following them, you'll make it—and you could just make it big. None of the rules involves opening a Swiss bank account.

Introduction

THESE ARE hard times for America—our economy racked by
both inflation and recession, our financial markets in shambles, some of our greatest industries on the very edge of
collapse. You must earn $3 today to buy what $1 bought in
1960—if recession doesn't wipe your job out altogether.

For that you can mostly blame the government, which has
done its best (or its worst) to destroy our money—not out of
malice and not as part of some grand conspiracy, but through
miscalculation, mischance, and plain stupidity.

We've had worse inflation—during the Revolution and
during the Civil War—and times were even harder during
the Depression of the thirties when every fourth American
was out of work. But never has economic distress lasted so
long or touched so many of us. And unless we're very careful, and very lucky, our economy could soon plunge into that
dark never-never land where only hyperinflation and deep
depression await.

I call it an "age of new money" because it's a time unlike
any we've known—or our parents, or our grandparents, or
any other generation in American history.

We could blame the oil nations of OPEC, and surely they
deserve blame. But inflation was well rooted in our economy

15

years before the price of oil went up, and we've done little enough in the years since to adapt our economy to higher oil prices.

It's harder to blame ourselves for wanting everything after a depression and a war in which we had little. Of course we want jobs and cars and homes and rich vacations and Medicare and clean air and a nation whose military might is second to none. We won't settle for less, but neither will we pay the higher taxes so we can have it all. We—the people and the government—have paid for these with borrowed money until there isn't a hope all our debts can ever be paid off.

Mostly we can blame our government for promising we could have it all when it knew we couldn't, and for trying to provide it all when it knew it shouldn't. The government's answer has been to print new money as fast as the presses would turn until our money has ceased to have much value —which is what inflation is all about. The value of anything lies in its relative scarcity, and in trying to satisfy everyone, our government has printed so much money that it's as commonplace as acorns on the ground.

We, as a people, permitted it to happen. But that's because we knew so little about money that we didn't understand what was happening until it was too late.

Had we known more about money, we'd have known that governments always destroy their currencies—and that money, when it isn't backed by gold or silver, has led to inflation in every country that ever issued it. It's an age of new money for us, but it's an old story elsewhere, and 1,000 years ago there were nations going through what we're going through today.

Had we known more about money, we'd have understood that even those who claimed to know everything about it— the wise scholars and those who make money policy for our economy—don't know very much either. Because we know so little we've taken too much on faith, and we're paying dearly for that.

And so, this is a book about money—not for the scholars and not for the makers of policy, but for the average person who doesn't like where we are, who'd like to know how we got here, how—and when and if—we'll get out, and how to get by until the age of new money ends.

I've tried to explain what money is—and what it isn't—and how the government manages (and mostly mismanages) our money. The Federal Reserve makes our money and the government spends it, and we lurch from inflation to recession because the making and spending of money has gone out of control. There's the history of money, starting with cows and seashells, and a look at the great government presses and stamping machines that produce our money.

The age of new money has swallowed everything. The great banks that guard our wealth have changed more in the past 20 years than in the 2,000 years before that—which is only a prelude to how they'll change as old, restrictive laws come tumbling down, and as electronic money comes in. In time, impulses in a vast computer network will replace checks and credit cards, and instead of your visiting your bank, the bank will come to you through your TV set.

The stock and bond markets have turned treacherous in this age of new money, and we've turned to other markets that thrive in uncertain times: markets in which you bet on the future price of everything from a carload of wheat to 100 shares of common stock. The oldest of markets has become the hottest of speculations: the market for gold is in such frenzy that a week's salary for an average worker will buy a single coin no bigger than a poker chip.

The age of new money has swollen the shadowy markets in which Eurodollars and petrodollars trade, and in which OPEC controls enough wealth to buy up most of America. The world's trade routes today carry drugs and drug money, and there's the hidden world of hot money—of couriers called "money mules" who carry millions in cash to banking centers where no questions are asked.

There's the world of the very rich, in which tax shelters, tax havens, and tax lawyers make the age of new money endurable to those with wealth enough.

And then there's the money world in which most of us live —where times are hard and getting harder. But if you know enough about money, you can make it, and maybe even prosper, in the age of new money. There are five rules (they are spelled out in Chapter 17) for economic survival and none of them involves putting your money into Swiss francs. This is advice for those who don't want a Swiss bank account, and who probably wouldn't be welcome in a Swiss bank if they did.

President Reagan may yet turn our economy around, but other Presidents have promised much and delivered little. It took 15 years to get where we are and it may take 15 years more to set our economy right again. It's certain that the price of less inflation will be less economic growth, fewer jobs, and less of what we've come to expect from government. The only way to end our inflation quickly would be to cast the economy into deep, prolonged recession. Keep in mind that each time inflation has appeared to wane in the past fifteen years, it has roared back worse than ever. It takes a lot of faith to believe this time will be different.

When you finish reading this book you'll at least understand why there's an age of new money—and who to blame for it. And you'll know enough about money to plan your own economic survival until the age of new money ends.

Chapter 1

The Age of New Money
and How It Grew

FRESHLY PRINTED dollar bills stack up 233 to the inch, 2,796 to the foot. Counting its television tower, the Empire State Building is the tallest in the land at 1,472 feet. At the rate Americans spend money, we consume a stack of dollar bills 200 feet taller than the Empire State Building every minute of every hour of every day of the year. By the time the clock strikes midnight on New Year's Eve, we've gone through a tower of dollars 170,000 miles high—seven times around the world at the equator, two-thirds of the way to the moon.

And that's one way of looking at money: the awesome amount of it we spend on all the shoes and ships and sealing wax and all the cabbages and king-sized cigarettes we buy each year.

We live in a $2½ trillion economy—that being our gross national product, which is the value of all we produce in a year. It's the biggest and the richest economy the world has ever known, and in most years has been among the fastest growing. It took from the day the first settler landed until 1970 for the economy to reach $1 trillion and just seven years more to reach $2 trillion. At the rate our economy has been growing, we'll hit $5 trillion by 1990 and $10 trillion by early in the twenty-first century.

But there's another, darker way of looking at money: how much of it goes to pay for the inflation that has engulfed us. Most—sometimes all—of our economic growth now is illusory, the product only of inflation. We aren't spending more because we're buying more of everything, but because everything we spend on costs more.

Example: I make no more beanbags this year than last, but I charge 25 percent more per beanbag, and my sales dollars increase dramatically. If you count only the dollars, the economy has grown. If you look behind the dollars and count the beanbags, economic growth has been nil.

In 1979, our economy grew by $260 billion, of which one-quarter was real growth (we made a few more beanbags) and three-quarters was inflation (the cost of each beanbag went way up). In 1980, the economy grew by something more than $200 billion and every last cent of that was due to inflation (we made fewer beanbags, but the cost of each one rose out of sight).

Yet our government's standard response to inflation has been to push the economy into periodic recessions that inflict another sort of agony. Jobs vanish, companies fail, and our tower of dollars grows more slowly, with all the growth due to inflation. And our recessions, bad as they are, are no lasting cure for inflation. The inflation diminishes, but only for the instant, and then it returns, worse than ever. The terrible recession of 1974–75 was followed by worse inflation than before, and the 1980 recession didn't reduce inflation at all.

We can still joke about our plight. "Inflation is not all bad," quips Senator Alan Cranston of California. "It has allowed every American to live in a more expensive neighborhood without moving."

But that's gallows humor, and we feel the pain on every

level: psychologically because our feelings about money go back to our earliest childhood memories, and economically because for most of us times are hard and getting harder. This sense of pain, of having lost control over our economic destiny, can damage the strongest among us. When times get hard, crimes of violence, from rape to child abuse, increase. We drink more, more marriages break up, and if we can afford the fee ($70 an hour and up in New York), more of us seek psychiatric help.

To get by, the one-income family has become the two-income family, and now, warns Lacy Hunt, chief economist for Fidelity Bank in Philadelphia, "You are going to have to put teenagers to work." But when recession hits, the two-income family often becomes the no-income family, and jobs for teenagers vanish altogether.

The strength of any economy can be measured by the strength of its money, and when it comes to our money, nothing today is as it used to be. There's more money: the economy is bigger, our incomes are greater. But there's less money: it doesn't buy what it used to, and between inflation and recession, its purchasing power is being eaten away at a terrible rate. We still compete, connive, and conspire to get money, and we live in mortal dread of losing it. Some of us steal it, and some of us print our own, made bold because the penalty for counterfeiting is jail and not castration, dismemberment, or decapitation as it used to be. But we don't look upon money as we once did. Its possession doesn't comfort as it used to and the lack of it is more threatening.

Because it costs so much to get by, Americans have all but stopped saving. We put aside no more than 5 cents of each $1 earned, and when inflation rages we save even less —while the French save 18 percent of their income and the Japanese 20 percent. We, however, to survive inflation and recession, spend all we earn and then we borrow and spend some more. The American debt today—of government, business, and the public—is $5 trillion, which is twice what it was in 1975. The average consumer spends 23 cents of each after-tax dollar to pay off debts, and the interest on the national debt is now $65 billion a year. If we suddenly had to pay off our debts, all we could do is declare national bankruptcy.

By borrowing and spending so much and saving so little, we live today by stealing from tomorrow. We must pay for the future growth of America from what we save today, and so the future of America is precarious—all the more so because inflation will make everything cost more tomorrow than it does today. For such industries as steel and automobiles, tomorrow is already here, and both industries are in terrible trouble because neither can afford to replace yesterday's out-of-date equipment at today's prices. Each is losing out to rivals from other lands where people save and invest more than we do.

We can invest today and earn some of the highest returns in history. Yet, in most years, even those high returns don't match the inflation rate, which is one reason we've stopped saving. Further, no matter how much we earn, it's instantly diminished because inflation has pushed most of us into higher tax brackets. That's called "bracket creep" and it is one thing the 1981 tax cuts are supposed to remedy. And the 1981 law *will* help—cutting tax rates, dropping the top rate on capital gains to 20 percent. But the full benefits of the rate cuts won't come until 1984. The highest brackets will get the most benefits, and when it comes to taxing interest and dividends, the new law is harsher than the old.

Because our taxes are so high—the average American working three of every eight hours to earn enough to pay taxes—more of us deal in an underground economy where all transactions are for cash, and where the tax laws don't reach. Our spending in this underground economy is now $250 billion a year—one-tenth as big as our above-ground economy, and growing faster.

Some of our underground spending is on drugs, prostitution, and gambling, which have always lurked beyond the law. Two-thirds of it, though, is for transactions that are perfectly legal—cash paid to a doctor, a hot dog bought from a street vendor, an antique bought at a flea market—except that everything is in cash and not a penny is reported to the tax collector. When it comes to money today, we're all a tiny bit crooked.

Why It's an Age of New Money

There is, in fact, a new money today, as different from the old as Turkish taffy is from turtle soup, and the difference between new money and old money has nothing to do with when it was made or how long it has been in the family. The difference is partly a state of mind and partly the state of the world.

The old money flourished in the two decades after World War Two when the economy was healthy and the inflation rate low. The new money was born amid the economic turmoil that has plagued us for 15 years and that will plague us for many years more. And the government we count on to keep our economy healthy bears most of the responsibility for putting us where we are.

There's no great conspiracy at work. Our leaders haven't sold out to the Communists or the Fascists or the Trilateralists, or to anyone else. To manage our economy according to the designs of some grand conspiracy would require a level of skill our government simply doesn't possess. Neither, however, is there any real incentive for government to combat inflation for very long. To do so, government would have to promise less and provide less, whereas it's the nature of governments to promise more and provide more. The truth is, governments like inflation because it inflates tax revenues, giving them more to spend, more jobs to create, and more ways of pleasing the voters. When prices soar, you can't print more money to make ends meet, and neither can General Motors or AT&T. But the government can, and does every day, and for government, inflation is the biggest growth industry ever.

Even the promises of Ronald Reagan are no guarantee the age of new money will end any time soon. Assuming the President is serious about fighting inflation (which is no absolutely sure thing), the most he can do in the next few years is slow the advance in prices—diminishing the pain a little but certainly not eradicating it. Inflation can't be cured in a hurry without the wholesale breaking of promises government has made us over the years, or without giving us an economy where there's no inflation because there's no growth. And since some prices are beyond our ability to control at all—the price of food and of oil—it's possible that inflation will get worse, not better, no matter what the President tries to do.

Finally, even when inflation is rolled back, the age of new money will linger on—the legacy of decrepit industries, battered financial markets, and shattered lives haunting us for years as the Great Depression of the thirties haunted an earlier generation.

We've so far managed to avoid hyperinflation of the sort that swept Germany in 1923 and Hungary in 1946, when money ceased to have value and people spent a truckload of it to buy something tangible like a loaf of bread. And we still may avoid inflation of that magnitude. Hyperinflation doesn't just happen; it must be made to happen. It swept Germany in the aftermath of World War One, and it was inflicted on Hungary by Russia to punish it for fighting with the Nazis during World War Two. As inept as our government is in managing our money—and it's very inept—we're not yet on the edge of hyperinflation.

And we probably aren't on the edge of a new Great Depression. That depression was the result of a profound ignorance of economics, which is not the case today. We're dumb, but no longer that dumb—or at least not dumb in the same ways we were in the 1930s. The Depression became the Great Depression because we didn't know how to revive a stagnant economy. We have so much inflation today because we know very well how to revive a stagnant economy. What we don't know is how to slow an economy out of control. In the 1930s we forgot our car had an accelerator. Today we've forgotten it has brakes.

But we still could have either hyperinflation as our money runs wild or a depression brought on in the name of fighting inflation. And in order to avoid both hyperinflation and depression, we'll have to face a future of slower economic growth, higher unemployment, and a diminishing standard of living for most of us.

So uncertain is our economic future that nothing can be ruled out, and it's that very uncertainty that's so threatening. No one, including the government, which is supposed to manage our economy, and the Federal Reserve, which is supposed to manage our money, really knows what tomorrow will bring—or even when tomorrow will come.

At the heart of the old money was the deeply held belief that our money had value and would keep that value through the next day and the next month and the next year. But the new money has lost half its value since 1970—the dollar of 1970 being worth only 45 cents today—and it will continue to lose value each additional minute inflation rages. If our economy reaches $5 trillion by 1990, more than half the growth will be due to inflation—money that might as well be burned in a giant bonfire for all the good it will do us.

What cost a $1 in 1970 now costs $2.50, and, if things go on as they have, by 1990 it will cost $5. If you earned $15,000 in 1970, you needed $30,722 in 1980 to stay even. Had your income gone up by that much—104 percent—your federal income tax would have gone up by 134 percent and your

Social Security tax by 325 percent—the government getting its share (more, in fact, than its share) before you got yours —which is why government likes inflation.

By the end of the eighties, the way things are going, a family automobile will cost $15,000, four years at a fine private college $100,000, and a four-bedroom house in an average neighborhood $250,000. That still wouldn't be hyperinflation, but it would be getting close.

How We Became a Banana Republic

We adapt as best we can—and that very adaptation makes it harder still to banish inflation because it weaves inflation into the very fabric of our economy. Most labor contracts today contain a COLA, which isn't a soft drink but a cost-of-living adjustment so wages move up along with inflation (which, of course, adds to inflation). Social Security payments have gone up as fast as inflation in most years—faster than the salary of the average worker (and that also adds to inflation). The interest on savings, instead of being fixed, is now tied to the rate the Treasury pays when it borrows money. But the more we're paid on our savings the more lenders charge when we borrow (and that, too, adds to inflation).

This tying of wages, Social Security, and interest to inflation is called indexation, and it has been used in such high-inflation countries as Brazil and Argentina. In Argentina, for instance, you don't pay taxes on gains in income due to inflation. That we're obliged to use indexation at all today tells much about the state of our money. On one hand we have the biggest, most sophisticated economy in the world. On the other, we play by the economic rules of a banana republic.

The trouble with indexation is that once you start you can't stop, and the more you index, the more inflation becomes embedded in the economy. Not only are wages, Social Security, and interest rates indexed today, but also utility bills, auto prices, air fares, and a few thousand other things—the price of each going higher as costs go higher.

And so we have a mechanism in which prices go up more or less automatically—with nothing on the other side to bring them down when costs ease. So prices go up like a hot knife through butter and they come down almost never. Economic slumps should turn things around—wages coming down as jobs become harder to find and prices coming down as demand dries up. But since we fear the slump will be followed by even worse inflation, workers won't accept lower wages and companies won't accept lower prices. The expectation that inflation tomorrow will be worse than inflation today all but guarantees that inflation tomorrow will be worse than inflation today, until deep, deep recession brings everything tumbling down.

More of us respond to the age of new money by getting out altogether. We invest less in stocks and bonds because inflation erodes our money even when it's invested in the securities of America's greatest corporations, while recession destroys the earning power of those corporations. Instead we buy more "hard" assets—silver and gold, diamonds and land, arts and antiques—in hope they will keep their value, come what may. But every dollar put into gold—or into diamonds or Chinese snuffboxes or real-estate speculation—is a dollar that won't be invested in a new factory or a piece of machinery for the American economy.

And even investments in hard assets are no sure thing, because all our markets—even the ones that seem most secure—have turned wildly erratic in this age of new money. Fortunes have been lost in stocks and bonds—but fortunes have been lost in gold and silver and arts and antiques. For a fleeting moment in early 1980, silver soared to $50 an ounce. A few months later the price was $10 and the affairs of even one of the richest families in America—the Hunts of

Texas—were temporarily thrown into disarray. In the age of new money, nothing financial works as it should.

When Inflation Finally Ends

Neither does anything go on forever, and some day our inflation will end—perhaps because government and the people finally want it to end, but perhaps instead in the cataclysm of another Depression, or in the national unity brought on by war. For most people, the half-century after the Civil War was a time of depression that seemed as though it would last forever. But it ended—just as the Great Depression did. Our inflation didn't just happen. We—the government and the people together—made it happen, and if we want badly enough for inflation to stop we can make it stop.

But we may not like our post-inflation world because there will be much less of what we've come to expect government to provide. We may not like it because in the name of fighting inflation our government may seize the power to set the price of everything anyone sells, and the salaries of everyone who works. That might end inflation, but it might also end American democracy. Unfortunately, when inflation lasts too long and gets too bad, democracy tends to fall victim, and in scores of countries inflation has led to dictatorship.

Meanwhile we keep making more adjustments to inflation. Lenders are loath to commit money at today's interest rates because they believe tomorrow's rates will be higher, so more and more loans now carry rates that automatically move up in line with inflation. Already the old fixed-rate mortgage has all but vanished into the pages of history, and your next mortgage will have a rate that changes frequently —which, of course, is indexation creeping into still another corner of our lives. If you think the mortgage rate is too high, the lender may reduce it a little—in return for a share of your profits when you sell the house.

When the price of a home is higher than most people can afford, new financing gimmicks appear. In the future you may buy only the house, renting the land from someone else —which is already happening in California's wildly inflated real estate market.

Even if inflation ends, our money world will look quite different ten years from now than it does today because so much of our money world has been governed by laws so arcane and so punitive that they cry out for change. Long before 1990 the distinction between a checking account and a savings account will have vanished. There will only be "transaction" accounts, which pay interest and against which you can write checks. Instead of a set rate of interest, your account will have a return that varies according to economic conditions and how you instruct your bank to invest your money. By 1990 the distinctions among commercial banks, savings banks, and savings and loan associations will have vanished, and our financial system will consist of just a few gigantic, widely diversified institutions with offices all over the land.

In time there will be a newer money still—electronic money that will replace some of the currency and most of the checks we write each year. When the day of electronic money arrives for real—probably before the year 2000— most money will exist only as electronic blips in a vast, global computer system. You'll pay bills by punching keys on a computer terminal in your house or by talking to your television set. If your home base is Miami and you are dining in Seattle, you'll pay for your meal with a plastic card called a debit card, instead of a credit card. Before you finish your after-dinner mint, the money will have gone directly, and electronically, from your bank account in Miami to the restaurant's bank account in Seattle. The Bonnies and Clydes of 2000 will be electronic wizards bent on lifting your money out of a computer system. The bank dicks of 2000 will be electronic wizards trying to build theft-proof systems.

But that's getting ahead of the story. That's the *new* new money, and we're having trouble enough with the new money.

We've used money since the dawn of time, and some of the wisest economists have spent their lives studying it. We've given truly extraordinary powers to the agency of government whose job it is to create and manage our money —the Federal Reserve. Yet no one—not those wise economists and not even the Federal Reserve—knows for certain how money really works in the economy, or even how to define money.

That the Federal Reserve tries to manage our money without knowing how it works or how to define it explains much about why our economy is as it is. If you hunt elephants without knowing how to bring one down, or even what an elephant looks like, you're asking for trouble. Since ignorance never stops anyone in government from doing anything, the Fed (as it's known to friend and foe alike) keeps trying to manage our money with consequences that occasionally are whimsical but usually are disastrous.

Mostly the Fed creates too much money and we have inflation. Occasionally it creates too little and we have recession. Almost never in recent years has there been just the right amount of money in our economy, and so almost never in recent years have we known a moment's economic peace.

There are explanations for this: extenuating circumstances, unforeseen developments—of which the explosion in the price of oil is the most dramatic. In the Fed's defense, few foreign nations have done much better, dumbness about money being a universal malady these days. Even Germany and Switzerland, those bastions of "sound money," are creating too much money today. If they continue to do so, in time both will suffer what we are suffering today. But that other nations are in the same boat is cold comfort to the American people, who have endured 15 years of economic anguish with no more than vague promises of relief on the horizon.

And so it's time to learn all we do know about money— starting with the most basic and elusive questions of all: What is money and how does it work?

Chapter 2

What Is Money, What Isn't Money, and Why It Makes a Difference

MONEY IS admittedly complex stuff, replete with species and subspecies. Money is what you earn and spend. Credit is what you borrow and lend. Capital is what you invest in hopes of making more money—the successful result of such investment being the acquisition of more capital. If money runs short and credit isn't available, you must dip into capital, which is considered a bad thing to do. When you run out of money, credit, and capital, you're bankrupt, and a record 380,000 Americans went bankrupt in 1980.

Still, in trying to understand money, this much can be said with absolute certainty: Codfish isn't money.

To count as money, an object has to meet some basic tests.

It must serve as a unit of account, meaning we have to agree that the price of things will be set in terms of that object. We could go on a codfish standard in which everything would be priced in terms of codfish. Through the ages, people have used stranger things than codfish as money.

32

It must serve as a medium of exchange, meaning you'll accept it from me in exchange for goods and services. You're selling cameras and you price the camera I want at 100 pounds of freshly caught codfish. I hand over my codfish and you sell me the camera.

On two counts, then, codfish could be money. But money also has to be a store of value, meaning you must be able to store it for a time—say in a savings account—and then retrieve it without its having lost value. And that's where our codfish standard breaks down. You might count my codfish as valuable today, but a week from now you'd have second thoughts, and a month from now my codfish would be a stinking mess you wouldn't touch with rubber gloves.

Since an object must be a unit of account, a medium of exchange, *and* a store of value to count as money, and since codfish fails a basic test, codfish isn't money. Neither are plates of scrambled eggs nor toasted English muffins. You can assume the Mona Lisa will keep its value through the years, but how could you price cameras in terms of Mona Lisas? So the Mona Lisa isn't money either.

Some things clearly pass all three tests but still don't count as money because our government says they aren't money.

Gold is accepted in every corner of the globe and you can assume it will be as valuable 100 years from now as it is today. Countries have used gold as money for eons and a few still do today. But the United States hasn't used gold as money since 1933, and while gold may be money in some countries, it isn't money here.

Silver meets all the tests. It, too, has been used as money for eons and still is in some countries. But the United States hasn't used silver as money in a decade and it isn't money here.

What obviously does count as money for us is our currency and coin—without intrinsic value, being made of rag paper and base metals, but money because our government says so. The store-of-value side of our money is pretty iffy these days, but we make do.

More Money Than Meets the Eye

That definition of money is fine, as far as it goes, which isn't very far. There was only $115 billion in currency and coin at the start of 1981, which isn't much for a $2½ trillion economy.

One reason for the discrepancy is that money never sits still. It leaps from hand to hand—from buyer to seller and from lender to borrower—as fast as the ball in a pinball machine leaps from bumper to bumper—the speed with which money leaps from hand to hand being its velocity. My dollar in the morning becomes your dollar when I buy a pack of cigarettes, and someone else's dollar when you pay a bill at lunchtime.

Another reason is that currency and coin don't begin to cover what really counts as money today—not only cash, but any asset liquid enough to be converted quickly into cash. It would take weeks to sell your house for cash, and months to find a buyer for the Picasso that hangs in your front hall. You can turn other assets into cash in an instant. And once we begin looking for assets liquid enough to be turned quickly into cash, our money supply grows by leaps and bounds.

A check is a near-perfect substitute for currency, and the $275 billion in checking accounts at the start of 1981 is certainly liquid enough to count as money. We had $400 billion more in savings accounts, and while savings deposits are less liquid than checking deposits, they aren't off on the moon either. Time deposits are less liquid still because they're supposed to stay there, untouched, for months or years. But I'll get the deposit back, plus interest, some day, and I can have it right now if I'm willing to pay a penalty. And there were

$1 trillion in time deposits at the start of 1981, including $400 billion in six-month savings certificates, and $115 billion in big corporate time deposits ($100,000 and up left at banks for 14 days or more), which are called certificates of deposit.

A corporation will keep some of its assets in certificates of deposit, or CDs, because they pay a nice rate of interest and because a CD from a world-class bank—say Citibank—can be sold in minutes to another corporation with assets to invest. Surely that deposit is money. But a corporation might also put some of its assets into a Treasury bill—an IOU which the government promises to repay within a year. There were some $200 billion in Treasury bills at the start of 1981 and you can sell one even more quickly than a CD. If a CD is money, why not a Treasury bill?

If deposits in U.S. banks are money, what about deposits in their overseas branches? Those foreign deposits run into the billions of dollars, and banks can bring the money home in the time it takes to send a Telex message.

What about money-market mutual funds, which invest in CDs, Treasury bills, international bank deposits, and other very liquid securities? Those funds held nearly $120 billion in the spring of 1981 and deposits in one of these were no farther away than a checkbook, since the funds let you withdraw your assets merely by writing a check. Is that money or isn't it?

Why It Matters

If all this sounds like the splitting of academic hairs, recall that the Federal Reserve is supposed to provide just the right amount of money to our economy—not so much that we go off on an inflationary spending spree, and not so little that our economy falls into recession. That being the case, the Fed certainly should know what counts as money and what doesn't.

In fact, the Fed doesn't know. Through the years it had come up with five different ways of counting money—each tagged with its own letter "M" (for money). M_1 counted only coins, currency, and checking accounts at commercial banks. M_2, M_3, and M_4 each added another wrinkle. M_5 counted all that plus time and savings deposits at commerical banks *and* thrift institutions—which is the generic name for savings banks, savings and loans, and credit unions.

That was how things stood until 1980, and it wasn't a very satisfactory way of doing things. If you have five different ways of counting money, how can you ever be sure which one is best? Not only was M_1 $380 billion, and M_5 $1.7 trillion, in early 1980, but growth rates among the different measures of money were vastly different.

It was troublesome enough when the Fed at least knew which sort of deposit fit into which M. But then the lines among checking, savings, and time deposits began to break down, as did the line between commercial banks and thrifts.

The law stated plainly enough that only commercial banks could offer checking accounts while thrifts couldn't, and it said no institution could pay interest on a checking account. Then, in the mid-1970s, New England thrifts invented the NOW account, which stands for Negotiable Order of Withdrawal. These were savings accounts against which you wrote what looked like a check but which was a NOW. Commercial banks and credit unions countered with their own versions of NOW accounts, and suddenly there was chaos.

Congress finally jumped in and wrote what, for want of a more infelicitous name, was called the Depository Institutions Deregulation and Monetary Control Act of 1980. Among other things, this act legalized NOW accounts for all institutions (only for consumers, though—not for business). Instead of separate checking and savings accounts, there are to be only NOW, or transaction, accounts.

And now the Fed was really at sea—trying to count money five different ways and with all those neat distinctions among institutions and accounts gone by the boards. So the Fed cast out all the old Ms and started again.

Unfortunately, it merely replaced the old Ms with five new measures. These start at M_1A (coins, currency, and checking accounts) and run to L, which tries to count all our wealth that could be quickly converted into cash (every conceivable deposit in every sort of institution, plus Treasury bills, and even savings bonds).

Presumably having five new measures of money is better than having five old ones, but it isn't much better. As before, the differences between the five are staggering: M_1A totaling $390 billion at the start of 1981, while L came to nearly $2½ trillion. Further, while M_1A grew by 5 percent in 1980, L grew by about 10 percent.

Finally, the Fed still doesn't count all that might be counted as money. I can pay with cash or a check, or I can use a credit card. Most cards provide a credit line, and as long as I stay within the limits of that credit line, I can charge things until the cows come home. If a checking account is money, why not the billions of dollars in unused credit-card lines, which are every bit as liquid? And what about the unused credit lines companies have at their banks? Companies contract for loans before they need the money, and all a company has to do to turn the credit line into spendable money is start writing checks.

Put it all together and you do get a comprehensive measure of our money, which you won't find on any list put out by the Fed. Obviously you want to count all deposits at all institutions, plus cash, plus money in money-market funds, plus foreign deposits of U.S. banks, plus those unused credit lines of companies and consumers. Now you have a measure of money that covers everything liquid enough to matter.

It's an orphan among measures of money without an M to call its own. Time and the turmoil of the age of new money may produce something better. Call it what you will, though, it's more complete than anything the Fed offers and it's endorsed by such serious students of money as David Jones, economist for Aubrey Lanston & Co., a big New York dealer in Treasury securities.

Meanwhile the Fed keeps trying to get by with five different measures of money, and that's where we get into trouble. If the creator of our money can't decide what money is, how can it ever hit on the right amount for our economy?

Finally, since our money today is backed only by the best wishes of the government, the Fed can create it without limit.

There was a time when gold was our money and our money supply was limited to the gold we had in our vaults. There was a time, more recently, when our money had to be backed by gold: 25 cents in gold for every dollar in the money supply. But we haven't used gold in our money since 1933—or silver since the late 1960s. Not since the 1960s has our money been backed by either gold or silver. Today we have what's called "fiat money": intrinsically worthless, unbacked by precious metals, money only because the government says it is. Today the government says bits of rag paper are money. Tomorrow it could say turnips are money— bringing wealth to those wise enough to grow turnips and poverty to the rest of us. And the turnip might be a better bet, since it has some intrinsic worth while our paper money has none.

When a currency isn't backed by silver or gold, and when there's no gold or silver in the money supply, the only limits on how much money a government can create are prudence and common sense, and neither is a commodity that governments have in great abundance.

In theory it's anachronistic to limit our money supply to our holdings of gold and silver. In theory we're wise and mature enough to manage our money without tying it to precious metals. But theory is theory and fact is fact, and, in fact, our money has been out of control since the backing of gold and silver was taken away, and fiat money came to stay.

Since the gold backing came off the dollar, the Fed has created money three times as fast as when the dollar was backed by gold. It is hardly coincidence that consumer prices have gone up more than six times as fast since the gold backing came off the dollar as before.

If the supply of money is infinite, warned John Stuart Mill, the nineteenth-century economist, philosopher, and all-around genius, prices will be infinitely high. Today's inflation isn't infinity, but it's getting there. Indeed, since the world began, every time a country has opted for fiat money the result has been inflation—all promises to curb inflation notwithstanding. We're the latest in a long line that began a millennium ago when the Mongol conquerors of China offered fiat money and started the world's first recorded inflation.

Monetarists vs. Keynesians in Mortal Combat

Even if the Fed could define money with absolute precision, it would still be caught up in a second great debate over money: how it works in the economy. Here the battle lines have been drawn for half a century between those who believe the cost of money is most important (no matter how much money is around, we'll borrow only when it's cheap), and those who believe the quantity of money is most important (we'll borrow and spend more because there's more money around, with the cost of money a secondary consideration).

The contestants in this long-running debate are two camps of economists. In one corner are the monetarists—worried about the supply of money and led these days by Professor Milton Friedman, the 1976 Nobel laureate in economics. In the other corner are the Keynesians—worried about the cost of money, and still fighting under the banner of their late and much-lamented leader, the brilliant English economist John Maynard Keynes.

There are, in addition, countless splinter groups, and then there's a new force to be reckoned with—the supply-side economists, who care for neither the monetarists nor the Keynesians, and who count Ronald Reagan as their most prestigious convert. We'll get to the supply-siders in a moment, since they could loom very large in our economic future. But first, to set the stage, we'll watch the monetarists vs. the Keynesians in mortal combat, with our economy as the battleground.

Monetarists tend to be politically conservative and they are believers in the adage "Government that governs best governs least." Their view is that, except in matters of national defense, government should be as close to invisible as possible. They oppose compulsory union membership, government regulation of most things, and would, if permitted, repeal all the years of the twentieth century since 1933.

Keynesians tend to be politically liberal and believers in the adage "Governments that govern least don't know a good thing when they see it." They favor unions, government regulation of nearly everything, and would, if permitted, repeal nearly all the years of human existence before 1933.

Monetarists see the economy as inherently stable. Point it in a given direction and, like a bowling ball, it will follow a straight line unless otherwise disturbed. Those who manage the economy, say the monetarists, should point it in the right direction, give it the proper amount of shove, and then stand clear. All attempts by government to interfere with the free functioning of the economy will lead to disaster.

There is, say the monetarists, a "right" amount of money for the economy at any given moment. If money is created beyond that level, we'll immediately spend it, because money always burns holes in our pockets. If the economy is in a recession, this extra spending will help pull us out—but if we just keep creating money, ultimately the increased spending will reach a point where the demand for goods and services exceeds the supply. When too much money chases too few goods, prices are bid higher, and the result is inflation. If too little money is created, spending will dry up, unsold goods will pile up on shelves, and the result will be recession.

Further, say the monetarists, not only is the economy inherently stable, but so is the velocity of money—which, put most simply, is the speed with which we pass it from hand to hand. In other words, we'll all tend to move our money around the economy in a pretty predictable way—we don't save it all one week and spend it all the next. Because velocity is both stable and predictable, this argument runs, a change in the supply of money will change spending, and the level of economic activity, by a pretty predictable amount, and in a pretty predictable amount of time.

Finally, the monetarists believe the Federal Reserve can control with considerable precision how much money there is in the economy. If there's too much money, or too little, it's because the Fed through malice, mischance, or malfeasance has created too much or too little. All the Fed need do, given the inherent stability of the economy, and the inherent stability of velocity, is decide on an appropriate level of money growth and do all it can to keep money growing at that rate. If the Fed wants the economy to grow by 6 percent a year, after inflation, it should increase the supply of money by a nice, steady 6 percent a year. Then all other economic matters—inflation among them—will take care of themselves.

How the Fed defines money is less important to the monetarists than that it settle on a single definition and work from there. It's the commitment to stability that monetarists want from the Fed, and quibbles over defining money merely make it easier for the Fed to avoid making that commitment.

The cost of money is of interest to the monetarists, but not of great interest. Nor, they argue, should it be of great interest to the Fed. What happens to the cost, they say, is merely a consequence of what happens to the supply. Creating too much money will at first reduce the cost because there's so much around. In time, as inflation takes hold, the cost of money, along with the cost of everything else, will go up. By controlling the supply of money, say the monetarists, the Fed would also be controlling the cost.

John Maynard Keynes Arrives on the Scene

The monetarists ruled the world of economics from early in the nineteenth century until the 1930s. Then came an event so awful it seemed to defy all the rules of economics. That, of course, was the Great Depression—the most awesome economic calamity in American history. There had been depressions before—panics, they used to be called—and each time the economy had recovered. In the 1930s, things just kept getting worse and worse.

The non-monetarist explanation of the Depression is that because of such things as the stock-market crash, a shell-shocked public simply stopped borrowing, spending, and investing money, even though money could be borrowed at less than 1 percent a year. The Fed can create the first dollar, but that dollar will only grow into many dollars when banks create new deposits. New deposits come into being when banks make loans, and banks make loans only when there are borrowers.

The monetarist view, in turn, is that the Fed didn't create enough money quickly enough—particularly since bank failures were destroying money at a prodigious rate. As evidence, the monetarists note that the nation's money supply shrank by 27 percent between 1929 and 1933.

In any event, by 1933 the economy was in darkness: 25 percent of a work force of 52 million unemployed, 85,000 American businesses and 9,000 banks with more than $7 billion in assets had failed. At that point, from out of the east (actually from Cambridge, England) came John Maynard Keynes with a whole new set of economic rules.

To the monetarists, monetary policy—how the government creates and manages money—is supreme. To Keynes, it was fiscal policy—how the government collects and spends money—that was supreme. Economies aren't inherently stable, said Keynes, nor is the velocity of money. Nor can the economy be managed merely by having the Federal Reserve adjust the money supply. There are times, said Keynes, when the public is too stricken to borrow, spend, and invest on its own. At such times, the government must get things moving again by making use of its own ability to borrow, spend, and invest. Priming the pump, it was called—the government taking the first steps to encourage the rest of us to follow.

Monetarists were aware of fiscal policy. They just didn't think it was very important—nor do they today. Fiscal policy can shift money from pocket to pocket. The government can decide, for instance, to spend more on cities and less on defense. A cut in taxes will give government less to spend and taxpayers more. But, they argue, unless the Federal Reserve creates more money, all fiscal policy can do is play games with a fixed amount of money. As a device for regulating the economy, fiscal policy can't hold a candle to monetary policy.

To Keynes, of course, just the opposite was true: changes in government taxing and spending were the best way to speed up or slow down an economy, or change its direction altogether. The cost of money was very important to Keynes because if money was very expensive, no matter how much there was around, people wouldn't borrow, spend, or invest. Keynes didn't banish monetary policy altogether. Its main job, though, would be to make sure money was priced cheap enough to produce the desired amount of borrowing and investing.

America never embraced more than a bit of Keynesian economics during the 1930s, and Roosevelt was a less than enthusiastic follower of Keynes. The two met once, and neither thought much of the other. It took the massive spending of World War Two to end the Depression.

Still, Keynes shaped the thinking of a generation of economists, and they shaped the thinking of a new generation of political leaders. Keynes's activist approach to managing the economy, and his endorsement of fiscal policy, was adopted by America and by almost every other industrial country as soon after the war as they could adopt any peacetime policies at all.

At first there was a great popular outcry, worldwide, that government must do whatever had to be done so there would never be another Great Depression. There was also the recognition by politicians that hand in hand with more government borrowing and spending went more government power, the capacity to promise more to the voters, and the ability to create more jobs for the faithful.

At first glance, fiscal policy does seem superior to monetary policy in some very basic ways.

Monetary policy is inherently passive. The Fed can create the initial dollar, but only when someone borrows, and a new bank deposit is created, will that first dollar begin to grow into many dollars. Fiscal policy, by contrast, is active —the government jumping in and borrowing and spending to make things happen.

Further, it takes months for changes in the supply of money to have any real impact on the economy, while changes in fiscal policy are felt the instant the government puts more money in our pockets.

Finally, monetary policy is a veritable atomic bomb among economic weapons. Use it and nearly everyone feels the consequences. Reduce the supply of money and except for those with the absolutely strongest claims on money—the federal government and the biggest corporations—everyone has to do with less. Fiscal policy, it was argued, could be precisely tailored to do specific things to specific slices of the economy. Give business a tax credit for money spent on new factories and business will build new factories. Cut individual income taxes and consumers will spend more. Make the interest on a home mortgage a tax deduction, with no comparable deduction for those who rent, and a lot of people will move from city apartments to suburban homes. Give people a tax deduction on the interest on a loan and everyone will borrow more. Provide a tax break for those with blond hair and America will turn blond overnight. Economists began to talk seriously about their ability to ''fine tune'' the economy, as though it were a racing car or a violin.

And so the role of government in postwar America has been to borrow and spend and borrow and spend some more to satisfy every need, real or perceived, within the American economy. There have been endless new spending programs, and endless fiddling with the tax laws, to aid this group or that group, and there isn't a corner of our economy where government hasn't intruded. And for a long time it worked. The triumph of Keynesian economics was the 20-year boom that followed World War Two in which we had high spending, low unemployment, and a rate of inflation that seldom went over 2 percent a year.

Inflation Changes the Rules

If the triumph of Keynesian economics was to take an economy knocked flat by Depression and produce our postwar economic miracle, it would seem that its weakness has been its failure to produce solutions appropriate to the age of new money. Yet that isn't fair to the memory of Keynes. The real weakness of Keynesian economics today doesn't lie in the teachings of Keynes, but in the insistence of economists upon worshiping his name while refusing to play by his rules. Government must borrow and spend more when things are soggy, said Keynes. And that we surely do. Government must borrow and spend less when things are booming, said Keynes. And that we surely do not. Presumably John Maynard Keynes is whirling in his grave at the sins being committed in his name.

Borrowing and spending less would reduce government revenues and government power, and so government does too much of both nearly all the time, whether it's good for us or not. President Reagan, of course, has promised to both borrow and spend less. But other Presidents have promised the same and failed to deliver, and it will be years before we can make a final judgment on Reagan's willingness—and ability—to deliver. He wouldn't be the first to tumble into one of the abysses that the age of new money offers in abundance.

Another answer is to raise taxes—cooling down the economy by taking some money out of the public's hands. But none of us wants higher taxes, and so government doesn't do that either.

A stable monetary policy wouldn't hurt. But even passionate Keynesians concede the Federal Reserve creates too much money most of the time—except when it creates too little.

Our standard response to inflation, which is to shove the economy into recession, plainly isn't the answer. Not only does recession hurt too much, but far from curing inflation, each recession carries within it the seeds of worse inflation to come.

Government spending invariably goes up during a recession. There are unemployment and welfare payments, and innumerable programs to minimize the impact of the recession on this or that group. Congress will always create new programs to help out. But tax revenues fall during recessions and this combination of more spending and reduced revenue produces gigantic federal budget deficits. We've run $400 billion in deficits in the past decade—money which the Treasury must then borrow—and a lot of that $400 billion has come from recessions. And then—and the reason there's an age of new money—the Federal Reserve, instead of creating money by design and according to plan, invariably creates money according to how much the Treasury must borrow to cover its deficits.

Two things must happen before inflation gets to where our inflation is now: the demand for money by the government and everyone else must build to excessive levels (which it has), and the Fed must create enough new money to satisfy that demand (which it has).

Neither law nor common sense dictates that the Fed must create enough money to cover the government's deficits. Both law and common sense dictate that the Fed create only enough money to promote a stable and sound economy, even if that means telling the Treasury to go fly a kite. Then the Treasury, in financing its deficits, would have to draw from the same pool of money the rest of us use. The Treasury, with its strong claim on what money is available, would get what it needs, while some of the rest of us would have to do without. There would be yelps of anguish from those borrowers chased out of the markets by the Treasury. In time those yelps would become so strident that government might be forced to mend its fiscal ways—finally being obliged to borrow less and spend less, which is precisely what our economy needs.

It was the yelping of those victimized by the age of new money, as much as anything else, that put Ronald Reagan in the White House with a mandate to cut government borrowing and spending. But each dollar spent by government is in fulfillment of a promise made to one group or another through the years, and if we don't much like the age of new money, we like it even less when promises are broken. The chances are really very slim that President Reagan can get government to mend its fiscal ways for very long. Yet unless he does, there isn't a prayer of getting the Fed to mend *its* monetary ways. And unless the Fed mends its monetary ways there isn't a prayer of rolling back inflation.

The fact is, the Fed never tells the Treasury to go fly a kite, even though it's sufficiently insulated from political pressures to do just that. Instead, the Fed is forever railing against profligate government, forever warning about too much Treasury borrowing—and then, totally ignoring the lessons of the past, forever creating enough money to satisfy the Treasury and everyone else. The mightier the oath the Fed swears never to do it again, the more certain you can be the Fed will do it again—and again, and yet again.

Only when inflation overwhelms us does the Fed stop creating money. But then we fall into recession, and since recession produces both gigantic budget deficits and cries of pain from those hurt by it, the Fed quickly resumes its old ways, creating new money until printing presses threaten to melt.

How the Fed Looks at Money

One would expect the Fed, as manager of our money, to be monetarist to the bone. Instead it has been unremittingly Keynesian through the postwar years, worrying mostly about the cost of money and seldom about the supply. The reason the Fed creates too much money too much of the time is that it believes by doing so it will keep the enormous demand for money—from the Treasury and from everyone else—from pushing the cost of money to the skies. The resultant inflation does, of course, push the cost of money to the skies. When that happens, as it invariably must—too much money causing inflation, and the inflation sending the cost of money shooting up—the Fed never seems to understand why.

The Fed further believes the economy is inherently unstable and must perpetually be manipulated to make it work—meaning that the damage done by errors in policy is compounded because policy is applied erratically. William McChesney Martin, Jr., who ruled the Fed from 1951 to 1970 had the view that the Fed's role was "one of leaning against the winds of inflation and deflation—and with equal vigor."

The Fed is always pushing interest rates up and then bringing them down, and it's always creating more money, and then less money, and then more money again. Far from playing the passive, stabilizing, soothing role the monetarists demand, the Fed is always in motion, leaning first this way and then that as it tries to make the economy behave. When the economy, understandably enough, doesn't behave, the Fed blames it on dark forces and the imperfection of man and goes right on leaning.

It has now played this active role of leaning against the winds for three decades—forever fiddling with the cost and the supply of money—with little enough positive to show for it. It's blamed, and with good reason, for touching off every major postwar inflation, including the latest one, and also for producing every postwar recession, including the latest one. Had the chairman and the six governors who rule the Federal Reserve System done nothing but play marbles over the years, the result could scarcely have been worse.

In its defense, the Fed argues it has constantly been the victim of unforeseen economic developments—meaning it has seldom been sure which way to lean at any given moment. It kept creating too much money in the face of the inflation that accompanied the Vietnam War because it was never told the true cost of the war. It was similarly caught unaware when the anchovies vanished from the waters off the coast of Peru in the early 1970s. Anchovies, it turns out, are used as cheap animal feed. When they vanished, the cost of feeding an animal went up; and so did the cost of meat, and so did consumer prices generally. The disappearance of the anchovies was just a minor episode in the rise of inflation. Unfortunately, the Fed seems not to have seen the inflation coming at all.

How could the Fed be blamed for not anticipating the horrendous rise in the price of oil in the 1970s, when no one else saw it coming either? Once oil prices did go up, the Fed was left racing to catch up with an inflation that had gone out of control. Once it did catch up, in 1979, it then created so little money that the economy fell into recession. In late 1980, to help us out of the recession, and to pay for the huge budget deficit caused by the recession, it was again creating enough money to fuel a dozen inflations.

What seems to have escaped the Fed's notice is that there will always be the unexpected to catch you if you don't watch out, and any policy that pretends otherwise will fail. To run a policy in which the Fed always leans against the economic winds requires an ability to spot those winds while they're still gentle zephyrs. And that, in turn, requires an ability to forecast the economic future that no one, inside the Fed or out, has developed or is likely to develop. And since what the Fed does now won't hit the economy for months, it won't know it has failed until it's too late to avoid the consequences of that failure. At that point the Fed must turn itself around, and we must wait months for the impact of that turnaround to show up in the economy.

The beauty of the monetarist argument is that, by heeding it, the Fed could get out of the guessing game altogether. Instead of constantly trying to outguess the economy, the Fed could play a passive role, spending all of its time simply keeping the nation's money supply growing at a steady rate. Once money growth was stabilized, interest rates would stabilize, too, and once again we would know true economic bliss. That would make for high unemployment among the hundreds of economists who work for the Fed, but it might make for a more stable economy.

In truth, the Fed can't control the money supply from day to day, or even from week to week, with any great precision. Neither is the velocity of money—the rate at which we move it around the economy—as stable or as predictable as the monetarists claim it is. What is also true, however, is that the Fed can control the money supply from month to month with sufficient precision to do the job, and velocity is not as wildly erratic as the Fed likes to pretend it is. In sum, the Fed may not be able to achieve perfection, but it surely can —and surely should—do a lot better than it does.

It's possible the Fed is changing, but don't count on it. Until the late 1960s the Fed worried only about the cost of money and ignored the supply completely. When economist Arthur F. Burns succeeded stockbroker Martin as chairman in 1970, he took a baby step toward monetarism. The Fed still concentrated on the cost of money, but at least it paid some attention to the supply.

On October 6, 1979, the current chairman, Paul A. Volcker, went a step further. Henceforth, he said, the Fed would concentrate on controlling the supply of money even if it meant letting interest rates run wild.

It's too early to judge this latest turn, but it doesn't look good. For all its promises the Fed still seems as concerned about the cost of money as about the supply, and in trying to maintain some control over both, it has, in fact, lost control over both. Interest rates have turned wildly erratic, just as Volcker said they would: first the highest rates in history, then a dramatic plunge in rates, and then a sudden jump in rates again. But growth in the money supply has been as erratic as ever—first too much, then too little, and then too much again. And so the economy continues to swing back and forth, from inflation to recession.

The Newest Team in Town

And that has opened the door to the supply-side economists, who offer their own cure for our distress.

The real problem, say the supply-siders, is that government has concentrated on stimulating demand so the demand for nearly everything now exceeds the supply and we have inflation. Supply hadn't kept up with demand, they argue, because it takes investment to produce more, and our tax code offered no incentive for anyone to invest. Earn more and your tax rate went up as you crept into higher and higher brackets. Save money and the government taxed the interest on your savings. Invest and your dividends were taxed, and so were any gains you made on the investment of your capital. If the tax rate were zero, say the supply-siders, the government would collect no taxes. But if the tax rate were 100 percent, the argument goes, government would also collect no taxes because there would be no incentive for anyone to save or invest or even work for a living.

Their answer is to cut taxes to the bone. As taxes fall, they argue, our desire to work, save, and invest will be rekindled because we can keep so much more of what we earn. The resultant surge of investment will soon bring supply back into line with demand and the major source of inflation will be eliminated. Government revenues will initially fall as tax rates fall and there must be some hefty cuts in government spending to offset that drop in revenue. In time, though, as we all work harder and earn more in response to those lower tax rates, government revenue will swell to a point where there no longer will be a budget deficit. And with no budget deficit to finance, the Federal Reserve can devote its all to keeping money growing at a nice, steady rate—appropriate to our economic needs.

Most economists, monetarists and Keynesians alike, sneer

at the supply-siders, and the ease with which President Reagan got his tax cuts through Congress left them more than a little uncomfortable.

And indeed, while supply-side theory is beautiful to behold, it's also replete with perils. We all want lower taxes. But unless government spending is cut to keep pace, all that lower taxes will do is fatten the budget deficit and give the Federal Reserve reason to create enough new money to create a lot more inflation. And it's hard to be very optimistic about government's cutting spending in any real way over any extended period of time. Promises must be broken, vast programs must be scrapped, and a lot of people and a lot of institutions must be told to do with less.

Also, unfortunately, it is not possible to prove the supply-side theory without trying it out, and paying the price if it fails—more theorizing while our money burns.

And that takes us back to square one: how little we know for sure about our money. And so it's time to set down what we do know—beginning with how money began.

Chapter 3

If the Buck Stops Here,
Where Did It Start?

IN THE beginning there were seashells—also cows and sheep
and stones and salt and silver and gold and a hundred other
things that have served as money to someone, someplace,
sometime, ever since a caveman swapped a juicy hunk of
brontosaurus steak for a stone ax, and so invented commerce.

For a rule of thumb, try this: If someone thinks it has
value, if it can be moved from place to place without undue
difficulty, and if it doesn't smell too bad after a few days in
the sun, it has at one time or another been used as money.

Wampum—strings of beads made from shells—became
the money of Massachusetts in 1641. In Colonial Virginia,
tobacco served as money (the price of a bride from England
being 100 pounds of choice tobacco). In nineteenth-century
Russia, platinum was of so little value that it was used to
make lesser coins. In Civil War United States, coins vanished and we used postage stamps as small change. If the
report of a 1979 U.S. government task force is accepted,
the one-dollar bill will vanish forever, a victim of inflation,

to be replaced by the two-dollar bill and the one-dollar coin.

We call it money because Juno, Queen of the Heavens, consort of Jupiter, was the favorite goddess of ancient Rome. Among her talents was an ability to warn of impending danger. And so she was known as Juno Moneta—Juno who warns. When the Romans built their mint, they put it in the temple of Juno Moneta on the Capitoline Hill. From *moneta* came our words for mint and for money.

Our money (and that of 20 other countries) is the dollar, and we call it that because in 1516 silver was discovered in a corner of Bohemia known as Joachim's Valley or Joachimsthal. The counts of Schlick, who owned the mine, used the silver to mint a one-ounce coin called a Joachimsthaler. It was of such high quality that in short order the Joachimsthaler—soon shortened to "thaler"—became a hit throughout Germany.

In money, as in anything else, it pays to advertise. Other states, seeking to promote the fineness of their coins, took to calling them thalers until, in time, thaler (or dollar, depending on the language of the issuer) became the accepted name for almost any one-ounce silver coin.

One such coin was the Spanish dollar, known more familiarly as the "piece of eight," which simply meant it was a one-peso coin worth eight reales. Spain dominated world commerce in the seventeenth and eighteenth centuries, and the Spanish dollar served as the coin of international trade, as the U.S. dollar does today. Since England refused to share her own coins with the colonies, the most common coin in Colonial America was the Spanish dollar. When the colonies became the United States they kept calling their money the dollar.

"The dollar," wrote Thomas Jefferson, "is a known coin and the most familiar of all to the mind of the people." It was years before we minted enough coins to satisfy demand, and the Spanish dollar and the U.S. dollar circulated side by side in America until well into the nineteenth century. If George Washington really threw a silver dollar across the Rappahannock, the coin he threw was a Spanish dollar.

Other countries must settle for less romantic origins for their money. In Britain it's a pound because it originally was a pound of silver. The mark, the lira, and the peso, among others, were all originally weights. Even the Biblical shekel —now revived as the money of modern-day Israel—was a weight of metal, not a coin with a fixed value.

Still, if Spain gave us the dollar, Rome did the most to flesh out our lexicon of money. Dime is from the Latin *decimus,* meaning one-tenth, and cent is from *centum,* or $\frac{1}{100}$th. Coin is from *cuneus,* meaning wedge (the first dies the Romans used to make coins being wedge-shaped). Capital is from *caput,* or head—meaning head of cattle, since cattle were widely used as money. Salary is from the Latin for salt, since Roman soldiers got at least part of their pay in salt. A slacker was someone not worth his salt.

But the Spanish dollar provided one familiar slang word for money. Each piece of eight was made to be broken into eight pieces, with each piece worth ⅛th of a dollar. One bit was worth 12½ cents, two bits, 25 cents.

According to legend, the South is called Dixie because the $10 bills issued by banks in French-speaking New Orleans carried the word *dix*—which is French for ten. A $10 bill is a sawbuck because the earliest U.S. paper money used Roman rather than Arabic numerals, and people thought the X for $10 looked like a sawhorse, or sawbuck.

I'll Give You 100 Cows for Your Farm

Why we have money is plain enough. Pure barter has its limitations, and it's too messy to cut a cow in half.

Barter works well enough when a community is small and its wants are simple. You have an ax and I have some corn, and we swap. But say I raise tomatoes and you make shoes. My shoes wear out in December and you make me another pair. I can only promise to give you tomatoes when the crop comes in next September. Or try it another way. I raise tomatoes and you make shoes. You want my tomatoes but I bought a pair of shoes last year and what I need is a new knife. You have to swap some shoes with the knifemaker in order to buy my tomatoes.

Finally, barter breaks down completely in the face of trade with outsiders, and as the economy becomes more complex. (How many Cadillacs must General Motors swap to buy an IBM computer?) As trade developed and economies got complex, barter had to give way to something else—not coins, which came later, or paper money which came later still, but objects that could be used in trade and also serve as stores of value. Seashells probably came first, and animals were probably the most commonly used. One cow would buy a wife, three cows a farm, and your wealth was measured by the size of your herd.

But then you were in trouble if your cow died, or if you traveled to another country where cows were so plentiful it took 50 to buy a wife and 100 to buy a farm. You pushed cows when the seller wanted salt. And what happened when you wanted to buy something that costs only half a cow?

The answer was to use something other than cows. Metals were an obvious choice—gold and silver when available, but at times copper and iron. As long as the object had perceived value it would do.

"Perceived value" is the key phrase here. People had to regard the object as having some intrinsic worth. Wampum served nicely as money as long as it was hard to produce. You had to find the right sort of seashell, a white shell being three times as valuable as a black shell. Then a portion of the shell was broken off, smoothed and rounded, and a hole drilled through the shell, since wampum was normally carried on a thong. With all that hard work, the finished product was worth having. Then came tools of iron, which did in minutes what took human hands hours to do, and the value of wampum diminished to a point where it could no longer serve as money.

So: First came a cow, and then came an object that could substitute for a cow, and then, at some moment in history, that object became a coin. China and Egypt probably used coins more than 4,000 years ago and India almost certainly did 2,000 years ago. The first precious metals used as money were not in the form of coins. You got a lump of gold or silver, which had to be weighed to determine its value.

The first coins of which examples still exist appeared around 700 B.C. in the kingdom of Lydia in western Turkey. Gyges, the king, built a mint that turned out coins of a natural alloy of gold and silver found in local streambeds, and called electrum. Lydia next produced the first gold coins about 150 years later. The king then was Croesus (the one we say people are as rich as), and his mint turned out a bean-shaped lump of gold with the heads of a lion and a bull on one side and a double square on the other. It might not have looked like what we think of as a coin, but it was an object of given value, issued under the authority of a monarch. A cow was worth what you could get for it. Even a hunk of gold had no fixed value and you were at the mercy of the seller's scale. A Lydian gold stater (which is what it was called) had a set value, and if you didn't like it, go argue with King Croesus.

With the Lydians leading the way, the world went over to coinage, which raised another sort of problem: every ruler wanted to issue his own coins. Your territory might be no bigger than a football field, but you weren't much of a sovereign if you didn't have your own coinage. By medieval times, trade choked on the thousands of different coins that circulated through Europe—each with a different value, depending on how much gold or silver a ruler felt like putting into his coins. Among all nations, only Britain had a single coinage—a tribute to the Norman conquest that united the country after 1066.

A coin, once issued, was then subject to a variety of nefarious practices, despite penalties that ranged from the the inhumane to the unthinkable. Counterfeiting a coin that bore the likeness of a sovereign was considered treason and counterfeiters were punished by whatever sort of torture amused the ruler.

Besides counterfeiters, there were clippers who pared the edges of a coin for the gold or silver, and sweaters who dumped coins into a bag and shook them violently to loosen a few particles of metal. A coin might start life as an ounce of silver and then have half that silver clipped or sweated away. The face value of a coin meant nothing, and once again merchants hauled out their scales and weighed each coin, just as people had weighed metal before coins came along.

Gresham Said It All

Still, the most egregious crimes against money were invariably committed by governments themselves—which gets us to debasing. Say that I'm the Count of Oink, a small principality in Central Europe. I have 1,000 ounces of silver which I can turn into 1,000 Porkers (which happens to be the name of my coins, each shiny, new Porker containing one ounce of silver. Or I can put half an ounce of silver into each coin, still call it a Porker, and toss you in my dungeon if you don't like it. Oink has 1,000 new Porkers, I pocket 500 ounces of silver, and a new chapter has been written in the long history of debasing the currency.

It was all compounded by that bit of fundamental truth known as Gresham's Law because, while others said it first, it is attributed to Sir Thomas Gresham, financial adviser to Queen Elizabeth I. Bad money drives out good, said

Gresham. As soon as I put my Porkers with half an ounce of silver into circulation, hoarders will grab up any old Porkers containing a full ounce of silver and either sock them away or melt them down—one ounce of silver bullion now being worth two of the new, debased Porkers.

When the United States stopped minting silver coins in the 1960s and switched instead to an alloy of copper and nickel, it was assumed the old silver coins would continue to circulate for years. In fact, collectors and hoarders grabbed all the old silver coins they could and almost overnight they vanished from sight. In early 1980 those old silver coins were selling for 30 and 40 times their face value. Thanks to the current high price, we have more than enough gold in our vaults to replace all our coins and paper money with coins of gold. But if we tried it, hoarders would grab the gold coins, and the paper money and the intrinsically worthless alloy coins would continue to circulate.

Most coins, through the ages, were of silver, gold being too rare to use in coins. Then came discoveries of gold in the nineteenth century in California, Australia, Russia, and South Africa, and gold became the world's money and the gold standard the world's monetary system.

Today, in America and almost everywhere else, coins are of neither gold nor silver but of base metals. We stopped using gold coins when we went off the gold standard in 1933. In 1965 we dropped silver from all coins except the half-dollar, whose silver content went from 90 percent to 40 percent. In 1970, the last silver went out of the half-dollar and we've used only that copper-nickel blend ever since.

The Tawdry Tale of Paper Money

The history of paper money is even more cloudy than that of coins—and far more tawdry, too. Governments typically issue paper money when there isn't enough gold or silver in the vaults to issue hard money, and hand in hand with paper money goes inflation as surely as night follows day. More people have been duped out of their wealth by government issues of paper money than by all the flimflam artists since the beginning of time.

"Paper money is like dram drinking," said Thomas Paine a long time ago. "It relieves for a moment by deceitful sensation, but gradually diminishes the natural heat and leaves the body worse than it found it."

Marco Polo found thirteenth-century China, then ruled by Kublai Khan, using money made of mulberry bark. The bark was pounded into a pulp, rolled out in sheets, and cut into different sizes by denomination. A merchant might not like swapping real goods for mulberry bark, but Kublai Khan said it was money and no one was going to trifle with him. Predictably, in short order China had the world's first recorded inflation.

We don't use mulberry bark, but we do use pieces of rag paper that are money only because the government says they are. When we quit the gold standard in 1933, we still kept 45 cents of gold for each dollar in the money supply. That was reduced to 25 cents in 1945, further modified in the mid-1960s, and dropped altogether in 1968. In 1968 the Treasury also stopped redeeming paper money with silver, and in 1971 the last link between precious metals and the dollar was broken when President Nixon stopped selling our gold to foreign nations that had the dollars to buy it. In theory our money is now backed by Treasury securities but in practice the government can—and does—print all the money it wants.

Countries—ours and all the others—start off with the best of intentions. They issue coins of precious metals, and when they issue paper money—usually during wartime—they always promise that someday the paper will be paid off with precious metals. Then the stocks of silver and gold run down while the need to keep cranking out money increases. Grad-

ually the coins become base metals and the promise to redeem the paper money with precious metals is forgotten.
And then, almost without anyone's noticing it, the printing
presses turn faster and faster and suddenly the country is
awash in money and—in time—racked by inflation. Presumably it needn't happen this way. In fact, in the whole monetary history of the world, there are few instances when it
hasn't.

Item: The prim and proper Bank of England—the Old
Lady of Threadneedle Street, and the original central bank
from which all others (including our own Federal Reserve)
are copied—came into being because King William of Orange needed money. Because the money couldn't be raised
from taxes, William created the Bank of England, which
obligingly printed all the money he needed. In no time at all,
England had a raging inflation going.

Item: The first paper money in the New World was printed
by the Massachusetts Bay Colony in 1690 to finance a futile
expedition to conquer Quebec. Soldiers were paid in paper
money and promised eventual payment in hard coin, to be
provided out of tax collections. There was no tax collection,
and no coins, and in a short time no value to the paper
money, either.

Item: To finance the Revolution, the Continental Congress
in 1775 issued paper money in the amount of 2 million Spanish dollars—promising the war would be short and the
money retired through tax collections. The war was long,
again there was no tax collection, and by 1779 there were
some $242 million of these "Continental" dollars at large.
By 1780 it took $80 in Continentals to buy $1 worth of silver
—the currency then costing more to print than it was worth.
The flood of paper money gave the nation its only taste of
hyperinflation, and "not worth a Continental" became part
of the vocabulary.

Item: To finance the Civil War, Congress authorized $150
million of U.S. notes—the first paper money issued by the

U.S. government. The notes were done in green ink, and so were called "greenbacks." Again it was promised that the war would be short and the paper would, in time be redeemed with hard money. Again the war was long and only a portion of the outstanding greenbacks were ever redeemed. We issued $450 million of them during that war, and by 1865, a $1 greenback was worth 35 cents in gold. The inflation that accompanied the Civil war wasn't as bad as the inflation that accompanied the Revolution, but it was bad enough.

Item: The government promised that the Vietnam War would be short and would cost so little it could be financed out of normal tax revenues. But the war dragged on for a decade and mostly it was paid for by printing more and more money. The resultant inflation dogs us to this day.

In fact, the monetary history of the United States is the monetary history of the world, squeezed tight. It took the world an eon to go from barter to printing-press money. It took us less than four hundred years to make the same journey.

The American Experience

Barter worked well enough for the first settlers and well enough for the pioneers who trekked West. And when barter gave way to something else, the colonists were endlessly creative in finding substitutes for cash money: not only wampum and tobacco, but also rice, cattle, wheat, animal skins, pitch, and a dozen other things, with musket balls commonly used as small change. When real money came along, it was mostly foreign—the Spanish dollar being the most widely used.

British policy was to keep gold and silver at home, and further, to keep the Colonies from coining their own money. Independent from the start, the Colonies did what they could to circumvent this policy. Massachusetts, for instance, began minting "Tree Shillings" in 1652. When Britain ordered Massachusetts to quit, the Colony kept minting them, stamping each one 1652. Thirty years later, Massachusetts still was making Tree Shillings, dated 1652. Still, it was an imperfect system, and the Revolution was fought as much to gain our own monetary independence as to win political independence from Britain.

The first United States coin was the Fugio cent of 1787, which legend says was designed by Ben Franklin—but which probably wasn't. It was copper, about the size of a present-day half-dollar, and featured the sun, a sundial, and the Latin word *Fugio,* which means "I fly," referring to the passage of time. The coin further bore the strange admonition "Mind your business."

Sobered by the inflation wrought by that first try at paper money—the Continental—the drafters of the Constitution said that only the federal government could make coins, and no one could print paper money. The federal government duly limited itself to coins until the Civil War. But early on came an interpretation of the Constitution that said state-chartered banks could print paper money (all banks being state chartered until 1863), and print it they did in vast and marvelous profusion.

Government coins of gold and silver mostly circulated in the East, and the paper money issued by Eastern banks usually had some worth, since the banks would redeem the paper with coins. Almost no silver or gold came West—and there the story was quite different. Each new Western town got a bank, and each new bank printed paper money backed by nothing more than the best wishes of its president. A $1 bill from a New York bank might be worth 99 cents in Boston or Philadelphia and 95 cents in Pittsburgh. A $1 bill from a country bank in Michigan might be worth 30 cents in New York.

When you borrow today, you get a deposit in a checking account. But checking accounts didn't come into general use until a century ago, and until then, when you borrowed money you got currency, which is how currency was put into circulation.

Bank notes in the early nineteenth century came in all colors, shapes, and sizes, featuring portraits of everyone from George Washington to the banker's favorite niece. Since few Western banks could redeem their bills with gold or silver, the game was to make sure no one ever tried to redeem them. One way was to caution the local citizens that any attempt to redeem the money would cause the bank to fail, and that funny money was better than no money at all. Another was to circulate the money so far away from the bank that it would never come home—a practice called "wildcatting," since the money was put into circulation out in the wilderness, where the wildcats howled.

By the Civil War, there were 7,000 kinds of paper money circulating from 1,500 banks—some of them sound enough, some of them having long ago failed, and some of them never having existed at all. Some were as phony as $3 bills, and some *were* $3 bills, the range of denominations of those early bank notes being limited only by the imagination of the bank that created them. No banker or merchant did business without a volume known as a "bank note reporter" at his side to tell him which bills were worth money and which were merely worthless.

Today I walk into your store and pay for something with a $20 Federal Reserve note. It isn't as good as gold, but it was printed by the United States government and you accept it without question. But say I walked into your store in Red Bud, Illinois, in 1860 to buy a plow. I hand you a $10 bill from the Leander S. Smith Bank of East Overshoe, Ohio, a $5 bill from the Linus R. Smith Bank of North Cornstalk, Iowa, a $3 bill from the East Bank of the Wabash, and a $2 bill from the North Bank of the Ohio. They look like money. They feel like money. But are they money? It was you and your bank note reporter against the thieves and scalawags of the land.

The government tried to control things with the First and Second United States Banks. Neither lasted very long—the First Bank from 1791 to 1811, and the Second Bank from 1816 to 1832. Each served as banker for the government and each tried to enforce some discipline on our money by accepting only bank notes backed by gold or silver. Each bank was opposed by a variety of interests, from those who simply didn't like big banks to those who felt a government bank had an unfair advantage over private banks. More deeply, each bank foundered because of a fundamental conflict that would plague America until well into the twentieth century: the clash between the commercial East with its gold and silver and the agricultural West and South, which had little of either.

In 1863, Congress passed the National Bank Act, establishing the first national banks. These were (and still are) private, commercial banks chartered by the federal government, as opposed to state banks whose charters were (and still are) granted by the states. Only national banks could print money and every national bank note had to be backed by federal bonds, bought by the banks, and deposited with the U.S. Treasury. For more than a half-century, all paper money consisted of national bank notes, except for some Treasury gold and silver certificates, and except for the remnants of those greenbacks printed by the government during the Civil War. They were never recalled in full, but in time the amount allowed to circulate was limited to the odd sum of $322,539,016. That amount, now called United States notes, is still in circulation, as a strange adjunct to our paper money.

The Crime of '73 and the Cross of Gold

The clash between East and West resumed after the Civil War, but with one important difference. Thanks to silver strikes out West, it was now the "golden" East and the "silver" West. From that conflict came the rise of Populism and the most unforgettable speech in American political history.

As before, gold stayed in the East, and the South and West had to get by as best they could. Congress brought the fight to a boil in 1873 by casually dropping silver from the coinage —thereby putting America on the gold standard. There was gold aplenty, thanks to strikes in California and elsewhere, and seemingly no need for coins of silver. In 80 years, the U.S. had minted only 8 million silver dollars and Congress in 1873 thought it was doing no more than writing into law what was already an accomplished fact: that the U.S. was on the gold standard, with all coins of gold.

As usual, Congress got its timing wrong. It wrote the Act of 1873 just as new supplies of silver were pouring in from Western mines. Suddenly there was plenty of silver, and the nation's biggest potential buyer—the U.S. Treasury—was out of the market.

Further, 1873 was a year of financial panic, highlighted by the collapse of the nation's premier banking house, Jay Cooke & Co. of Philadelphia. Unemployment soared, businesses failed, and—as usual—it was the agricultural West and South that felt it the most. And now the silver states and the farming states found themselves united in common cause. The silver states wanted the Treasury back in the market as a buyer. The farming states wanted silver restored to the money supply to ease the depression. The two camps joined together, called themselves Populists, and the Act of 1873 the "crime of 1873."

The basis of Populism, in a money sense at least, was that the gold standard was the Devil's work, designed to enrich the East and pauperize the rest of the land. Populists pointed to a sharp drop in the money supply when silver was removed from the coinage—and to a companion drop in farm prices. One caused the other as surely as night followed day, they argued. Increase the money supply through the unlimited coinage of silver, they said, and the resultant growth in the money supply would return plenty to the land.

Populism's greatest voice was William Jennings Bryan of Nebraska, and no one ever stated the Populist credo more forcefully than Bryan did at the Democratic convention of 1896 in Chicago. "Having behind us the producing masses of this nation," thundered Bryan, "we shall answer their demands for a gold standard by saying to them: You shall not press down upon the brow of labor this crown of thorns, you shall not crucify mankind upon a cross of gold."

At the finish, Bryan flung his arms wide and dropped his chin to his chest. For a moment there was stunned silence and then there was pandemonium. Bryan won the Democratic nomination in a romp.

He lost the election, of course, to William B. McKinley— attacked not only by the Republicans but by the pro-gold forces of his own party. Twice more he ran for the Presidency, losing each time. Silver scored occasional victories through the years, but we stayed on the gold standard until Franklin D. Roosevelt took us off in 1933.

The Coming of the Fed

To solve the problems of economic booms and busts— specifically the financial panic of 1907—the U.S. instead created the Federal Reserve in 1913. It opened its doors the following year as the nation's first central bank since the Second Bank of the United States died eighty years before.

There were still those who feared the power of a strong government bank, and the Fed wasn't a central bank in the sense that the Bank of England was. The headquarters in Washington was weak and the real power rested with the dozen regional Federal Reserve banks around the country —in particular with the Federal Reserve Bank of New York.

Not until the 1950s did Washington become the unchallenged center of the Federal Reserve System.

The Fed's basic job was to manage the nation's money—making sure there was always enough to sustain the economy, but not enough to cause inflation, and that money moved around the country according to design rather than the fortunes of commerce. If money moved from West to East through the normal channels of trade, the Fed would provide enough money to the West to keep it healthy.

The Fed would also handle the intricate job of clearing checks—getting them from where they'd been cashed to the bank that had the money on deposit. The Fed would take command of the nation's gold stock—gold in those days still being the very foundation of the money supply. Finally the Fed would act as lender of last resort to banks in need, providing them with short-term loans to tide them over until things got better. In short, the Fed was given vast control over the economy, and that spelled an end to true nineteenth-century-style capitalism and marked the beginnings of our modern-day managed economy.

National banks continued issuing paper money until 1929, and the Treasury issued certificates backed by gold into the 1920s and certificates backed by silver into the 1960s. But after 1913 the real money of America was the Federal Reserve note, and today, except for the handful of United States notes, it is our only money.

Chapter **4**
The Printing of the Green

THESE DAYS, the presses at the Bureau of Engraving and Printing in Washington go *thunk* every two seconds and each *thunk* turns out a sheet of 32 bills. If the Bureau is printing $100 bills—the largest denomination made today—that's $3,200 per *thunk*. There are 12 presses and they run 24 hours a day seven days a week to satisfy our growing hunger for cash.

We write 40 billion checks a year and we collectively own 500 million credit cards, but still we use more cash than ever before. On March 1, 1981, the wallets and change purses of America held $119 billion in bills and $12 billion in coins. That's $575.62 for every man, woman, and child in the land —twice what it was in 1971, and ten times the amount in 1941. The Federal Reserve puts the money into circulation, but it is manufactured by the Treasury: the currency by Engraving and Printing, the coins by the mints in Philadelphia and Denver.

We use more coins because there are more vending machines, and those machines consume a lot of coins. The Treasury hopes to replace the dollar bill with the Susan B. Anthony dollar coin (possibly a forlorn hope because the public's acceptance of the coin has been nil). One reason is that the coin would last ten times as long as a dollar bill. Another is the hunger of those vending machines. With a dollar coin, a vending machine could stock more—and more costly—items. Or, inflation being what it is in this age of new money, maybe what costs a quarter now will soon cost a dollar.

We use more paper money, as opposed to checks and credit cards, for a number of reasons. The dollar, for all of its problems, is still the world's most widely used currency, and many dollars wind up abroad in the international banknote market. The Treasury further knows that billions of dollars are smuggled overseas each year to avoid the police and the tax collectors.

Finally there is our booming underground economy where at least $250 billion in cash is spent each year on everything from a hot dog from a street vendor to a shot of heroin from a drug pusher. At least 75 percent of all cash transactions are for $1 or less, 95 percent of them for $10 or less, and it is rare for legitimate commerce to use anything bigger than a $20 bill. When the authorities spot a trail of $100 bills, they pretty well know they are onto something illegal, and that the something illegal probably involves drugs.

However we use the money, the Treasury must provide it in whatever quantities are needed. So each of the 12 presses at Engraving and Printing turns out 90,000 sheets of 32 bills per day. In the course of a year, the Bureau produces some 4 billion bills—more than half of them $1 bills—with a total value of about $35 billion.

It costs the Bureau about two cents to print a bill, whether it's a $1 bill or a $100 bill, and that's what the Federal Reserve pays when it buys them from the Treasury to put into circulation. But mounting volume has taken its toll, and veterans at Engraving and Printing say the quality of our money today isn't what it was a generation ago. The work is still handsome, fine-detailed, and difficult to counterfeit. But, say the old-timers, the money used to have more depth—more of what they call "feeling."

The two big mints—Philadelphia and Denver—are every bit as busy. In fiscal 1978 the two mints together produced 12 billion coins with a total value of $487 million. In volume the penny was the leader at 9½ billion. In face value, the quarter led, at a total value of $199 million. In producing these coins, the mints used 42,000 tons of copper, 1,681 tons of nickel, and 1,634 tons of zinc.

Besides making our coins, the mint also does contract work for a fee for foreign governments. Through the years it has produced more than 11 billion coins for 40 foreign governments including Australia, China, Cuba, Greenland, Haiti, Korea, Nepal, Panama, Peru, the Philippines, and the former Dutch East Indies. It takes on these foreign jobs when there is excess capacity at the mints, using not only the mints at Philadelphia and Denver but also the U.S. Assay Office in San Francisco (which used to be a mint), and the bullion depository at West Point, New York, where the government stores some of our silver and gold. There were also mints in Carson City, Nevada, Charlotte, North Carolina, Dahlonega, Georgia, and New Orleans, but all were long ago shut down.

Finally, the mints produce an array of medals of various sorts and sizes: medals for each President, Secretary of the Treasury, Director of the Mint, for various national heroes, and to commemorate great events in American history. The most popular medal nowadays—probably the most popular medal ever—is the one struck to honor John Wayne. It was authorized in 1979 and within a year the public bought 350,000 of them.

Beyond that, the facility at West Point produces the new ounce and half-ounce gold medallions that went on sale in mid-1980. The medallions aren't coins, but do offer Americans a chance to buy small quantities of gold from a reputable domestic source. The first medallions featured painter

Grant Wood on the one-ounce piece and singer Marian An-
derson on the half-ounce piece. They were to be replaced by
Mark Twain and Willa Cather in 1981, Frank Lloyd Wright
and Louis Armstrong in 1982, Alexander Calder and Robert
Frost in 1983, and John Steinbeck and Helen Hayes in 1984.

The mint turns out to be a good deal for the taxpayers. It
makes coins of base metals and sells them to the Federal
Reserve at face value. It further profits from its work for
foreign governments, from the sale of medals and medallions, and from the sale of special coin sets for collectors. It
cost $147 million to run the mint in 1978 but it earned $565
million—handing $418 million back to the Treasury. The
mint used metal costing $40 million to make coins with a face
value of $487 million, which is a pretty nifty deal any way
you look at it.

Why We Sort Of Like Our Money

By and large, we're content with our money, even if it's a
puzzlement to foreigners, who wonder why all our bills are
the same size and color. In most countries, bills of different
denominations differ in size and color as well. One reason
our bills are uniform in size and color is that it's cheaper to
make them that way. Another is that, since we must study
each bill to determine its denomination, we are more likely
to spot counterfeit money.

At any rate, there's no great outcry to change our money,
and all attempts to do so have been resisted furiously by
the public. The $2 bill, resurrected in 1976, was a fiasco, and
the Anthony coin is shunned as being too close in size to the
quarter. The Treasury hopes to persuade Congress to change
the color of the Anthony dollar from silver to bronze, but the
coin's future is still uncertain. The Treasury has also exper-
imented with Braille markings on bills to aid the blind, but
found the raised bumps wore down too quickly, and that it

was too easy to add bumps to make a $1 bill feel like a $20 bill.

Changes in our money are coming, though. The Treasury wants to make the penny of something cheaper than the present blend of copper and zinc, and it has looked at pennies made of aluminum and steel. The half-dollar is seldom used these days, and if a metallic dollar comes to stay, the half-dollar will have to go, because cash drawers have only five coin compartments. To add a sixth compartment in order to handle pennies, nickels, dimes, quarters, half-dollars, *and* dollars would mean redesigning billions of cash drawers. The cash-register industry did that once, adding an extra bill compartment to handle the $2 bill. Since the drawers meant for the $2 bill have mostly gathered dust, there is great resistance to any more changes.

We're probably content with our money because it's very simple, whereas it used to be very complicated. We have used coins of silver, gold, various alloys of copper, zinc, and nickel, and, for one year during World War Two, of steel. We've had coins ranging in denomination from a half-cent to $50. Our paper money has included notes of the First and Second United States Banks, of several thousand state banks, of several thousand national banks, United States notes, Treasury gold and silver certificates, and Federal Reserve notes.

The last half-cent was made in 1849, the last two-cent piece in 1872, and the last three-cent piece in 1889. There have been no gold coins since 1933—which took care of all denominations of coin over $1. Today we have the copper-zinc penny, the nickel-copper nickel, and all other coins made of a three-layered copper-nickel sandwich called "clad." The design of each coin is selected by the Director of the Mint and approved by the Secretary of the Treasury. Unless Congress says otherwise, the design of a coin then stands unchanged for 25 years.

From the welter of paper money of the past, we now have

only the seven Federal Reserve notes—$1, $2, $5, $10, $20, $50, and $100—and that oddity called the United States note, which is what is left of the greenbacks issued to finance the Civil War. All United States notes today are $100 bills —new ones issued as old ones wear out—with the number in circulation as close to the statutory $322,539,016 as the Treasury can get.

Federal Reserve note or United States note, the country has nothing bigger than a $100 bill today. There used to be notes of $500, $1,000, $5,000, and $10,000—and for a brief time even a $100,000 note. In 1945 the Fed decided there wasn't enough demand for them, and it ordered that no more be printed. In 1969 the Fed ordered them out of circulation, and we've made do with our current array of bills since then.

The rest of our paper money was simply phased out of existence. The notes of the two United States Banks died when the banks died. Notes issued by state banks were banished with passage of the National Bank Act of 1863, which authorized National Bank notes. All National Bank notes ultimately gave way to Federal Reserve notes.

The Treasury issued gold certificates from 1882 to 1928, redeemable in gold coins—and silver certificates from 1878 until the 1960s, which were redeemable first in silver coins and then in silver bullion. The gold certificates vanished when the U.S. went off the gold standard in 1933. The last silver certificates were issued in 1963, and the Treasury finally stopped redeeming them for silver in 1968. Until 1963 all $1 bills were silver certificates. The first $1 Federal Reserve notes were issued on November 26, 1963, and there have been nothing but Federal Reserve notes since.

The U.S. got its first coin—the Fugio cent of 1787—some years before it got its first mint (which opened in September 1792), and that first coin was made by private contractors. The first mint was in Philadelphia, and Congress authorized it to turn out cents and half-cents of copper; dollars, half-dollars, quarters, dimes, and half-dimes of silver; and eagles ($10), half-eagles ($5) and quarter-eagles ($2.50) of gold.

Local gold discoveries next led to the opening of the mints at Charlotte and Dahlonega in 1838. Both were shut by the Civil War. The New Orleans mint also opened in 1838, was seized by the South during the Civil War, went back to minting U.S. coins after the war, and was finally shut in 1909. The San Franciso mint opened in 1854, after the California Gold Rush, and operated as a mint until 1955. It officially became an assay office in 1965 and now, as indicated earlier, mints medals and an occasional coin. The Denver mint opened in 1906 and in most years produces more coins than the Philadelphia mint.

As mints go, ours is regarded as one of the best, turning out some very handsome coins and a few oddities as well. Collectors regard the 1907 double eagle ($20), designed by sculptor Augustus Saint-Gaudens, as the most beautiful U.S. coin, and one in top condition today would fetch $15,000.

The highest-denomination coin—also the biggest and heaviest—ever made was the Panama-Pacific $50 gold piece to commemorate the 1915 Panama Pacific Exposition in San Francisco. There were two types—round and octagonal— each more than 1½ inches across and each weighing 2½ ounces. Some 3,000 were minted, but in a day when $25 a week was a handsome salary, the demand for a $50 gold piece was pretty small, especially since the coin was too big and heavy to carry comfortably in a pocket. Only 1,100 got into circulation, the rest being hauled back to the mint and melted down. A round Panama Pacific $50 gold piece (of which only 483 got into circulation) would fetch $80,000 today.

Nowadays the mint is simply a mass-production operation, the romance having vanished from the American coinage when first gold and then silver vanished from our coins. It's hard to wax romantic about coins made of cupronickel alloy.

A penny is a mix of 95 percent copper and 5 percent zinc. A nickel is 75 percent copper and 25 percent nickel. All other coins, including the Anthony dollar, are made of clad, which is that three-layered sandwich of copper and nickel. The metals for pennies and nickels are simply blended together into a metallic pudding—the result being a strip of the approximate color of a new penny or nickel. Each of the three layers in a strip of clad is made separately—the outside layers of 75 percent copper and 25 percent nickel and the center layer of pure copper. The three layers are fused together to make the sandwich.

All these metal strips are fed through rolling mills to bring them to the approximate thickness of the finished coin. Next the strips go through a blanking machine that punches out blanks (or, more precisely, planchets) roughly the size of the finished coins. The blanks go through an annealing furnace to soften the metal, then through rotating cylinders filled with chemicals to clean and burnish the metal, through a washing process, and finally into machines that dry them.

An "upsetting machine" produces the raised rim around the edge of each coin. Next, under incredible pressure (from 40 tons for a penny to 170 tons for the old "cartwheel" silver dollars) the design is stamped on both sides of the coin at the same time. The coin is held in place by a collar and the ridges of the inner surface of the collar produce the ridges on the outer rim of each coin. Originally the ridges were to discourage clipping—paring a little silver or gold from the edge of a coin. Since there is no silver or gold in our coins today, the ridges exist as much for tradition's sake as anything—though mint officials say that ridges also make it easier for a blind person to tell a coin from a slug.

Finished coins are counted, bagged, weighed, and shipped to the district Federal Reserve Bank that will put them into circulation. Pennies go $50 to the bag, nickels $200 per bag, and everything else, from dimes to dollars, $1,000 per bag.

The Secrets of Our Paper Money

Since the government has made paper money only since the Civil War, the Bureau of Engraving and Printing is a far newer operation than the mint. It was started in 1862, with its first home in the basement of the main Treasury Building, next door to the White House. The current building, a sprawling, five-story blend of functional and neoclassical, was built in 1914. It stands on Fourteenth Street in Washington, under the shadow of the Washington Monument and just a stone's throw from the Potomac River. Across Fourteenth Street is the Annex, built in 1936, where postage stamps are printed. In fact, the Bureau prints some 800 different items from money to invitations to White House functions.

A lot of meticulous work goes into the making of plates for bills. The printing process is known as intaglio, and while printing by photo-offset would be a lot cheaper, it would not produce such high-quality bills, and counterfeiters would have a field day.

With any new bill, an artist prepares a model, which must gain the approval of the Treasury Secretary. Then engravers reproduce the design on soft steel with a tool known as a graver. One engraver will do the portrait, another the lettering, and so on—a specialist for each feature of the bill. The final product is a die; this is used to make the plates which actually will do the printing.

Each plate is good for 250,000 or so impressions, and then must be recoated with chrome before being put back into use. If a plate wears out or cracks, it is melted and the metal used again. In the intaglio process, the ink is forced onto the paper under enormous pressure, creating a three-dimensional effect which is a protection against counterfeiting. If you get a brand-new bill, run your finger over the surface and you can actually feel the tiny ridges of ink.

The Bureau makes its own ink, the formula being a closely guarded secret. The paper has been made by Crane and Company of Dalton, Massachusetts, since 1879, and while the precise formulation is a secret, it's made of 25 percent cotton and 75 percent linen, with red and blue fibers woven in to make it difficult to reproduce. The paper comes to the Bureau on skids, each one containing two stacks of 10,000 sheets each, each sheet 24.81 by 22.13 inches. The dozen presses, running full tilt, will gobble up 27 skids of paper each day.

Security is tight at the Bureau, as befits a building from which comes $35 billion in money each year. The public is permitted to watch the printing process—but from behind glass, a floor above the printing floor. The printers themselves seem pretty blasé about it all, and while there is obviously an essential order to things, the skids of paper about to become money, and the stacks of partially printed bills, seem to be left in haphazard fashion about the place. The presses themselves aren't very imposing—squat, blue objects that look as though they might print a small-town newspaper. But the plates have a fine, silvery sheen, and look quite handsome.

Only once in recent years has an employee succumbed to temptation. In 1954 a worker stuffed $160,000 in $20 bills into his pants, substituting scrap paper for the missing bills. The Bureau uncovered the loss, the Secret Service—guardian of the nation's money—caught him, and all but $25,800 was recovered.

Each bill is worked over three times as it makes its way from rag paper to money. First the back is printed in the familiar green ink and then the bills are set aside for a day to dry. Next the front is printed—again by the intaglio process, but this time in black ink. Finally the Treasury seal, the serial number, and the symbols for the Federal Reserve Bank that will issue it are printed on the bill—this time using offset.

When the fronts and backs are finished, the sheets of money are trimmed to size and then cut into two half-sheets of 16 bills each. Then the sheets go to a room where examiners scan every sheet for defects: unexamined sheets piled on the right, perfect work in the middle, and defective bills on the left. It would seem a job better left to sophisticated electronic scanners, but the Bureau's human scanners do a better job—each one able to check 12,000 to 14,000 sheets a day. Fingers fly, eyes peer, and the sheets fly across the examining tables so fast they seem to blur. Roughly every tenth sheet has a defect and must be replaced.

The serial number and the marks of the appropriate Federal Reserve Bank are added by the Bureau's favorite toy, its COPE machine (Currency Overprinting and Processing Equipment). The COPE machine also cuts each half-sheet into individual bills, forms the bills into stacks of 100, and binds them with a paper strip. The finished stacks of bills drop into a great revolving carousel of trays—32 trays in all, each able to hold 4,000 bills. Finally the bills go into the vaults, and then out to one of the dozen Federal Reserve Banks.

Each Fed Bank orders currency as needed and each bill bears the name and letter of the bank that ordered it. The lineup is this:

Bank	District Number	Letter Symbol
Boston	1	A
New York	2	B
Philadelphia	3	C
Cleveland	4	D
Richmond	5	E
Atlanta	6	F
Chicago	7	G
St. Louis	8	H
Minneapolis	9	I
Kansas City	10	J
Dallas	11	K
San Francisco	12	L

The Fed buys both coins and bills from the Treasury. Commercial banks, in return, buy them from the Fed and put the money into circulation.

Worn-out money goes back to a Federal Reserve Bank to be replaced with new money. Old or damaged coins are returned to a U.S. Assay Office and melted down, the metal to be used again in new coins. Old or damaged bills are destroyed by the Fed—usually by burning for several hours at temperatures that reach 1,800 degrees Fahrenheit. Sometimes, though, the Fed shreds the bills for use as mulch, and it has tried turning worn-out bills into insulating material.

Funny Money

When it comes to making money, governments have had the franchise for at least 2,500 years—right back to the Lydians. Still, people keep on making their own, despite all those nasty penalties for counterfeiting through the ages—castration being one of the milder ones. The ancient Chinese took another tack, though. When they uncovered a particularly gifted counterfeiter, he was put to work at the royal mint.

Because modern-day coins in virtually every country are made of base metals, there is little percentage in trying to counterfeit them. Counterfeiters turned out $22 million worth of phony bills in 1978, according to the Secret Service, of which $18 million was seized before it was circulated. The same year, counterfeiters turned out only $3,115 worth of phony coins.

Potentially more profitable is the business of counterfeiting rare old coins, or of altering the face of a coin to increase its value. Say I have a 1916 "Mercury" dime—a misnomer, since it is actually supposed to be a representation of Liberty. Still most people call it a Mercury dime. The dime I have has no mint marking on it, meaning it was made in

Philadelphia, which produced 22 million dimes in 1916. The value of my dime, in tiptop shape, would be $75. In Denver, though, they made only 264,000 dimes in 1916. If I could add a tiny D to the face of the dime, an unwary collector might pay $5,000 for it.

Or say I have an 1854 gold dollar minted in Philadelphia. In top shape, it might be worth about $1,000. The same dollar minted in San Francisco, with an S on it, would be worth about $2,500. If I could turn the S into a D for Dahlonega, Georgia, the coin might be worth $5,000. In 1854 the New Orleans mint made 46,000 half-eagles ($5 gold pieces)—each today would be worth about $2,000. The mint mark for New Orleans was an O. But the San Francisco mint made only 268 double eagles in 1854, and if the O could be turned into an S, I would have a genuine rarity and I could name my own price.

Actually I couldn't, since only a serious collector or a dealer would bid on my coin, and it would be spotted as a fake in about five seconds. Further, while the coins may be old, counterfeiting is counterfeiting, and I'd have the Secret Service to contend with. Yet the value of old U.S. coins has soared in the past few years, and the practice of trying to hike the value of old coins goes on. Indeed, circumstance breeds its own crimes, and in the summer of 1980 the Secret Service was busy tracking down counterfeiters of Kruger-rands—the one-ounce gold coin from South Africa that has been widely sold in the U.S. In August 1980, the Secret Service said it had already seized $5 million in phony Kru-gerrands and was on the trail of phony British gold sover-eigns, which also were being sold in the U.S.

The counterfeiting of coins requires a fairly high level of skill, but the counterfeiting of paper money no longer does. The image of the crafty old engraver patiently turning out plates capable of fooling the experts is very much out of the past, and the name of the game today is photo-offset. The typical counterfeiter is someone with access to offset equipment. The bill is photographed, the image is transferred to a metal plate, and *voilà*—instant money.

One way the Secret Service combats this is by setting down rigid rules about photographing money. You can publish a photograph of money, but it must be in black and white, and it must be less than three-quarters, or more than 1½ times the size of the genuine article. The photograph must be for publication and the printing plates must be destroyed after use. If you load your camera with color film, photograph a dollar bill, and enlarge it to life size, you have broken the law.

Counterfeiters favor $10 and $20 bills, as they're the ones most frequently used in day-to-day business. Counterfeit money is most likely to be passed in establishments such as grocery stores, drugstores, and bars, all of which handle lots of money fast. Counterfeiters avoid banks and racetracks because the people who handle money there are trained to spot phony bills.

Counterfeiting is a decidedly low-pay proposition, even if we do use more money than ever. That's because photo-offset produces instant, but discernibly phony, money. No counterfeiter can produce the special paper used in our money and offset can't produce a bill of high enough quality to pass a close inspection. The three-dimensional effect created by intaglio printing is absent and counterfeit bills look and feel flat. The lines and details aren't as sharp, and the colors aren't as crisp as the real thing. The Secret Service regards the intaglio process as the best defense against counterfeiting and would be deeply upset if we opted for photo-offset in printing our money.

Most counterfeiters are caught pretty quickly, and only one phony bill in ten ever reaches the public. The biggest haul of counterfeit money was $16 million seized in New York in 1974. Counterfeiting all but vanished during World War Two—either because of patriotism or because all potential counterfeiters were in service.

The Secret Service got the job of safeguarding our money on July 5, 1865, making it the first general law-enforcement agency of the government. Not until after the assassination of President McKinley in 1901 did it get the job of protecting our Presidents.

It hasn't given up protecting our money, but the job of protecting people has gotten very big. Besides the President and his family, it protects past Presidents, other government officials, visiting dignitaries, and, most recently, Presidential candidates.

But even the Secret Service can't stop the government from making its own funny money, as it does on occasion. In the fall of 1980, an electronic banking machine in California began feeding out $20 bills perfect in every respect— except that Engraving and Printing had somehow left off the serial number and the Federal Reserve Bank seal. The innocent turned them in to the bank in exchange for perfect bills. The wise sold them to collectors who were said to be paying $1,000 apiece for the flawed notes.

Chapter 5
How the Fed Manages—and Mismanages—Your Money

WHAT THE Bureau of Engraving and Printing in Washington produces is money. What the mints in Philadelphia and Denver produce is likewise money. But the Treasury produces neither currency nor coins until the Federal Reserve tells it to, because, of all the agencies of the government, only the Fed can make money—and it doesn't make it the way the rest of us do. The Fed makes money out of thin air, which is a nice trick if you can do it (and the Fed can).

I make money working for *Business Week*. You make money flying a jet airplane or removing tonsils or playing linebacker for the Dallas Cowboys. Except for the unemployed and the outrageously rich, we all make money working at one sort of job or another.

But when we talk about making money, it's just a figure of speech. We don't make money in the sense of creating something that didn't exist before. We merely pass around money which the Federal Reserve has already created.

When I say I make money working for *Business Week*, I mean that each month the company that owns *Business*

Week shifts money from its bank account to my bank account. Years ago it would have given me a pay envelope filled with bills and coins. Until a few years ago it wrote me a check. Now the money is automatically transferred from one account in a New York bank to another.

Business Week got the money by selling advertising and copies of the magazine. Companies pay for their advertising with money from the sale of products or services. Someone —maybe you—gave money to a company by buying one of its products. To complete the circle, say you got your money because I paid you $100 for filling a tooth. All of us working together have moved money around the economy, but at no time did we create money.

At any given moment there's a fixed amount of money in our economy and we're all obliged to share it. If there's too much, relative to demand, we'll all go on a spending spree, and the result is inflation. If there's too little, relative to demand, we'll put off purchases, and soon the economy will slip into recession. Ideally there's always just enough money to avoid both inflation and recession.

Whether it's the right amount or not, we have to make do because none of us can make more than minor modifications in the supply of money.

We can change what a given amount of money will do to the economy by changing its velocity—by slowing down or speeding up the rate at which we spend it. I could remove money from the economy altogether by burying it in my backyard or moving it to a Swiss bank account (but there's a good chance the Swiss bank would move it right back by investing the money in the U.S. stock market).

But only the Fed can change the basic equation, because only the Fed can create new money—money which didn't exist until the moment the Fed created it. And only the Fed can cause money to vanish the moment it gets tired of having it around.

Congress created the Fed in 1913 to end the haphazard

arrangement by which the government created some of our money (by minting coins and occasionally printing currency), and national banks the rest. Congress hoped, by putting all money creation in the hands of the Fed, to stabilize the U.S. financial system and end the long cycle of economic booms followed by what in those days were known as "panics." There were panics in 1819, 1837, 1884, 1893, and a particularly grim panic in 1907, which led to the creation of the Fed. We called it a "depression" in the 1930s because "panic" sounded so awful. Because that depression was so awful, we started calling them "recessions." We'll call them recessions until there's a Great Recession, and then we'll call them something else.

The Powers of the Fed

The Federal Reserve does a lot of things. It supervises the 5,600 banks that are members of the Federal Reserve System, and while only one bank in three is a member of the System, those member banks have 70 percent of the $1½ trillion in U.S. banking assets. The Fed further is supposed to maintain the economic health of the U.S. by maintaining the money supply at the right level—even if it isn't sure how to define money, has only the haziest idea of what constitutes the right level, and seldom seems able to control the money supply at all. Still, Congress has given the Fed some awesome weapons, and it makes use of all of them in trying to manage the nation's money.

The Fed sets the basic interest rate—the discount rate. Among its jobs, the Fed acts as "lender of last resort" to the financial system—ready to lend money to financial institutions when all other sources have failed. This lender-of-last-resort function makes the Fed comforting to have around. True, it didn't prevent the collapse of 9,000 banks during the Depression, but it has gotten better. When the Franklin National Bank in New York—then 20th biggest in the country —failed in 1974, the Fed provided nearly $2 billion to keep it afloat until a rescue merger could be arranged. When the collapse of the Penn Central a decade ago threatened to topple many financial institutions, Fed officials stayed on the telephone through a weekend assuring banks that any needing help would get it. And banks tapped the Fed for $1 billion over the next month.

Even a healthy bank will occasionally run short of money. Then it will turn to the Fed and borrow for a day or two, the rate it pays being the discount rate. There's a real discount window at each Federal Reserve branch, and a needy banker must appear, hat in hand, to convince the Fed he needs the money. Banks are supposed to manage their affairs so they don't run short, and when one does, the Fed wants to know why.

By raising the discount rate, the Fed can make it more expensive for a bank to borrow at the discount window. The bank, in turn, will charge more when it lends money, and it probably will make fewer loans so it doesn't run short again. In time the higher cost and reduced availability of money will act as a drag on the economy. Or the Fed can go the other way, cutting the discount rate and enabling banks to pick up some bargain-basement money at the discount window. Bankers can then charge less when they lend and they can make more loans, and that will tend to revive the economy.

Until 1980 only the 5,600 member banks could borrow at the discount window. Then, in that monumental piece of legislation called the Depository Institutions Deregulation and Monetary Control Act of 1980, the Fed was made lender of last resort to all institutions that accept deposits—40,000 of them, including all banks and all thrift institutions. In one swoop the Fed greatly increased its grip on the whole U.S. financial system.

Granted, the discount rate isn't what it used to be. Bankers have proven infinitely clever in finding sources of funds in time of need other than the discount window. They can tap their overseas branches and they can borrow from corporations by selling certificates of deposit. And they can borrow for a day or two from banks that have extra money around in what is called the "federal funds" market. The federal funds rate—the rate paid when banks borrow from one another—is far more important than the discount rate today, since on any given day $10 is borrowed in the federal funds market for every $1 borrowed from the discount window.

But, as it happens, the Fed not only controls the discount rate—it also has near-absolute control over the federal funds rate, and a lot to say about all interest rates. Finally, even if little money is borrowed most of the time from the discount window, the discount rate still plays an important function as a signaling device for the Fed. When the Fed raises the discount rate it's signaling the economy—bankers and borrowers and investors and everyone else—that it thinks things have gotten out of hand and it means to slow them down. A cut in the discount rate usually is a signal that the Fed wants to speed up the economy.

A Fed chairman could accomplish the same thing by announcing the change in policy on national television. But hallowed tradition calls for central banks to signal changes in policy by changing the bank rate—which is what the discount rate is called in most countries—and the Fed, our central bank, hews strictly to tradition.

Besides controlling interest rates, the Fed also sets the level of reserves banks must hold against deposits.

Prudence dictates institutions that take deposits must hold part of those deposits as surety that when people want to withdraw their money there will be money to be withdrawn. Since not all bankers are as prudent as they might be, the Fed tells them how much to hold in reserve.

It's unlikely that everyone would withdraw their money

the same day, so a bank doesn't hold $1 in reserve for each $1 on deposit. Bankers instead hold a fraction of each deposit in reserve, which is why it's called a fractional reserve system. In 1981, banks held 3 cents in reserve for each $1 in a consumer savings account, and between 7 cents and 16¼ cents for each $1 in a checking account. The 7 cents was at smaller banks and the 16¼ cents at big banks—big banks tending to get big corporate customers that can move millions in and out of an account in the twinkling of an eye.

Banks can count any cash they have around as reserves. Mostly, though, reserves are kept on deposit at the nearest Federal Reserve Bank, of which there are the dozen regional banks, plus 25 branches. In early 1981, the 5,600 banks that were members of the Federal Reserve System held some $40 billion as reserves against deposits.

Since a bank need keep only 16¼ cents or less as a reserve against each $1 of deposits, each reserve dollar can support several dollars of deposits. And since new deposits come about when banks make loans—the borrowed money being deposited in a checking account—each additional dollar of reserves permits banks to make several dollars of new loans. How banks gain those new dollars of reserves comes later in the chapter. For the moment, merely appreciate what drastic things the Fed can do to the banking system—and the economy—by ordering banks to hold more, or less, in reserve. Raising the level of reserves a bank must hold against deposits would suddenly freeze a lot of money that previously had been available for lending. Lowering the level of required reserves would suddenly free money for lending that previously had been frozen.

In fact, we are fast heading toward a grand change in the level of required reserves, because the Fed in 1980 won the monetary equivalent of the charge up San Juan Hill—its foes driven from the field in full flight and in total disarray. That, too, happened when Congress passed the Depository Institutions Deregulation etc., etc., etc.

As with the discount rate, the Fed's authority to set reserve levels used to be limited to its member banks. For years the Fed complained that its ability to control our money was impaired because so many institutions were beyond its reach, subject not to the Fed's reserve rules but to those of the states in which they operated. As noted elsewhere, the Fed's ability to manage money is impaired by a great many things—but no matter. It sold its case to Congress, which responded with the Depository Institutions etc., etc., etc., etc. Now the Fed is to set reserve levels not only for member banks but for all 40,000 depository institutions in the U.S. Henceforth all will march to the Fed's drumbeat, even if the Fed is beating a quickstep when it should be beating a dirge.

Congress merely bowed to the inevitable when it passed the 1980 Act, because the distinctions among the various kinds of financial institutions are fading, as are distinctions between checking and savings accounts—all accounts either having become, or soon will become, transaction accounts. Instead of the hodgepodge of reserve levels for different kinds of accounts, there will simply be a 3 percent reserve on deposits up to $25 million, a 12 percent reserve on deposits over $25 million, and a 3 percent reserve on big certificates of deposit. These will apply to all institutions that take deposits—banks and thrifts alike—member banks having until 1984, and all other institutions until 1988, to fall into line.

So the Fed can control the cost of money, and its word is law on how much institutions must hold as reserves against deposits. Its third key weapon, and the one with maximum impact on the economy, is its unique ability to create new money. More precisely, the Fed creates new bank reserves which the banks will turn into money, which is why those reserves are sometimes called "high-powered money."

The new bank reserves come about through the Fed's open-market operations, which involve the buying and selling of government securities in the marketplace. Banks will use the new reserves to make new loans, which, in turn, will produce new deposits. And those bank deposits become money the instant they are created.

The open-market trading desk at the Federal Reserve Bank of New York does the buying and selling, based on instructions from the most important policy-making body of the Fed—the Federal Open Market Committee, or FOMC. The FOMC meets formally once a month in Washington and consults daily by telephone to decide how much money the economy needs and what price people ought to pay for it. The New York trading desk implements those decisions.

During 1979, the trading desk traded some $750 billion of government securities, making the Fed the biggest investor in the world. The interest on the government securities the Fed owns produced $9.4 billion in income in 1979—32 percent more than in 1978—of which $700 million went to operate the Fed and the rest went back to the Treasury. Since the Fed has so much to say about interest rates—and since the higher rates go, the more the Fed earns—its ability to control its own profits is an advantage any private corporation would give its eyeteeth to have. But since most of what the Fed earns in a year goes back to the Treasury, it has no incentive to push rates up just to make a profit and no one has ever accused it of doing so.

Since the Fed has only a hazy idea how much money should be in the economy at any given time, can't measure money with any precision, and isn't sure how changes in the money supply affect the economy, the decisions made by the Federal Open Market Committee have a dreamlike quality to them. Undaunted, the Fed keeps plugging along and the economy keeps careening from inflation to recession and back to inflation.

How the Fed Makes Money

Let's for the moment say the Fed has decided to create more money because it thinks there is too little around relative to demand, and that the cost of available money is too high. Banks are hard-pressed to satisfy the demand for loans. To get more money, they are borrowing heavily in the federal funds market and paying dearly when they do so, and so they are charging dearly when they lend. Because money has become so expensive, there's a good chance business activity will slow, and the Fed thinks just a little new money will turn things around. There will be more money available, the cost of borrowing will come down, and while economists disagree over which is more important—having more money or having cheaper money—all agree that when you have both, something is going to happen.

To create the money, the Fed, through the open-market trading desk in New York, will purchase some government securities from one or more of the three dozen commercial banks and securities firms that are in the business of buying and selling government securities.

The Fed always deals in government issues rather than those of private companies so it doesn't have to explain why it bought General Motors bonds instead of AT&T bonds. Other agencies of government sell securities, but the Fed almost always deals in U.S. Treasury issues because they are the most plentiful and the market for them is so vast. In the course of a year, some $4 trillion in Treasury issues will change hands. Banks, corporations, insurance companies, pension funds, money-market funds, and foreign governments all invest in Treasury issues, and there is someone buying or selling a Treasury issue every moment of the working day.

The Fed will usually buy Treasury bills—issues that mature in less than a year. That's partly because the bill market is so big—60 percent of all Treasury issues traded each year are bills—that a transaction can be wrapped up in two seconds. It's also because the Fed is most concerned with controlling short-term rates, since most business borrowing is short term. Sometimes, to even out its impact on the market, the Fed will buy Treasury notes (maturing in between one and ten years), and very occasionally it will buy Treasury bonds (which mature in more than ten years).

Let's say the Fed on a certain day will create money by adding $1 million to the reserve level of the banking system, and it will do that by purchasing $1 million worth of Treasury bills from one or more of the government bond dealers. Like the rest of us, the dealer has a bank with which it does business. And that bank, in common with all banks that are members of the Federal Reserve System, must maintain a reserve account at its nearest Federal Reserve branch.

To pay for the $1 million in bills it has just bought, the Fed simply adds $1 million to the reserve account of the dealer's bank. The dealer is Lapis, Lazuli & Co. and the bank the Seventh National. With a stroke of the Fed's pen (nowadays with a few strokes of the keys of a computer) the Seventh National has gained $1 million in reserves that didn't exist an instant before. Lapis, Lazuli & Co. has parted with $1 million in Treasury bills, but its checking account at Seventh National has been credited with a $1 million deposit.

As to where the Fed got the $1 million in the first place—it created it out of thin air. If we tried it, the bank would first chide us about writing checks with insufficient funds, and shortly it would call the cops. But we can't create money and the Fed can. Let there be money, says the Fed, and suddenly there is.

By creating these new reserves, the Fed has made it unnecessary for the Seventh National to borrow from other banks in the federal funds market, and the reduced demand for federal funds has, in turn, reduced the federal funds rate.

Other banks can now borrow federal funds for less, and if they can borrow for less, they can lend for less, too. By adding or taking away reserves, the Fed can put the federal funds rate precisely where it wants at any moment.

Finally, since each dollar of reserves can support several dollars' worth of deposits, and since new deposits come about when banks make loans, the $1 million in new reserves the Fed just created will allow the banking system to make several million in new loans. And since deposits count as money, the $1 million in new reserves will add several million dollars to our money supply.

What the Fed creates, it can also destroy. Say the Fed thinks there's too much money in the economy and the price, in turn, is too low. The banks have so much money they're dragging in citizens off the streets and forcing them at gunpoint to borrow. We're all borrowing, and the economy is beginning to reel from the inflationary consequences of too much money chasing too few goods. The party is getting raucous and the Fed wants to quiet things down.

Now the Fed will remove reserves from the banking system—that, in turn, pushing the federal funds rate higher. Instead of buying Treasury bills, the Fed will sell $1 million. Once again the dealer is Lapis, Lazuli & Co. and the bank is the Seventh National. The Fed will collect its $1 million by charging the reserve account of the Seventh National, which in turn will deduct $1 million from the checking account of Lapis, Lazuli. Lapis, Lazuli will have $1 million in Treasury bills, but $1 million in reserves which existed only a second ago is gone.

Since that $1 million in reserves was the base for several million in bank deposits, the Fed has actually removed the underpinnings from several million in loans (and from several million dollars of money). Now the Seventh National must scramble for cover. It will hold off on new loans until someone brings new deposits to the bank, or it may call in some outstanding loans. When the Fed creates $1 million in reserves, making money easier, the impact on the money supply and the economy is greater than that, and when it destroys $1 million in reserves, making money tighter, the impact on the money supply and the economy is greater than that.

When the Fed Speaks, Everyone Listens

The whole process of money expansion—how the banks go about creating several dollars of money from each dollar of reserves the Fed provides—will be explained in detail in Chapter 6. For the moment, we'll deal with the mechanics —and the politics—of the creation of high-powered money by the Fed. It is worth studying in detail, because, except for the defense of the land in wartime, it's the most important function carried out by government.

So crucial is the Fed's role in the economy that its pronouncements on money are studied religiously by everyone with a stake in the financial system. When money is scarce and the cost is high, it's considered bad for the stock market. The cost of borrowing money to invest in stocks—buying on margin—becomes so high that fewer people will chance it. Also, interest rates in time get to a point where the return on a Treasury bill (or any other security bought because of its return) becomes higher than the return on stocks.

The Fed announces the amount of money in the economy at 4:10 P.M. every Friday. Let the money supply grow too rapidly, relative to economic conditions, and stockmarket investors, fearful the Fed will counter with tighter money and higher interest rates, will sell off in droves. On October 6, 1979, the Fed announced a slew of moves (a higher discount rate, higher reserves required on some kinds of deposits) all aimed at fighting inflation, and the stock market lost $50 billion in a month. By the same token, a Friday report showing a drop in the money supply will send stock prices up on the assumption the Fed will soon make money easier and cheaper.

There's an element of madness in this. The Fed reports on only two of its five measures of money each week, neither of which may be valid. Further, the Fed can offer only a rough approximation of the supply of money, based on some preliminary calculations. It's common for the numbers released one week to be revised substantially the next. In October 1979, for instance, the Fed kept reporting big gains in the money supply even after it announced all those anti-inflation moves. To all appearances, the Fed was doing all it could, but the supply of money was still growing at an inflationary rate.

Actually a clerk at a New York bank had goofed in reporting his bank's financial position to the Fed. Somehow the Fed missed the error and into the money supply went the errant numbers. A chagrined Fed later had to admit at least $3 billion in money it had reported as existing didn't exist at all. Millions of shares of stock were sold, and countless other decisions were made on the basis of numbers worth less than the paper they were printed on. When the Fed revised its numbers, showing a much smaller gain, the stock market duly rallied—which was cold comfort for the investors whose losses had contributed to the $50 billion bloodbath.

Finally, assuming the Fed's definitions of money are correct, and assuming no one has erred in preparing the money supply report, there still will be some very erratic movements in the money numbers from week to week. The reasons are technical but the conclusion is obvious. Trying to guess what the Fed is up to on the basis of one (or two or three) weeks' money numbers is like trying to decide who won a baseball game from the score for a single inning.

It would help if the Fed simply came out and said what it was doing. But again there's that code (or conspiracy, depending on your paranoia level) among central bankers that nothing is ever said straight out. Henry Ruess, former chairman of the powerful House Banking Committee, has been known to gnash his teeth and accuse the Fed of talking not in English but in the language of flowers.

Fed officials argue that if they came right out and explained exactly what they were trying to do, sophisticated investors would do better in translating that into hard investment decisions than would the majority of investors. But investors who can pay for it get some very sophisticated interpretations of what the Fed is up to, and some of the highest salaries on Wall Street go to economists who specialize in translating the meanderings of Fed policy into investment advice. It's poetic justice that among the biggest losers in October 1979 were the very banks and brokers who employ these economists.

It is more likely that the central bankers never say anything flat out because they are themselves confused, and to speak plainly would make that clear to everyone. Economist Sherman J. Maisel was lured away from the University of California in 1965 to serve on the Federal Reserve Board. After leaving the Fed, a bemused Maisel wrote of frequently finding his colleagues arguing "over the merits of a policy without ever having arrived at a meeting of the minds as to what monetary policy was and how it worked."

If You Don't Like It, Too Bad for You

If you don't like what the Fed is doing with money, however, you are invited to stick it in your ear. The Fed these days is accountable to few and beholden to no one. Other decisions made about the economy by government must be ratified by Congress, but not those made by the Fed.

In the early days, the Secretary of the Treasury and the Comptroller of the Currency—both Presidential appointees—sat on the Federal Reserve Board. Both went off the board in 1935 and since then all seven Fed governors have been independent of any other government agency. During World War Two and after, the Fed was totally subservient to the Treasury, functioning only to make it possible for the Treasury to borrow at the lowest possible cost. That ended with the "accord of 1951" by which the Fed was set totally free, and free it has been ever since.

Each Fed governor is appointed by the President for a single 14-year term. Because a governor can't be reappointed, there's no point in currying favor with the President to win another term. The terms are staggered so one expires every two years—a governor appointed to fill a term left open by death or resignation serving only the unexpired years of that term. Because seats on the board open only every two years, a President can appoint only two governors per term, making it very hard for a President to pack the board.

Only the chairman of the Fed faces a potential problem with tenure. While he's a Fed governor, appointed for 14 years, his term as chairman runs only four years, after which he must be reappointed by the President. Still, when it comes to job security, if you can't be a federal judge, become a governor of the Fed.

Congress, in recent years, has gained a modest degree of overseeing the Fed—the sole result of years of trying to police the Fed's power. Fed officials must go before Congress in February and again in July to explain their goals for growth in the money supply and their expectations about the economic outlook. The Fed is further supposed to explain why all previous estimates of money-supply growth were wrong—as they mostly have proven to be. But since what's done is done, Congressional overseeing amounts to little in the real world. The Fed can say, "Gosh, guys, we blew it and we sure are sorry," and there isn't much Congress can do about it.

Yet because Fed governors are appointed and not elected,

they're a comfort to have around. If harsh things must be done to the economy to control inflation, both the White House and Congress can remain saintly in the eyes of voters by letting the Fed do it all.

What must be said about the Fed is that it means well. Its leaders may be dense or confused or both, but apparently they aren't venal. There have been some flat-out incompetents among the governors and chairmen, but there have been no scoundrels, and the Fed is probably the most scandal-free agency in the government. Considering the influence every breath by the Fed has on the investment markets, anyone at the Fed who wanted to make use of inside information could make a killing in the market. That no one has done so (or at least no one has been caught) is a tribute to the caliber of people the Fed has attracted through the years and to the strong sense of propriety that pervades the organization. It may not know what it's doing, but the Fed has kept its image as a class act.

It's generally conceded that President Carter erred in his first choice as Fed chairman—businessman G. William Miller—and did better with Paul Volcker, his second selection. Miller had a successful career running Textron, the giant conglomerate, but he had no central banking experience and not much money sense. He fumbled along for 18 months and then was named Secretary of the Treasury, a position in which talking with one's foot in one's mouth is considered a plus for the job.

Then Carter turned to Volcker, a former high official at Chase Manhattan Bank, a high Treasury official in the Nixon-Ford years, and finally president of the very powerful Federal Reserve Bank of New York. Miller is remembered as an amateur in a job that was too big for him. Volcker is widely respected on Wall Street and at the banks, and by central bankers from other nations as well. Monetary policy has been no better under Volcker than it was under Miller, but Volcker gives a lot of tone to the place. In late 1980, of

course, Volcker's future was cast in doubt by the election of
Ronald Reagan, who might want his own man at the Fed as
soon as he could put him there.

Volcker and the other six governors who together make
up the Federal Reserve Board reign over the greatest concentration of wealth in the world—the 40,000 institutions
that now fall under their sway having some $2½ trillion in
assets.

The board meets each morning to pass on such things as
bank applications to branch, merge, or make acquisitions.
Any of the twelve regional banks can propose a change in
the discount rate, but it must be approved by the board in
Washington. And it's the board that sets reserve levels for
depository institutions.

No one has ever accused the Fed of using its power capri-
ciously. It draws on the advice of hundreds of economists
within the Federal Reserve System, plus that of bankers and
economists from outside the system. In setting monetary
policy, the Federal Open Market Committee goes through
one of the most exhaustive decision-making processes in
government, as it settles on rates of money-supply growth
and levels of interest rates for the economy.

On the FOMC, besides the chairman and the other governors, are the presidents of the 12 regional banks (Boston,
New York, Philadelphia, Richmond, Atlanta, Cleveland,
Chicago, St. Louis, Kansas City, Minneapolis, Dallas, and
San Francisco), of whom five at any given time are voting
members. The president of the New York bank is always a
voting member and always the vice-chairman. The chairman
of the Fed is, of course, chairman of the FOMC.

The meeting is usually the third Tuesday of each month
and the place is the second-floor boardroom at Fed headquarters in Washington. It's useless trying to get in unless
you belong: outsiders aren't welcome. A Fed official is asked
what would happen if the President of the United States
wanted to sit in on an FOMC meeting. The answer is the

request would be regarded as an unwelcome intrusion and turned down.

In Which You Join the Fed

Still, imagine yourself a governor of the Federal Reserve System, which isn't such a bad job. Your job is secure for fourteen years, you earn $55,400 a year ($60,700 if you're chairman), and you have a handsome office in one of the nicer quarters of Washington. The State Department is just kitty-corner, and magnificent Georgetown is a pleasant stroll away. Were you president of the New York Fed, you'd do even better, earning $125,000 a year—but still being a Fed governor is a pleasant life. (Volcker, by moving from New York to Washington, took a monumental cut in pay.)

Your duties aren't too onerous: the daily board meeting, the monthly meeting of the FOMC, and lots of time to sit around and think about the sins of the past. Fed governors are much-sought-after public speakers. Miller was unusually loquacious for a Fed chairman—willing to speak often, and to be quoted. Volcker, in common with most chairmen, speaks only when he has something important to say.

Whatever a Fed chairman says in public is analyzed and interpreted, both at home and in foreign capitals. A frown from the chairman can send the financial markets tumbling and a smile can launch a rally. In June 1965, then-chairman William McChesney Martin, Jr., said in a speech that he saw disturbing similarities between the stock market then and the market of 1929. Martin, who had become president of the New York Stock Exchange when he was thirty-one, was thought to know a thing or two about stocks, and the stock market plunged. Miller never got the idea that *everything* he said would be studied as carefully as messages from the Oracle of Delphi, and much of what he said was pretty naive.

Fed governors tend to be economists or bankers, and

Miller is seen as proof that businessmen seldom make good central bankers. On the other hand, the Fed has had very few first-rate bankers or economists on its board. Soundness, not brilliance, is plainly what is wanted.

Central bankers tend to be sober, serious types, but the Fed has had its share of fun-loving sorts. J. Dewey Daane, a governor in the 1960s, while in Spain to attend an international banking meeting, once leaped into a Spanish bullring and spent a few minutes sparring with the bull. Martin, chairman from 1951 until 1970, was a top-notch tennis player, and as soon as the morning board meeting ended, he would race from his office and get in a few sets on the Fed's own courts, which then stood across the street. An annex to the Fed now occupies the ground, and while there are tennis courts in the neighborhood, they are, a Fed official sniffs, "public courts."

The FOMC meeting is serious business, though, and as a member of the committee you turn your thoughts to the financial health of the Republic as you approach the Federal Reserve building on Constitution Avenue. The building is very solemn—a low, block-square expanse of white marble that looks like nothing so much as a vast mausoleum.

Inside there is more marble and a hushed solemnity that is contagious. You find yourself talking quietly and treading softly. The boardroom is up a grand stairway—more marble and a lot of gleaming brass. At the top of the stairs is a rotunda in which a guard sits. He's there to guard the governors since there's nothing in the building worth stealing except secrets. The Fed bank in New York holds billions in cash and securities and its vaults hold the world's biggest gold hoard. The only money in the Fed building in Washington is whatever employees have in their pockets. This is the headquarters, where decisions are made; the product is handled out in the field.

Beyond the rotunda is a cross-corridor, and on the far side of the corridor is the boardroom with the chairman's office next to it, and the offices of the other governors and the senior staff lined up on either side. The boardroom is as handsome and elegant a room as you'll find anywhere—a monument to restraint and good taste. It is 56 feet long and 32 feet wide—half the size of a basketball court—with a 23-foot ceiling. The room is dominated by the boardroom table, a slab of mahogany 30 feet long. Comfortable armchairs line both sides of the table, and dangling above the table is a chandelier that weighs a half-ton. At one end is a vast, wood-burning fireplace that's sometimes used during receptions, but never during meetings. The walls are beige, the ceiling white and beige. On the floor is a rich, deep carpet in a pleasing shade of brown. On the Constitution Avenue side there are three great windows that reach nearly from floor to ceiling, with draperies in gold brocade.

The whole room was redone several years ago as part of a $12 million renovation of the whole building. One improvement was to double-glaze the windows to keep out the noise of planes flying in and out of National Airport a few miles away.

The Fed is superbank and this is superboardroom—meant for serious discussion and profound decisions. Presumably Fed governors sometimes talk of baseball or the weather or even crack a dirty joke or two, but it's impossible to think of them doing so in this room. A man who has attended meetings for years says he has never heard a voice raised in anger. That, too, would be unthinkable.

This day, as usual, the FOMC meeting will begin at 9:30. Most out-of-towners arrived the day before and spent the night at the Watergate Hotel, which is close by. The banks in Philadelphia and Richmond are close enough for their presidents to just breeze in for the day.

There's a precise order to how the men (joined in 1978 by the first woman governor, economist Nancy Teeters) array themselves around the table. The chairman and the Secretary of the Open Market Committee are at the head. Next is the president of the New York Fed as vice-chairman of the FOMC. Then come the other six governors, three on each side of the table, and then the presidents of the regional banks, also on either side of the table. The few chairs that remain are for economists from the Fed's Washington staff and for officials of the New York trading desk. Along the walls are chairs for economists from the regional banks.

Each place has a microphone, a brown folder marked "boardroom," and an ashtray. Arthur F. Burns, chairman of the Fed from 1970 to 1978, was a pipe smoker and there were ashtrays on the boardroom table. Miller was a non-smoker who banned smoking from the room, and the ash-trays vanished. Volcker is a cigar smoker (of rather cheap cigars, given his station) and the ashtrays are back.

Green Books, Red Books, Blue Books

Fed economists have been getting ready for this meeting almost since the last one ended, preparing the small moun-tain of material each member is expected to master. There is first the Green Book (so-called because it has a green paper cover), circulated a week before the meeting with a mimeo-graphed update the Friday before each meeting. It contains the best estimates by Fed economists of the economic out-look, here and abroad.

There is next the Red Book (red paper cover), put together by the regional banks and describing economic conditions around the country. The regional banks are anachronisms today—holdovers from 1913, when Congress created a dozen regional Federal Reserve banks instead of one mono-lithic central bank. Regional banks clear checks, distribute currency and coin, keep the reserve accounts for the com-mercial banks in the region, and run the discount window for these banks. They also do research that's supposed to pro-vide the Fed with insights into regional economic problems.

It isn't clear how much the Fed gains from this, but still the Red Book appears the Thursday or Friday before each meeting.

Finally, there's the Blue Book (blue paper cover) which provides up-to-the-minute financial data and discusses the various policy options open to the FOMC. It's terse and is not completed until the Friday night before a meeting.

Each meeting opens with a look at the international financial situation (invariably bleak) offered by the New York Fed, which handles international financial transactions for the Federal Reserve System, and, indeed, for the whole U.S. government. The New York Fed is the prime defender of the dollar in international markets, the U.S. financial agent for foreign governments, and the caretaker of the gold that foreign governments have acquired from us through the years —most of which has been left for safekeeping in New York.

Next comes a review of the domestic economy, with everyone in the room free to ask questions. Fingers are waggled, noted by the Secretary of the FOMC, and the questioners are called upon in turn.

Then there's a review of what the New York trading desk has done since the last meeting, then a review of the various policy options open to the Fed at the moment, and then a coffee break.

After coffee comes the guts of the meeting: the debate over the policy the FOMC will adopt, stated in terms of desired rates of money-supply growth and ranges in which the federal funds rates will be allowed to trade. Were a meeting to degenerate into bickering, it would happen now. Seldom do the members of the FOMC speak with one voice, and most policy decisions are adopted with a few dissenting votes. The seven governors are a disparate lot, representing differing political and economic philosophies and different parts of the country. No Federal Reserve district, for instance, can have more than one governor at a time. The regional bank presidents are selected by their boards of directors, which are heavily weighted toward local banking interests, and so they tend to be pretty conservative, politically and economically.

Where the Fed Goes Awry

Dissent there may be at these meetings, but seldom is there out-and-out division. There's a great homogenizing process within the Fed—an institutionalization that swallows all—and whatever beliefs its officials held before they joined up, most seem to have embraced the beliefs of the Fed after they did so. Think of it as a private club with secrets and rituals unknown to the world at large, and a membership sworn to keep it that way. All may not like the rules of the club, but all, once initiated, seem willing to play by them. The names and faces at the Fed have changed through the years, but the errors of policy go on—the seven current governors of the Fed making the same errors their predecessors did a decade ago.

Even that doesn't say it all, and the reason why the Fed does so badly so often lies deeper still. Partly it's that inability to come down solidly on one side or the other of the cost-vs-supply argument over money. And then there's the matter of pressure from without. Everything the Fed does touches all of us so acutely that we all want the Fed to follow our own favorite brand of policy, and even the Fed's independence has its limits.

Say for purposes of illustration that you have just become the chairman of the Federal Reserve, charged with keeping our economy sound by keeping our money sound.

You can manage the supply of money if you're willing to say, "To hell with interest rates." You can manage interest rates if you're willing to say, "The hell with the supply."

Being of tolerably sound mind, and being keenly aware of the failings of your predecessors, you decide you will control the supply of money, letting interest rates go where they may.

You appreciate that it will be painful for a while—America's great corporations, the buyers of homes, the buyers of cars, and even the U.S. Treasury obliged to pay more for money. Not all will appreciate what you are doing and your office is close enough to Constitution Avenue that some unhappy borrower can easily peg a rock through your window. If rates go high enough, maybe mobs will form. Yet you will suffer these slings and arrows because in the long run the U.S. will be the better for your having taken control of the money supply.

"In the long run," said John Maynard Keynes, "we are all dead." You never make it to the long run because those pressures begin to pile up at once.

You tighten the money supply, and the cost of automobile loans goes up, and suddenly the entire Michigan Congressional delegation assembles at your door and warns that you are about to push the whole U.S. auto industry over the edge.

You tighten the supply of money some more and mortgage rates go to the skies and 5,000 men in hardhats assemble at your door and announce you have just killed the U.S. construction industry.

You tighten some more and platoons of somber bankers appear at your door and proclaim that 1,000 banks with $100 billion in assets stand on the very brink of collapse. Now there are mobs in the streets, and rocks bounce off your window like raindrops off the flowers of spring.

And finally the President summons you to the White House. (And keep in mind that all Presidents want the same thing from the Fed, whatever they say in public. Every President wants every penny of the federal budget deficit financed, with no would-be borrowers turned away for want of funds, and all of that done without budging up interest rates an inch.)

So the President talks about the weather, and asks about the wife and kids, and tells you his dream for a greater and more glorious America. Then he explains he will surely lose the next election if interest rates don't come down, and he casually asks you if you want to go down in history as the Fed chairman who drove an incumbent President from office. Independent you may be, but no one is *that* independent.

You return to your office, mull for a while, and at the next meeting of the Open Market Committee you convince all that interest rates have gone a trifle high and that maybe just a little more money in the economy wouldn't do anyone a bit of harm. Tomorrow, you reason, will somehow take care of itself.

Be all that as it may, it is your job this day as Fed chairman to smooth away what differences there are within the FOMC and to produce a consensus. Once a clear majority emerges, there's a vote, and although the nation doesn't know it yet and may not until the results of the meeting are made public a month or so later, it now has a monetary policy for the next month—probably the wrong policy, but a policy just the same.

More precisely, there's a policy directive from the FOMC to the trading desk in New York on monetary policy for the next month. Then a date is set for the next meeting, and the governors and the regional bank presidents adjourn for lunch.

You wouldn't want to be caught on a desert island with only the FOMC directive to read. It runs about a dozen pages, starting with a dry discourse on the current state of the economy and the financial markets, followed by an equally dry discourse on what the FOMC hopes to do to the economy and the financial markets, followed by operating instructions for the New York trading desk.

Typical is the directive of February 1980. The committee (wrongly as it turned out) saw the economy still expanding.

"Staff projections prepared for this meeting," says the document, "suggested that growth of nominal GNP would slow much less in the current quarter than had appeared likely a month earlier, and growth over the remaining quarters of 1980 was expected to vary relatively little from the first-quarter pace. The projections continued to suggest that real GNP would contract moderately during the year. . . ."

Nominal GNP means economic growth without regard to how much of it is due to inflation. Real GNP is what's left after growth due solely to inflation is removed. The committee had concluded that GNP, however measured, would behave itself in 1980. Having concluded that, the FOMC told the New York trading desk to keep the money supply growing at a 4½ percent to 5 percent rate, provided it could also keep the federal funds rate within a range of 11½ percent to 15 percent. Should anything go awry, the directive concluded, please call the chairman at once.

Presumably the chairman got a lot of telephone calls because nothing worked as the FOMC expected it to. Even as the February meeting was going on in Washington, the economy was tipping into a short but intense recession—a recession the Fed never saw coming. The whole U.S. economy (nominal GNP) actually shrank in the second quarter. Real GNP, instead of contracting mildly, took its worst tumble in postwar history, the economy, once inflationary growth was pared away, shrinking at an astonishing 10 percent rate in the second quarter.

Furthermore, it would be some weeks before the Fed understood we were in a recession, and during those weeks it made one horrendous goof after another.

Thanks mostly to a surge in food and energy prices, inflation suddenly got a lot worse. There isn't much that the Fed can do about surging food and energy prices. Nonetheless, it tried to battle the inflation by pushing interest rates up at a hasty clip—which threw the financial markets into a panic. And then, on March 14, 1980, in tandem with President

Carter's umpteenth anti-inflation program, it raised interest rates some more and slapped on rules that made it harder for business and consumers to borrow money—those who could afford to borrow at all.

If the Fed missed the boat in February, what it did on March 14 was overkill on a grand scale. At that point the economy was clearly in a recession and what it needed was a little tender loving care. What it got from the Fed was a fast one-two to the gut. Instead of the money supply growing at a 4½ percent to 5 percent rate, as the FOMC had ordered, the money supply was now shrinking at a distressing rate and would continue to shrink well into the spring. Between that shrinking money supply and what the Fed did on March 14, it guaranteed the recession would be a brutish one.

Through it all the Fed never seemed to grasp that it had created the recession and that what it was doing was making the recession worse. Once the Fed caught on, it then yanked us out of recession by creating money in prodigious quantities—starting the whole inflation-recession-inflation cycle all over again.

In the end, we got nothing worse for 1980 than the moderate contraction in real GNP the Fed had forecast back in February. The Fed could (and did) pat itself on the back for a job well done. What really happened, of course, was that the Fed first slammed the economy to the ground and then force-fed it back to vigorous recovery. Nor did the recession, nasty as it was, slow inflation one bit. The Fed has had some bad years before, but 1980 was something else again.

The New York Story

In any event, once the FOMC's directive is written, the story shifts to downtown New York and to the towering, neo-Florentine palace that the Federal Reserve Bank of New York calls home. The trading room is on the eighth floor of the building, and while the average person hasn't the foggiest idea the room even exists, its role in our economic lives is crucial.

The trading room is tastefully done in orange and beige—or was in 1980. A new, bigger, and more imposing room is now in the planning stages. There are ten traders—men and women, black and white. In return for trading $750 billion worth of securities each year, they earn between $13,500 and $33,500 a year, depending on experience.

They are anonymous people—simply voices on the telephone to the traders for the government bond dealers. It's quite possible for a Fed trader to deal with the trader at a Wall Street firm for years—trading trillions of dollars of issues over that time—without their ever meeting face to face. Actually, it's common for someone to work for the Fed for a few years and then go on to a Wall Street house, where a trader in Treasury issues might make $250,000 a year.

What the desk in New York got from Washington was a very broad statement of policy aims. It's up to the desk to make the necessary jiggles, day by day, to hit the targets the FOMC has set. The desk has been told, in effect, to drive the car at an average 50 miles per hour. To do that will mean sometimes racing 70 miles per hour, and sometimes bringing the car to a dead halt.

The Fed has proved it can always hit an interest-rate target by buying enough securities (and so feeding new money into the banking system) when the federal funds rate is rising to bring it back down, and by selling enough securities (and so pulling money out of the banking system) when the federal funds rate is falling to bring it back up. All it takes to control rates is money—sometimes, unfortunately, a great deal of money. Or, if the Fed were willing to forget about trying to control the cost of money, it could, through its exclusive franchise to create high-powered money, control the money supply with at least fair precision.

To hit an interest-rate target while keeping money growing at the desired rate is far more difficult—not so much patting your head while rubbing your stomach as trying to play a tuba while riding a bicycle. Why the Fed believes it can do both—in the face of all evidence to the contrary—defies rational explanation. The Fed, as noted elsewhere, hopes to do better in controlling the supply of money now that it's willing to surrender some control over rates. It plainly isn't willing to surrender enough control over rates, and now the Fed has lost control over both the cost of money and the supply.

Be that as it may, the trading desk still is the very front lines of monetary policy and will remain so indefinitely— perpetually snatching defeat from the jaws of victory.

The desk starts to come alive around 9 A.M., although it will be several hours before it makes its first trade. By the time the officials who run the desk arrive, it's known how well the dollar is doing overseas. The desk next finds out how the U.S. financial markets are opening, and about the financial position of the banks. Are the banks so flush with reserves that there will be little demand for federal funds, or so strapped that the demand will be enormous? Desk officials sharpen their feel of the market by consulting each morning with representatives of a different group of government-bond dealers.

By 11:15, New York has a good idea of what it will do that day. Now it's ready to get down to business, and that means the daily conference call around the Fed system at which an actual strategy for the day is set. In New York the call is handled by the System Open Market Account Manager— these days a veteran of both the Treasury and the Fed named Peter Sternlight. In Washington, the call involves someone from the research staff, usually joined by a Fed governor and, in tense times, by the chairman. Also on the line each morning is a regional bank president who is a voting member of the FOMC. Everyone gets in his two cents, and by the time the phones are hung up, there's agreement on what the desk will do next.

On this day, say the demand for bank loans is a little stronger than the Fed would like to see it. Further, the federal funds rate is low enough that banks will want to borrow all they can so they can lend some more. So the Fed will push the funds rate a little higher, to a level where some banks will no longer find it worthwhile to borrow. To accomplish that, the desk will sell $500 million worth of Treasury bills. Reserve accounts of banks will be charged to pay for those bills, and those reserves will disappear from sight—and from the economy.

Each trader has a telephone console with direct links to every government-bond dealer. The traders are quickly told what the Fed wants to do—sell $500 million of bills at the highest price it can get. The selling (and the buying on another day) is handled through the "go-around." The traders grab their phones, fingers punch buttons, and within a minute or so each bond dealer has been asked to bid on Treasury bills for sale by the Fed. The dealers never know how much the Fed is selling, simply that it's selling. A minute or two more, and the dealers call back with their bids. On this day, say the dealers offer to buy $2 billion of bills. The Fed quickly decides which bids it will accept, the dealers are notified, and a half-billion dollars of bank reserves are on their way to oblivion. By selling bills, the Fed has reduced the total supply of reserves among banks and that, in turn, has pushed up the federal funds rate by a little bit. Loans that might have been made before will not be made now, and a tiny amount of inflationary pressure has been removed from the economy.

The same go-around would be used if the Fed were buying, and accomplished as quickly. On some days, that one trade would do it for the desk. Other days the Fed might be in the market several times—sometimes trading for itself, sometimes for the account of a customer, which almost always is a foreign government.

There are further refinements the Fed can make. A purchase or sale of bills is for keeps. It can also add or take away reserves for just a day or two. It can do a repurchase agreement, or "repo." Here it will contract with a bond dealer to buy Treasury issues for cash with the dealer agreeing to buy the securities back at a slightly higher price in a day or two. The dealer has borrowed money for a couple of days at a competitive rate, while the Fed has put reserves into the financial system for a couple of days. Or it can do a matched sale, or "reverse repo"—selling securities to a dealer for a few days and so pulling some reserves out of the banking system for a short time.

Presumably, as the Fed concentrates less on stabilizing interest rates and concentrates more on stabilizing the money supply, there will be new wrinkles and refinements.

The basic function of the desk won't change, though. This is where money is born and where it dies—perhaps the most important room in the nation after the Oval Office of the President. At times it's even more important than the Oval Office, since the best-laid economic plans of the President could come a cropper there if the Fed creates too much or too little money. If all works as it's supposed to, the result is economic bliss. More often, the trading desk is the breeding ground for inflation and recession.

Chapter **6**

Why You Can't Make Money Grow Like Magic and Your Banker Can

GROW THE perfect lawn, and still, one fine spring day, a lonely dandelion will appear. Ignore it and suddenly your lawn will be dotted with more dandelions than you can count. Let the Federal Reserve create one lonely dollar, and before you know it the banking system has turned it into many dollars through the magical process known as "multiple expansion."

No single bank works this magic, but the banking system can and does, every day. And while the average banker would have a hard time explaining this, it isn't as mystifying as it sounds.

Recall that the Fed doesn't create money in the sense of something you can carry in your pocket and spend, but rather it creates new bank reserves—high-powered money —which won't become money until a bank makes a loan and creates a deposit. It fattens the reserve accounts banks keep with their local Federal Reserve bank when it pays for securities bought by its open-market trading desk.

Having created high-powered money, the Fed steps aside. It's up to the rest of us—bankers and borrowers working in concert—to turn each high-powered dollar into lots of real, spendable dollars. The only limit on how many new dollars can grow from each high-powered dollar is that a fraction of every dollar must be set aside as a reserve. If banks could make full use of every high-powered dollar, with nothing held back in reserve, they could create new dollars until the world ran out of zeros.

The process of turning high-powered money into real money begins when someone wants to borrow from a bank with enough idle reserves to make the loan. Once upon a time you actually got gold or silver or currency when you borrowed. For more than a century, though, you've gotten a deposit in a checking account. The only limit on the bank's ability to lend is that it must have enough reserves to back the new deposit created by the loan.

If no one wanted to borrow, the new reserves created by the Fed would remain unused—monetary Cinderellas no one invited to the ball. What turned the Depression of the thirties into the Great Depression was that no one wanted to borrow —no one wanted to turn a dollar of high-powered money into several dollars of real money. As noted elsewhere, different theorists offer different theories as to why no one wanted to borrow. Still that's ancient history, and finding borrowers hasn't been a problem for a long time. Nor, most of the time, has the Fed been shy about providing banks with sufficient reserves to make new loans—the $5 trillion Americans owe to someone else being proof enough of that.

How You Help Make Money

So there you are, you and your friendly neighborhood banker, at the very heart of the creation of money—in the front lines of that process called multiple expansion.

Picture this: It's a beautiful, spring morning. The birds are singing, the sky is dotted with fleecy clouds. In just a week you're off on the vacation of your life—two wonderful weeks in American Samoa, and every penny you have in the world is pledged to pay for that vacation. Yet this morning you leap from bed unsatisfied. You know, before this day ends, that in order to make your vacation complete, you must possess a Whiz-Bang camera with electronic flash, telephoto lens, and motor drive. The cost of a Whiz-Bang camera with electronic flash, telephoto lens, and motor drive is $837.50. If someone turned you upside down and shook you, they'd be lucky to find $5. But you and your banker are going to work some magic. Together you're going to create money.

You hop in your car, drive downtown, and call upon Jeremiah Flintheart, the loan officer of the Seventh National Bank. You're known at the bank as it holds the mortgage on your house and the title to your car. Flintheart knows you well, since he handled the loan in 1977 when you bought your dirt bike, and the loan in 1974 when you built a sauna. You have repaid both loans, are current on your mortgage and auto-loan payments, and are counted a valued customer of Seventh National.

Further, you're in luck because only yesterday the Federal Reserve decided the economy was looking a trifled peaked and so it fed some extra reserves into the banking system by buying $1 million in Treasury bills. That gave the banks another $1 million in high-powered money—new reserves that didn't exist until the Fed created them. Of that, $1,000 has been added to the reserve account of the Seventh National to be credited to the account of Lapis, Lazuli & Co., dealers in government securities.

Banks earn their money by lending it at a profit, and right now the Seventh National has some money it's itching to lend. Specifically, having gained $1,000 in new reserves, it will hold $162.50 as a reserve and lend out the remaining $837.50.

As it happens, $837.50 is exactly what you need, and in an instant, banker Flintheart has approved your loan and your checking account is now fatter by $837.50.

If you were to take that money home and bury it in your backyard, that would be the end of it. The creation of money from the new reserves the Fed provided would stop right there. But you aren't planning to bury it. You will spend it on that Whiz-Bang camera with electronic flash, telephoto lens, and motor drive, which costs $837.50.

You hurry to the camera store, buy the camera by writing a check, and hurry home. At lunchtime the camera dealer deposits your check in his account at the Third National, which is delighted to gain a new deposit in the amount of $837.50. The fractional reserve system is still at work, and of that $837.50 the Third National will set aside $136.09—leaving $701.41 which can be loaned.

At that point I appear, having just seen the most amazing bicycle in the whole world—24 speeds, titanium frame, the works. It costs $701.41, of which I haven't a penny. But I do have a friendly consumer loan officer at the Third National who is only too glad to loan me the $701.41. I hasten off with my money, and within moments, having paid for the bike with a check for $701.41, I am pedaling away for dear life.

We're still dealing with that $1,000 in reserves which the Fed put into play when it paid Lapis, Lazuli for the Treasury bill, and which became money when banker Flintheart made you the loan. But now that $1,000 has bought a camera for $837.50 and a bike for $701.41—$1,538.91 in all.

But we are not yet done. The bike dealer deposits my check at his bank, the Fifth National. Of the $701.41, the bank will hold $113.98 as a reserve against this new deposit, leaving $587.43 to lend to someone else. At that point your cousin Elmer appears at the Fifth National with an insatiable yen for a power mower with all the attachments, which costs $587.43, including tax. Enriched by a loan for $587.43 from the Fifth National, Elmer hastens off to buy the power mower.

We're still dealing with that $1,000 in high-powered money created by the Fed. But now the $1,000 has bought a camera outfit for $837.50, a bike for $701.41, and a power mower for $587.43—or $2,126.34 in all.

Nor is that the end of it. The hardware-store owner who sold Elmer the mower deposits the check for $587.43 in his bank, the Ninth National. Setting aside $95.46 as a reserve against the deposit, the Ninth National has $491.97 to lend. Money creation goes on and on—each incremental increase smaller than the last, but multiple expansion happening just the same. The original $1,000 could grow to $5,000 and more, and while the arithmetic will change as the new reserve levels mandated by the Depository Institutions etc., etc., etc. come into play, the basic process will not.

A bank could invest the money rather than lend it, but that wouldn't stop multiple expansion. Banks buy Treasury bills because they're a supersafe investment and because the market is so vast they can be sold in an instant should a big borrower happen along in need of a loan. Banks also buy municipal bonds—those issued by cities and states—because the interest earned on municipal bonds is exempt from federal income tax, and banks, like everyone else, want to pay as little in taxes as possible.

Still, the bank must pay for the securities it bought—crediting the account directly if the seller was a customer, or shifting reserves from its account at the Fed to the reserve account of another bank if the seller does his banking elsewhere. The act of transferring the money to someone else—whether by making a loan or by buying a security—would keep the money in play, allowing the process of creating new money to go on.

But There Are Limits

In practice, the banking system won't create $5,000 from each $1,000 in new reserves. There are too many variables, too many decisions by too many people.

The owner of the camera store might be working a tax dodge. Instead of depositing your check in his account, he might cash it and smuggle the cash to a numbered bank account in Switzerland. In that case, the process of money creation in the U.S. would stop, but the Swiss bank would put the money to work creating new money for the Swiss banking system.

There's further the matter of how fast money gets turned over. The faster we do it, the faster we will create money from high-powered money. If the camera, the bike, and the mower were all bought the same day, the process of money creation would be very rapid. Actually there would be lapses between each transaction, since it takes time for each check to clear and for each loan to be approved.

When a company borrows from a bank, it doesn't mean to use all the money. Banking practice dictates that a portion of the money—maybe 20 percent—will stay in the account as a "compensating balance." (Class helps. If you're a loan shark, it's called vigorish. If you're a banker, it's a compensating balance.)

Finally, no bank can afford to lend to the absolute limit of its reserve position, since it never knows how much its reserve position will be drawn down on a given day. When a bank pays out cash it's reducing its reserves, since cash on hand counts as part of its reserves. Checks written on the bank and cashed elsewhere will come back through the clearing process to the nearest Federal Reserve bank. There they will be charged against the bank's reserve position. Because the bank can't know how much cash it will pay out or how many checks will land on its reserve position in a day, it has to leave some idle reserves just in case.

Banks must settle up once a week—proving to the Fed they have sufficient reserves to cover deposits. There are ways to make up for a shortage of reserves, and ways to find reserves to make more loans. A bank can borrow in the federal funds market, borrowing for a day or two reserves from a bank that has some extra reserves around. It can borrow from the Fed's discount window, paying the prevailing discount rate. But borrowing federal funds is mostly for the giant banks, and the Fed takes a dim view of banks that turn up too often at the discount window. Most banks simply allow themselves some leeway—never quite loaning up to the limit.

Money moves around a lot faster than it used to, thanks to modern-day transportation and communications and the use of computers. Checks, for instance, are cleared far more quickly than they used to be. In the coming age of electronic banking, transactions will be nearly instantaneous: You buy the camera for $837.50 and the dealer's bank account is instantly credited. That will speed up the creation of money—and compound the Fed's job of trying to manage it.

All caveats aside, you can draw certain conclusions about money creation. If you define money as currency and demand deposits, banks create $2.50 in money for every $1 in high-powered money. If you take the broadest possible definition of money, banks create $11 for each $1 of high-powered money. The Fed may not always choose to act on that knowledge, and often, in fact, it likes to pretend it has no idea of how much money can be wrung out of each high-powered dollar. The truth, once again, is the Fed can control the level of reserves in the banking system with great precision, and so it could control the money supply with at least some degree of precision. Why it argues otherwise is one of life's enduring mysteries.

So far we've talked only about money creation—multiple expansion. There's also the "uncreating" of money, which the Fed accomplished by removing high-powered money from the banking system. That, of course, is done by selling Treasury bills to a dealer in such securities. In selling $1 million in Treasury bills, the Fed will remove $1 million from the dealer's account with a bank, and $1 million from the bank's reserve account with the Fed.

That's high-powered money being wiped out: the $1 million supporting several times that much in deposits. When money is destroyed, things can get dire in a hurry. New loans won't be made, outstanding loans will be called in, and the banks will sell some of their holdings of Treasury and municipal issues to generate some fast cash.

There's a profound danger in the Fed creating too much high-powered money, as it does most of the time, because the financial system will quickly translate that into lots of real money, and too much money, relative to demand, is inflationary. But there's also a profound danger when the Fed stops creating high-powered money, as it did in early 1980. Then multiple expansion turns into multiple contraction, and we're all in the economic soup.

Chapter 7
Why the Government Is Dangerous to Your Financial Health

IT's A comfort to have the Federal Reserve around as all-purpose scapegoat, to be blamed for all that has gone wrong with our economy. And the Fed does deserve a goodly share of the blame: trying to manage our money when it doesn't understand how money works in the economy, trying to control the cost of money while the supply runs out of control. There have been days, weeks, months, even whole years, when the governors of the Federal Reserve should have collectively hung their heads in shame.

Tempting as it is, though, you can't put all the blame on the Fed. We employ others to manage our economy—the President and Congress—and they haven't done such a great job, either: spending and borrowing as though there were no tomorrow, to a point where tomorrow is no sure thing.

And then there's this grim thought for the age of new money (and for those betting on President Reagan to turn things around): It may be the American economy has grown so vast and so complex that no one can manage it. The Fed,

124

the White House, and the Congress may have failed because we've been asking them to do the undoable.

Vast our economy is, past the point of comprehension. It's three times the size of Japan's economy, four times that of Germany, eight times that of Britain, and ten times that of Canada. The interest on our national debt was $65 billion last year. In all the world there are scarcely a score of countries whose economies amount to $65 billion. The gross national product of Israel was $16 billion in 1979, which is what we spent on shoes. The gross national product of South Africa was $57 billion, and we spent that dining out.

But it isn't enough to grasp the awesome size of our economy. You also have to understand how complex it has become. Our $2½ trillion economy includes an Exxon and an IBM. It also includes a North Dakota wheat farmer, a Florida fisherman, and a New York City chestnut vendor. Managing our economy is a perpetual balancing act: trying to satisfy both Exxon and the chestnut vendor without doing irreparable harm to either.

Borrowers want low interest rates, lenders want high interest rates. Consumers want low food prices, farmers want high food prices. The oil-producing states of the South and West want higher oil prices, while the urban North wants lower oil prices. The elderly want Social Security indexed to inflation, but each hike in the Social Security tax means less for workers to spend and invest.

Everyone wants lower taxes, but no one wants government to spend less on their piece of the economy. We're all against inflation—until we're asked to take smaller gains in wages or profits to bring the inflation rate down. We all want more, even when there's no more to give, and our demands have never been more strident than in this age of new money. Ronald Reagan swept the land in 1980 by promising lower taxes and less government spending, and he got Congress to buy both in 1981. Yet to cut taxes without cutting spending is to threaten worse inflation than any we've known, and so the President must further cut the budget in future years. To the extent that he does keep cutting spending, however, he'll risk driving away potential voters when he's up for reelection; if we demand punishment for those who brought us inflation, we punish even harder those who seek to take it away.

When it comes to our economy, we're like kids in a toy store. There are marvelous things all around, and we want everything we see. I want a new car. You want a new split-level ranch house with four bedrooms and a patio. The Boston Red Sox want a new third baseman. General Motors wants a new assembly line. The Defense Department wants a new aircraft carrier.

It would take so much money to satisfy all our demands that the inevitable inflation would leave our money with no value at all. But to satisfy none of the demands would leave us sullen and mutinous and in a state of chronic economic depression.

All the diverse elements that make up our economy will sort through those demands, deciding who gets what. I get my car but your house must wait until next year. The Red Sox get their third baseman, but General Motors must make do with its existing assembly lines. The Defense Department doesn't get its aircraft carrier, but it gets a missile cruiser and a better combat boot. When the shopping spree is over, some of us leave the toy store smiling, some of us crying, and the economy rolls on.

Washington Calls the Plays

There was a time when the management of our economy was both decentralized and disorganized. The crucial decisions were made by bankers and businessmen around the country. Private banks created our money and decisions on how to spend it were made locally.

Today the crucial economic decisions are made in Washington by virtue of the massive role the government plays in the economy and by virtue of the Federal Reserve's exclusive ability to create money. Not only does the government spend so much—over $600 billion in the latest fiscal year—but the way it spends influences the whole economy. If it spends on guns, one sector of the economy will benefit—defense contractors, their employees, and the regions of the country in which defense industries are located. If it spends on the cities, quite another sector will benefit.

Washington also controls the other side of the equation—revenues—because it writes our tax laws. Individuals paid $244 billion and corporations another $72 billion in income taxes in 1980—not counting Social Security, excise, gift and estate taxes, or the taxes levied by state and local government.

We live in a complex national economy within a complex world economy, and the job of managing our economy involves a lot of people. The White House and Congress together give us fiscal policy—the way government collects and spends our money. The Federal Reserve handles monetary policy—managing the cost and availability of money. There are dozens of federal agencies whose decisions have vast economic consequences, from the Interstate Commerce Commission, which regulates the cost of ground transport, to the new Commodity Futures Trading Commission, which polices the burgeoning commodity markets.

The White House starts by sketching in broad strokes a master plan for our economy each year. The President and his cohorts decide how much the government will spend and how it will spend it—decisions shaped by the President's thinking on how fast the economy should grow, and at what rates of unemployment and inflation. The President and his advisers further decide how much they can pluck from taxpayers, and whether the tax laws should be changed to produce more or less revenue.

If the economy is weak, the President can ask for more federal spending. That should help the economy by more than the amount federal spending is increased, since spending begets more spending. The President could decide the economy needs lower taxes so more money stays in the hands of taxpayers. When John Kennedy became President in 1961, his economic advisers decided the economy had grown slowly in the late 1950s because taxes were too high. The result was the big federal tax cut of 1964. In the view of President Reagan's economic advisers, we need sharply lower tax rates now to get us to save and invest more in the future of our economy—inflation having pushed so many of us into such high tax brackets we have lost all incentive to do either. The result was the tax cut of 1981.

The President could decide the economy is running too fast and needs to be slowed down—through less government spending, or higher taxes, or both. Presidents have seldom opted for either less spending or higher taxes, but the remedy is there.

The President could decide the economy is fundamentally sound and needs no more than some fine tuning—a little less spent on defense and a little more on housing, or less for farmers and more for cities.

The job of drafting this economic master plan takes months and draws on virtually every unit of government. Each decision is both economic and political. How will Russia perceive a cut in defense spending? How will farmers vote if they're asked to take a smaller slice of the pie? If spending on the cities is cut, will a Harlem or a Watts go up in flames?

The master plan is unveiled in stages very early in the year. There's first the President's State of the Union message in late January, just after Congress reassembles in Washington. Presidents use the State of the Union message to outline economic policy in very broad terms.

There's also the annual Economic Report of the President, which is, more precisely, the annual report of the President's three-member Council of Economic Advisers (each of the three a ranking economist drafted to do temporary duty for the President). The President gets a few pages in the front of the report, which runs about three hundred pages, and Presidents use the space to boast about the robust health of the economy, even if it's only a few inches away from disaster. The meat of the report is the Council's assessment of where the economy has been, where it is, and where it's going. Since the economists who advise the President are invariably from the President's party, the report tends to be long on back patting and short on critical analysis. The past is never as bad as we remembered it and the new day adawning will always be cloudless and sunny.

And finally there's the federal budget, sent to Congress in late January for the fiscal year starting the following October 1. The State of the Union message and the Economic Report of the President are wishful thinking. The budget is the real thing: the cold, hard numbers on how much the government means to spend, how much it hopes to earn and how big will be the federal budget surplus (almost never) or the budget deficit (almost always).

The Following Is Pure Fiction

To simplify things, say the economy is doing very nicely this year, being in need of neither fiscal stimulation nor fiscal restraint. There's no sector of the economy crying out for help and no sector of the economy receiving such a disproportionate share of the national wealth that common decency requires some be taken away. The existing tax laws are judged to be sound and equitable and in no need of modification. And so the budget leaves the White House in a state of perfect balance: a precise match between how much the government expects to spend and how much it expects to earn.

The complete budget for 1981, with supporting documents, runs 2,400 pages, weighs nine pounds, and is 1,000 pages longer and twice as heavy as the Manhattan telephone directory. A lot of people have sweated blood preparing it, and some backs have been sorely strained carrying it up to Capitol Hill. The instant a budget reaches Congress it is attacked as though by lions, each member of Congress regarding it as a vile document in which the most deserving of projects have been slighted in favor of worthless ventures.

The government of Chutney, known far and wide as a hotbed of repression and ritual cannibalism, is to receive $100 million in military aid while not a penny has been set aside for the domestic growers of gladiolus bulbs. The military base in my state will be shut down, while the one in your state will be enlarged. Starting with the House and Senate Budget Committees, each and every page of the budget will be picked over until scarcely a page of the original document remains untouched. Hundreds of witnesses, from inside government and out, will be hauled before one committee of Congress or another. Each spending item in the budget must be authorized by Congress and the actual money to be spent must be appropriated, and that takes months.

By the time Congress is done—all the spending authorized, all the money appropriated, and the tax laws changed if necessary—it's usually about thirty seconds before the start of the new fiscal year. Now the government knows precisely how much it has to spend, and we taxpayers have been told if our rates are going up, coming down, or will stay unchanged.

The Administration's hopes and dreams for the economy are implicit in the budget it sent to Congress. Congress has had some thoughts of its own: adding some money here,

taking some away there—modifying, but for all the storm
and fury seldom changing in any dramatic fashion, the President's plan for the economy.

To the Federal Reserve falls the job of keeping the economy on course, day-to-day, through the new year, because
it's the government agency best equipped to do so, if it can
be done at all. It takes forever and a day to get a budget
through Congress, and while Congress can usually be per-
suaded to cut taxes, it will almost never agree to raise them.

By contrast, the Federal Reserve is a leaping gazelle—
able to move swiftly should the economy appear to be going
off track. It can create money or destroy it in the twinkling
of an eye. It can raise or lower interest rates at will. By
changing the bank-reserve requirements, it can suddenly
freeze or unfreeze a lot of money in the banking system.
Best of all, since Federal Reserve governors are appointed
for 14-year terms, they needn't fear reprisals from the voters. If harsh things must be done to the economy, both the
President and Congress are delighted to have the Fed do it
—and to take the heat ever after.

In our example, however, the Fed—given that perfectly
balanced budget in a tranquil economy—would do little
more than sit in Washington and think happy thoughts.
There's no federal budget deficit to be financed, so the Fed
doesn't have to create new money to finance it. The prevailing economic winds are gentle zephyrs, so the Fed doesn't
have to do much leaning.

And now that Washington has pointed the way, the rest of
us take over. It's our turn to make the economy our government has given us work. The President proposes, Congress
disposes, the Fed (in this example at least) reposes, and the
millions of entities that make up the economy, from consumers to multinational corporations, do the work. Banks determine which borrowers get money. Investors, by buying one
security and not another, determine which companies can
raise money in the capital markets. Customers decide which

businesses thrive and which don't. My employer raises my salary so I buy my new car. Your employer is finding times hard and there are no raises—and so no new house. Fans, by coming out to the ball park or staying away, decide whether Boston's new third baseman was worth the money.

And Now the Grim Reality

But so much for fiction—and the notion of economic tranquility and a perfectly balanced buget is, of course, total fiction. There hasn't been a moment of economic tranquility in fifteen years, and the federal budget has been in deficit in every year but eight since World War Two, and in deficit in every year but one (1969) in the past two decades. The cumulative deficits of the federal government in the past decade came to $400 billion and the total debt of the U.S. in early 1981 was fast approaching $1 trillion. Seldom in those 15 years has the Federal Reserve gained control over our money, and the economy has seen only inflation, broken by terrible recessions.

Our government didn't always operate this way, trying actively to manage the economy, running vast budget deficits, creating money by the carload. But fashions in government change.

To think like an economist you must know economist jokes. The hoariest economist joke of all involves the father who returns to his college to visit his son, who is now a student. Still around is the economics professor who first taught the father and now teaches the son. The father is amazed to find the final exam in economics is the same one he took years before. "I can't believe it," says the father to the professor. "You haven't changed a single question in twenty-five years."

To which the professor replies, "You didn't understand economics when you were a student and you don't understand it now. In economics, it isn't the questions that change, only the answers.''

The answer, pre-1929, was that government kept hands off the economy. The economy was seen as inherently stable—the monetarists firmly in command—and all attempts to tamper with it could only lead to disaster. No one liked depressions, but they were considered necessary evils, needed periodically to purge excesses from the economy. Depressions, it was further argued, would cure themselves, and they should be of no concern to the government. The role of government, under the rules of classic laissez-faire capitalism, was to be seen little and heard less—to appear only in times of war and to disappear as quickly as possible once the war was over.

Only in wartime did our government run a deficit, and it was a thrifty government the rest of the time. Just once between the beginning of our country and 1917, did federal spending top $1 billion in a single year, and that was in the Civil War year of 1865. Against our trillion-dollar debt today, the national debt was only $2½ billion when we entered World War One and only $72 billion as late as 1942. Because the government spent so little, except in wartime, it never had the opportunity to develop much influence over the economy.

The government always turned out our coinage, and in 1863 it created and took command of a national banking system. The Interstate Commerce Commission came along in 1887 and the antitrust division of the Justice Department in 1903. The Federal Reserve and Federal Trade Commission both appeared just before World War One. But these were the exceptions, and by and large government knew its place.

It was the Great Depression that changed everything: the economy a shambles, every fourth American out of work by 1933. It got so bad and lasted so long that the old rules went out the window and government was invited in. Franklin

Roosevelt came to balance the budget and stayed to sire an economic revolution.

The government quit being passive and turned active—heeding the advice of John Maynard Keynes that when the private sector couldn't do the job it was not only the right but the duty of the government to take over. Like a modest maiden, the government blushed becomingly, proclaimed itself unworthy of the honor—and then grabbed hold of the American economy with a viselike grip that hasn't relaxed for an instant ever since.

Initially the government made its presence felt mostly by creating new agencies to regulate the economy. In 1933 government won the authority to regulate banking and the securities market. In 1934 it took over regulation of communications—broadcasting, telephone, and telegraph—and housing. The next year brought the Wagner Act, which extended government regulation to labor relations, and the same year brought Social Security. And so it went—each year new federal agencies were created, and each year the government's sway extended over a new area of the economy.

In terms of reviving a stricken economy, the New Deal was a flop. At no time during the 1930s, despite the preachings of Keynes, did federal spending amount to 10 percent of gross national product. Now, it's 20 percent and more of GNP, when the need for massive federal spending is more debatable. There were still 10 million unemployed when World War II began, and not until we entered the war did the Great Depression finally end. Yet the pattern was set. The federal government would be allowed near-total control over the American economy. In return, the government promised that, whatever else it might do, it would guarantee we'd never suffer another Great Depression.

There was no need to formalize this during the war, with the nation basking in the prosperity that wars invariably bring. There was, however, deep concern that we'd fall back into depression once the war ended; and so the bargain was written into law with the Employment Act of 1946. It set as a basic goal of government policy the perpetual maintenance of full employment. The definition of full employment has changed through the years—4 percent unemployment was regarded as too high in the early 1960s, while 6 percent is considered full employment today—but government has done its best (or its worst) to live up to that promise.

There was no postwar depression. Consumer demand exploded, industry expanded to meet that demand, and for two decades we lived through a remarkable period of economic strength and low inflation.

There were a few troublesome intervals—during the Korean war, for instance, when inflation threatened to get out of hand. The late 1950s produced slow growth and 7 percent unemployment as the Federal Reserve battled an inflation that never went above 3.6 percent in any year and usually was far lower. Richard Nixon always blamed the Fed for creating a recession in 1960 that he believed cost him the Presidency. When Nixon became President in 1969 he picked a close ally to be chairman of the Fed—economist Arthur Burns.

John Kennedy became President in 1961, and to push the economy back to full speed, he brought along the "New Economics" and the most active Administration since the New Deal. Taxes were cut, business gained incentives to invest more, and the U.S. entered the longest period of sustained economic growth in history: nearly a decade without a recession. Unemployment fell from 6.7 percent of the work force in 1961 to 3½ percent in 1969. Yet inflation stayed under 2 percent through the first half of the decade and still was only 3 percent in 1967.

The Coming Storm

Pride, however, goeth before a fall. There's nothing like gentle breezes and dead-calm seas to convince the novice sailor he can sail with the best of them. Having had no recession for so long, and no inflation to speak of either, we convinced ourselves that we had finally learned to avoid both. Economists couldn't say for certain how they'd accomplished this, but none doubted they had.

In fact, the worst economic storm since the Depression was already starting to boil up, and the economists and the makers of economic policy were so busy congratulating themselves that they never saw it coming. The gentle breezes were turning into gales, the dead-calm seas were giving way to great roiling waves, and shortly we would all be engulfed.

The event, of course, was the Vietnam war—not the war per se, but how we paid for it.

Wars breed inflation unless great care is taken to counter it. More money is spent, peacetime standards of prudence are cast aside in the name of hastening victory, and—unless government works hard to check it—the nation goes off on an inflationary spiral. The worst inflation in American history came during the Revolution, the second worst during the Civil War—each time fed by vast issues of paper money.

We took strong measures during World War Two—strict controls on wages, prices, and profits; tough limits on borrowing and lending—and we escaped the war years with little inflation and the postwar period with only a couple of bad years. We were less careful during the Korean war, and for a time inflation got out of control.

During Vietnam we did virtually nothing to control inflation and we're still paying for that today.

Lyndon Johnson saw himself in a box—obliged to fight a

war and, yet, because it was an unpopular war, obliged to minimize the damage the war was doing to our economy. He tried to finance both the shooting war and his war against poverty, promising us both guns and butter when, in fact, we could only afford one or the other. Not until 1968 did he finally ask for higher taxes to pay for the war, and to offset the inflationary forces the war had unleashed. Worst of all, Johnson and some of his aides lied shamelessly about the true cost of the war—not only to the American people, but to those in government who were supposed to be managing the economy.

Only in 1966 did the Federal Reserve learn how much the war was really costing, and only then did it begin to tighten money to counter the emerging inflation, a measure that, says William McChesney Martin, Jr., then the Fed chairman, was a year too late. President Johnson's 1968 tax increase—actually a 10 percent surtax on top of the regular income tax—was three years too late.

And so the war was financed by running huge federal budget deficits, with the Fed, as usual, creating the money to cover those deficits—an approach that has bred inflation in every country that ever tried it. The deficit was $1.5 billion in 1965 and $25 billion by 1968. By 1968, the last gold and silver backing came off the dollar, allowing the Fed to create money at will—and create it it did, in vast and inflationary quantities, and with entirely predictable consequences. Consumer-price inflation averaged 1.4 percent between 1952 and 1964. The rate was 1.7 percent in 1965, 4.2 percent in 1968, and 5.9 percent in 1970.

Snatching Defeat from the Jaws of Victory

Even then we might have avoided all that ails our economy today. Instead, the past decade has been marked by an unbroken string of errors in judgment, unanticipated shocks to the system from within (the loss of control over the economy when everyone was busy with Watergate, being an example), unanticipated shocks to the system from without (the deadly spiral in world oil prices being the best example), and plain bad luck. Not for a moment in 15 years has either the White House or the Federal Reserve gained control over the economy, and not for a moment in 15 years have we known economic peace. We have now reached a point where, far from regarding inflation and recession as evils to be avoided, we seem to regard both as essential tools of government economic management.

There's a reason for running deficits in the federal budget. A depressed economy will benefit from the additional federal spending. But the government has gotten into the habit of always running deficits—in good times or bad. Take an occasional sip of whiskey, say doctors, and it's good for the system. Drink it day in and day out and you're a drunk. Our government has gotten itself drunk on deficits.

There was a $3 billion budget surplus in 1969—much of it done with mirrors, but a surplus just the same. That turned into a $3 billion deficit in 1970, followed by deficits of $23 billion in both 1971 and 1972. The deficit shrank in 1973 and again in 1974 (when we could have used more spending to avert recession) but exploded to $45 billion in 1975 and to $66 billion in 1976. In the Korean war year of 1952, total government spending came to $58 billion. In 1976, that was the size of the budget deficit.

Jimmy Carter said he would balance our budget by 1980 if we put him in the White House. The actual deficit in 1980 was $59 billion. In March of 1980, Carter promised a budget surplus for fiscal 1981. Within four months the White House was talking about a $30 billion deficit for 1981, and by the spring of 1981, President Reagan was fighting to keep the deficit below $55 billion. Reagan, in turn, was promising a balanced budget in 1984, and few enough forecasters regard that as likely.

That has left the Federal Reserve a lot of winds to lean against. But each time the Fed has leaned against those winds it has leaned the wrong way, taking every error of government and compounding it.

The Fed was slow to tighten in 1966 and too quick to make money easy during the mini-recession of 1967. It feared the 10 percent surtax in 1968 would slash consumer spending, and so it poured money into the economy. In fact, the tax hike had little impact on consumer spending and the extra money merely fed inflation.

Plainly the Fed was far too easy with money in 1972—one of the most controversial moves it ever made. It could have been an innocent mistake by a Fed that, as usual, misread the economic signs—or it may have been a conscious decision by the Fed to insure Richard Nixon's not having to seek reelection during a recession. Arthur Burns, Fed chairman in 1972, recoils in horror at the suggestion that his Fed was trying to rig the game for Nixon. Still, Burns was a Nixon appointee, and the top White House adviser on the domestic economy before Nixon tapped him for the Fed.

In any case, the economy boomed, Nixon won in a landslide, and then—the result of complicity or simplicity at the Fed—we got, first, the worst inflation in peacetime history, followed by the worst slump since the Depression. Since then the Fed has mostly created too much money for an economy again swamped by inflation, until late 1979 and early 1980 when it stopped creating money and we fell into the recession of 1980.

There are mitigating circumstances—reasons why government economic policies, monetary and fiscal, appear so dreadful. We aren't alone in the world. We must blend our economy with the economies of more than 100 other countries, some of them very big and powerful. Policy failures are often the result of forces at play in lands far from our own.

The best example, of course, is the oil price explosion

since 1973, which has been a shock to the world economy of a magnitude never before experienced in peacetime. Oil-consuming nations paid oil-producing nations $250 billion in 1980, of which more than $60 billion came from the U.S. We spent 200 years building an industrial system based on cheap energy, and now we must change because energy is no longer cheap. The process of change is proving both disruptive and very inflationary.

And yet, massive as this change is, it needn't be as inflationary as our government is permitting it to be. We could have both OPEC oil and less inflation if our government had forced us to settle for fewer of the other things of life. That would have been painful, but really no more painful than today's inflation, and by and by we would have adapted. Instead, the government deliberately inflated our economy —creating more and more money so we could have expensive OPEC oil and still live approximately as we had become accustomed to living.

And, of course, it's a policy doomed to failure. The resultant inflation is overwhelming our economy and, ironically, it's also driving the price of oil ever higher. OPEC is paid for its oil in dollars, and as inflation cheapens the value of OPEC's dollars, the oil countries demand—and not altogether unreasonably—that they be paid still more dollars for their oil. If OPEC is the villain, our government is an accessory after the fact.

Further, there's the fact that we're a most demanding people, with our demands having grown more insistent over the years. And when government ignores those demands we create powerful blocs government can't ignore. Labor is organized, and so is business, and farmers, and women, and blacks, and the elderly, and the environmentalists. Each spending program in our budget represents a hard-fought victory for one or another of these blocs and none will surrender to budget-cutting without a struggle that will tie the budget-making process in knots. Balanced against a President Reagan who won by promising less government spending are powerful forces that want more government spending still—which is why it's no sure thing that the President can put a lid on spending and keep it there for very long, and why the age of new money will be around for a long time.

A buzzword of our age is "entitlements," as in "I'm entitled to that." And it is not easy to dismiss those demands. Who can be against a better shake for the poor, more jobs for blacks and women, a higher standard of living for workers, a better way of life for the elderly, or a reasonable return on capital for business and investors? Obviously we want our air and our water to be pure, the products we buy to be safe, and our land made secure against our enemies.

But economists have a favorite saying, which is: There's no free lunch. Everything costs something, even if the cost isn't immediately apparent. It costs more to hire and train an unskilled worker. It costs more to build a factory that doesn't pollute. It costs a fortune to provide health care to the elderly, and a fortune-and-a-half to defend our country.

We could settle for less, which we really don't want to do. We could have all that our government has to offer, if we would pay for it through higher taxes—which we want even less. Instead, we have demanded that government pay for today by borrowing from the future, and the Federal Reserve create enough money to pay for the resultant budget deficits. Government, ever willing to soothe those who cast the votes, has cheerfully obliged us, and the Federal Reserve has cheerfully obliged the government. We do pay for it, of course, in the form of higher inflation and reduced purchasing power, but that's at one remove, and we don't always make the connection.

Since we want so much but won't pay the price, it's next to impossible for government to fight inflation for very long even if government wanted to fight inflation for very long. We say we want inflation banished—but only as long as we don't feel it personally.

We railed against inflation in early 1980, demanding less spending and a balanced budget from the White House. Then came recession, and in a twinkling we were demanding more government spending and lower taxes, and lots more money, to ease the pain. We gave Ronald Reagan a mandate in 1980 to banish inflation. But if the price of less inflation is far fewer goodies from our government—as it surely must be—President Reagan is apt to find it a higher price than even those who put him in the White House are willing to pay.

Chapter 8
The New Banking: or Why Your Banker Sells Money Like Kellogg Sells Cornflakes

BEFORE THERE was a new money there was a new banking —the new banking being parent to the new money. And no one caught the essence of the new banking better than Mills B. Lane, a Georgia banker of a decade and more ago, whose habitual greeting was a hearty "Can I sell you any money?" The banker as parsimonious flintheart, loath to part with a dime, belongs to the dim and distant past. Today's banker sells money as fervently as Kellogg sells cornflakes, and there's a new money because bankers have learned to sell it so well.

The Federal Reserve creates money and the banking system expands it, and while there has been a lot of creating lately, there has also been a lot of expanding. All of us together—government, business, and the public—owe the banks $1¼ trillion. Every penny of it is money a banker sold to someone.

And that doesn't include the billions loaned by nonbank affiliates of the giant banking companies, the billions charged on bank credit cards, the billions loaned abroad by foreign offices of U.S. banks, or the billions of dollars of equipment, from computers to jet aircraft, owned by banks and leased to customers for a fee. There would be no age of new money had the banks not paid for so much of it. But the age of new money has further shaped and refined the banks, and banking is as different today from what it was two decades ago as a roller coaster is from a pony-cart ride. And all that has happened is merely prelude to what will come next to banking as electronic money moves in and as the new rules set by the Depository Institutions Deregulation and Monetary Control Act of 1980 take over.

Banks are no longer merely banks. Most have become holding companies since Citibank of New York showed the way in 1968. A holding company owns one or more banks that do what commercial banks have always done: take deposits, make loans, and, through their trust departments, manage the wealth of the wealthy. But the holding company can also own a variety of other businesses that the Federal Reserve has ruled have at least some marginal link to banking: various forms of business and consumer lending, equipment leasing, insurance, data processing, travel services, and more.

A bank holding company can't own a steel mill, but it can —and probably does—engage in any business in which the basic ingredient is money. And even ownership of a steel mill can't absolutely be ruled out. Big banks abroad can do a lot of things U.S. banks can't, and owning a nonfinancial business (including a steel mill) is one of the things many foreign banks can do. What goes on abroad could well go on here some day.

Where banks do business has also changed. A bank used to be a local institution, operating in a neighborhood, or a city, or sometimes a whole state, but unable to reach beyond that. Banks in other countries operate nationwide, and banks of the great trading countries have long operated worldwide.

But state laws limit where U.S. banks can operate, and very few states have been willing to let banks from other states into their midst. (One notable exception is Delaware, which in 1981 launched an aggressive drive to get out-of-state banks to open up in Delaware.) And except for a few hardy pioneers, U.S. banks were slow to move overseas.

The rush of U.S. companies abroad, and the pivotal role the dollar plays in international commerce, finally drew U.S. banks overseas in the 1960s and 1970s. Now almost every big U.S. bank has offices overseas, and giant Citicorp—the holding company that owns Citibank—operates in more than 90 countries and two-thirds of its profits come from abroad.

No U.S. bank can yet operate across state lines, but the laws that prohibit this can't touch the nonbank affiliates of the holding companies. The typical holding company today may, in addition to its banks, own a small loan company, operating in a few dozen states; a commercial finance company, operating in a dozen more states; and a leasing company, operating in several more states. Citicorp, beyond its international outposts, operates in 41 U.S. states and the District of Columbia.

And bankers have learned other ways to sidestep those laws. A California bank, no matter how big, couldn't open a branch in New York. It could, though, operate a "loan production" office in New York, staffed with eager bankers who solicit loans in the backyard of the giant New York banks. Most big banks now operate networks of loan production offices around the country, and most also have "Edge Act" offices in cities far from home.

Senator Walter Edge of New Jersey sponsored the act in 1919; it lets banks operate offices in other states, as long as those offices do only international banking. California's Bank of America is itself part of a holding company called BankAmerica Corp., which vies with Citicorp for position as the largest holding company. Each has more than $110 billion in assets. In 1980, Bank of America created a new sub-

sidiary just to operate its Edge Act offices. Were that
subsidiary independent, its $7 billion in assets would make it
the thirtieth-largest U.S. bank.

The New Style of Banking

The feature of the new banking most central to the age of
new money is the change in the way banking is carried out.

Until the dawn of the new banking two decades ago, banks
took deposits from the thrifty of the community, and when
sufficient deposits were on hand, a loan would be made. The
banker might buy lunch for a favored customer, but that was
as far as it went. Bankers then were noted for prudence, not
imagination, and if a lunch for a businessman or a toaster for
the occasional consumer who wandered in wouldn't draw
deposits, plainly nothing would.

A number of things happened at about the same time to
change that. Banks finally had acquired some talented young
managers after the Depression years when only the intellectually stunted chose a career in banking. By the early 1960s
these young people were moving toward the top—eager to
change an industry that hadn't changed much in 2,000
years.

Further, the U.S. economy was starting the longest boom
in history as the 1960s began, and everyone wanted money.
For those with money to lend, it was the very best of times.
Yet in the rush to finance the boom of the 1960s, the banks
were in danger of being left behind. The interesting financing
deals were being done in the stock market. In the competition for deposits, the commercial banks found themselves
losing ground to the thrift institutions—the savings and loan
associations and the savings banks.

The government sets limits on what institutions can pay
for deposits, with the Federal Reserve's Regulation Q applying to commercial banks, and comparable rules from other

regulators applying to the thrifts. These rate ceilings will soon vanish, thanks to still another provision of the Depository Institutions Deregulation etc., etc., etc., but they were very much in evidence in the early 1960s. And because of the way rate ceilings were administered, thrifts could pay a little more for deposits than could commercial banks. The rationale was that thrifts performed the socially useful function of financing housing for the masses, while commercial banks mostly loaned to the titans of business (which is why they are called "commercial" banks). That interest-rate advantage alone gave the thrifts an edge in competing for deposits. Also, the growth potential of the thrifts attracted some choice entrepreneurial spirits, and they, in turn, built some gigantic thrift institutions—particularly in California with its soaring population and its insatiable demand for housing. By the early 1960s the thrifts were pulling in deposits like mad—much of that at the expense of the banks.

Even the dimmest among the bankers came to realize that consumers represented a lush new market, and so the commercial banks finally went after the financial business of the masses instead of concentrating on the financial business of business. The more forbidding aspects of the typical bank— the barred windows at the teller's cage, for instance—came down and the public was invited in. You greeted the teller, not through a barred window, but across an open counter, as though you were buying a pound of flounder. That made banks easier to rob, but it brought more people in, and while thrifts could pay more for deposits, at least the commercial banks were back in the ball game.

Ironically, as the public began streaming in, the banks started losing the deposits of their traditional customers, the corporations. No longer were corporations willing to leave their money in checking accounts, which earned no interest. A corporation with extra cash would instead buy a Treasury bill, which did pay interest and which could be sold quickly when the corporation needed the cash.

Now the banks needed some way of holding onto corporate deposits. Specifically, they needed something that would be as liquid as money in a checking account, and pay interest competitive with a Treasury bill. One fine day in 1961, Citibank—then still known as First National City Bank of New York—accomplished all that by inventing the negotiable certificate of deposit, or CD, which did for banking what the jet engine did for commercial aviation.

A CD is a piece of paper acknowledging that so much money ($100,000 or more) has been deposited for a set period of time (30 days or more until 1980, and 14 days or more since), and that the money, plus an agreed-upon amount of interest, will be repaid when the CD matures. The Fed's interest rate ceilings didn't apply to CDs, so a bank could pay depositors more than they could earn from a Treasury bill. It was a negotiable CD because it was a "bearer" certificate, meaning the money would go to whoever physically held the CD when it matured. That, in turn, meant the original owner could sell the CD to someone else with a minimum of bother. Wall Street soon created a trading market in CDs, and a corporation could sell a certificate of deposit almost as quickly as it could a Treasury bill.

Say Consolidated Buttermilk has $100,000 it won't need for a month or so. In an earlier day it might have let the money sit in a checking account, earning no interest. By 1961, Consolidated probably would put the money in a Treasury bill with a month left to maturity. But now it had another choice. It could buy a CD from Citibank (or from the other banks that quickly copied Citibank), which paid more than a Treasury bill and which, because it was a bearer certificate, could be sold the instant Consolidated needed its money.

So Consolidated Buttermilk would buy a 30-day CD with its $100,000. Should it need the cash earlier than expected, it would call a dealer in CDs who would quickly find a buyer —say International Can Opener. International Can Opener might hold the CD until the last of the 30 days were up, or it might, in turn, sell it to someone else.

In short order, corporations with extra cash became heavy buyers of CDs, and Citibank, by inventing the CD, changed all the rules of banking.

A CD didn't carry the name of the U.S. government, as did a Treasury bill, but it carried the name of a big bank, and that was good enough. And it paid more than a Treasury bill. Instead of patiently waiting for depositors to turn up, banks —armed with the CD—could go forth and buy deposits. And that buying of deposits is at the very heart of the new banking, and of the new money as well. The more money a bank bought the more it had to lend, and as banks became more aggressive in buying money, they became more aggressive in finding borrowers. In banking, deposits are counted as liabilities because they represent money that must in time be paid back to depositors. The assets of a bank are its loans and investments. The buzzword of the new banking became "liability management"—the act of buying deposits and then aggressively finding borrowers for the money.

A few years later, Citibank began offering CDs in the international banking markets and the new banking became universal. In time financial institutions of every sort devised CDs for every taste and pocketbook, including the wildly successful six-month savings certificate, where the cost of entry is $10,000, and the 30-month certificate where it is $100.

The CD brought in corporate and consumer deposits. Banks could buy the extra reserves of other banks in the federal funds market and that quickly went from being a nickel-and-dime affair to still another gigantic source of bought money for the banks. At any given moment these days, banks will hold about $250 billion in bought money— CDs, federal funds, and the like—meaning about 20 percent of all bank loans and investments are financed with bought money.

It's common today for a big-city bank to buy $1 billion and more a day from other banks and from corporations here and overseas. The money may come from the bank across the street or from a corporation half a world away. The money you borrowed from the local branch of your bank might have been part of a Japanese refiner's payment for oil from Kuwait. Many of the billions paid to OPEC for oil wind up in overseas branches of U.S. banks, which can transfer them home in a twinkling.

It is a perpetual balancing act—buying enough money to support the loans and investments in a bank's portfolio. Should a bank be unable to buy money in a given day, it would be in dreadful trouble. Indeed, the ability of the Federal Reserve to manage money is limited by its appreciation that the wrong move could suddenly dry up the market for bought money—much of which must be bought anew every day or two—and throw some big banks into chaos. And while the banks could not have financed the economic boom of the 1960s and 1970s without bought money, it's just another one of those developments that has helped institutionalize inflation in the economy—the banks bidding high to buy the money and so charging dearly when they lend it. When one builds on borrowed money, one is said to be "leveraged." The U.S. banking system is leveraged to the hilt —as deeply and perpetually in debt as the most profligate consumer.

Of all the jobs in a bank, buying money is the most taxing, intellectually and emotionally. At Manufacturers Hanover Trust Company in New York, that job falls to David J. Barry, an executive vice-president with 40 years at the bank.

How Manny Hanny Buys Billions

Manufacturers Hanover—Manny Hanny to its friends—is the fourth largest bank in the nation with some $42 billion in deposits. Its parent holding company, Manufacturers Hanover Corporation, has close to $50 billion in assets, and among all bank holding companies it trails only Citicorp, BankAmerica Corporation, and Chase Manhattan Corporation. Its headquarters is on Park Avenue, which is choice real estate.

On a given day, Manny Hanny will buy about $1.6 billion, and that's done at 44 Wall Street, in the heart of the financial district and some miles south of the corporate headquarters. How much it buys each day is determined by how much it needs to support its portfolio of loans and investments. Before the trading day begins, Barry will check on the money the bank has on hand, and he'll check with the chairman of the bank on loan demand.

Barry will buy CD money from U.S. or foreign corporations, depending on who will sell at the lowest interest rate. He'll buy federal funds from other banks that have them for sale. And he'll do repurchase agreements, or "repos," in which the bank sells securities from its investment portfolio to someone with cash, promising to buy those securities back at a slightly higher price in a day or two. The Federal Reserve also does repos, but to pull money out of the banking system for a few days. Manny Hanny does them to raise some short-term cash.

CD money, once bought, is there for at least two weeks while a purchase of federal funds, or a repo, is just for a day or two. The more CD money Barry buys, the less he has to fight the day-to-day battle of buying federal funds and doing repos. Still, Barry tries never to buy too much CD money in a day since those CDs will then fall due on the same day, and he doesn't want to face a day in the future when he might have to roll over those CDs—get companies to renew them—when corporations might not have much cash to invest, or when rates might be so high that Barry would rather not tie himself into them for two weeks.

There are eight traders at the bank, each earning up to

$60,000 a year, and with a bonus that can double that. That's far more than a trader on the open-market desk of the New York Fed can earn, but Barry regards the people at the Fed as order takers rather than traders. At Manny Hanny, a trader can buy or sell several million dollars' worth of securities without having to clear the deal with a superior. Traders at the Fed have no such freedom, all decisions about what to buy and at what price being made by the officers of the trading desk.

Traders at banks deal in astronomical sums each day—a trade in CDs running to $50 million and in federal funds to $200 million. For all that, the trading room at Manny Hanny seems placid enough to a visitor. The room is light and airy, with plenty of space around each desk. The walls are beige, the chairs on which the traders sit are a vivid orange. On each desk is a telephone console of the sort found on the desk of almost anyone on Wall Street who trades anything. There are other trading rooms on Wall Street—at brokerage houses where stocks and bonds are traded, for instance— where the din is simply awful. At Manny Hanny, though, it's more a muted hum.

On this day, in early 1980, however, things are far from normal in the trading room, and the bank will be buying no CDs today because none are for sale. Early in the day, the Labor Department reported a shocking jump in the wholesale price index and moments later the Federal Reserve raised its discount rate from the crisis level of 12 percent to the supercrisis level of 13 percent. Never has money cost as much in America as it does this day (though it will cost even more in the weeks ahead) and the markets are in shock. Interest rates are leaping around wildly, and until they settle down, no corporate treasurer will commit money for 30 hours, let alone 30 days. Whatever the bank needs this day will come from federal funds and repurchase agreements— very short-term money, in other words—and the bank will pay dearly for every penny it buys.

On this day, Manny Hanny needs $1.8 billion, of which $1.3 billion will come from federal funds and $500 million from repurchase agreements. The traders are seasoned veterans and they've seen markets in turmoil before. Still, trading markets work best when things are stable—which they clearly aren't this day. The markets are functioning, but nervously—everyone trying to make sense of what has happened. There's a lot of anxious chatter going on in the trading room: "Is the Titanic sinking?" sort of thing.

No one knows it, of course, but it will be a long time before the markets return to normal. A month later, the Labor Department will report still another awful jump in wholesale prices, President Carter will then unveil still another anti-inflation program, and the financial markets will writhe in agony. The prime lending rate of the banks, which is at 15¼ percent this day will reach 20 percent. On top of the 13 percent discount rate, the Fed will soon add a 3 percent surcharge for big banks that visit the discount window too often. The stock and bond markets will tumble, and except for bank loans, the whole process of raising money by U.S. business will grind virtually to a halt.

And then, with a suddenness that astonishes even such veteran bankers as Barry, interest rates, having flown to the heights, will plummet as never before in history, and then soar again until the bank's prime rate reaches 21½ percent.

Still, the day-to-day business of buying money will go on —men like Barry of Manny Hanny at the leading edge of the new banking and the new money. From being sleeping pussycats, once content to accept what came their way, the banks have become hungry tigers, prowling the world in search of money and in search of buyers for that money. From being reluctant lenders to the few, commercial banks have become aggressive lenders to the masses.

The Roots of Revolution

Yet if it all seems to have happened so quickly, the revolution in banking was a long time coming. Its roots go back to all the repressive laws Congress has passed through the ages, that have made banking both the most overregulated and the most evasion-prone industry in the land.

Banking is overregulated because there are so many regulators and so many rules. It's evasion-prone because there are too many regulators and because so many of the rules are so punitive and so archaic they beg for evasion. Each phase of the banking revolution involved the discovery of a loophole, of a way around regulators and regulations.

A bank may be either state-chartered or a national bank. If it is a national bank, it's regulated by the Comptroller of the Currency, who is an official at the Treasury. If it's state-chartered, it is regulated by the authorities of its home state, there being as many sets of banking rules as there are states.

But every national bank must also be a member of the Federal Reserve System, and most large state-chartered banks also choose to be members. Further, the Fed is the primary regulator of bank holding companies, whether the bank part of the holding company is national or state-chartered. There is also the Federal Deposit Insurance Corporation, which insures deposits up to $100,000 in nearly all banks. The FDIC has some say in the affairs of insured, state-chartered banks that are not members of the Federal Reserve System, while the states alone supervise state banks that are not insured by the FDIC. And then there's the Depository Institutions Deregulation etc., etc., etc., Act of 1980, by which the Fed became lender of last resort to, and setter of all reserve requirements for, all institutions that take deposits, no matter who else regulates them.

There is, further, the McFadden Act of 1927, which says

that even national banks must follow state law when it comes to opening branches. Banks in California, New York, and many other states can operate statewide, but in some states they can operate from only a few offices or just one. Bank of America, the largest in the land in terms of deposits, has 1,100 offices throughout California. (Citicorp, the holding company, is larger than BankAmerica, the holding company; Bank of America, the bank, is larger than Citibank, the bank.) Continental Illinois in Chicago is seventh largest, and it can operate only three offices—all within two miles of one another.

No U.S. bank can yet do a full banking business—taking deposits and making loans—in more than a single state, which flies in the face of both geography and common sense. The New York metropolitan area embraces New York, New Jersey, and Connecticut. The Chicago area includes Illinois, Indiana, and a corner of Wisconsin. But no New York bank can open a branch in New Jersey and no Chicago bank can open a branch in Indiana. New York banks advertise heavily in newspapers and on the air even though half their audience lives in states where the banks can't operate. And while Congress tackled everything under the sun with the Depository Institutions etc., etc., etc., etc., it couldn't bring itself to tackle branching.

The restrictions on branching are archaic, unreasonable, and, lately, ludicrous as well, because a new class of bank has entered the U.S. market that is essentially outside existing regulation: banks from abroad. The biggest foreign banks have long had offices in the U.S., and a few even have had full-scale branches—mostly in New York. Beginning a decade or so ago, many of the foreign banks began buying, or opening, banks around the country—which was possible because their foreign ownership made them immune to U.S. banking rules. No U.S. bank can operate a nationwide banking chain, but many foreign banks now do, and that rankles American bankers.

Even now, in the early stages of electronic money, a bank branch is not what it used to be. Most big banks now operate automatic teller machines, at locations far removed from the main office. You slip in a plastic card and you can make deposits, or withdraw cash, or find out how much you have in your account. Still more sophisticated machines are on the way and in time they will do just about everything a flesh-and-blood banker can do. In 1974, James E. Smith, then Comptroller of the Currency, ruled electronic banking terminals weren't branches and so their placement wasn't bound by state branching laws. Under that ruling a New York bank could flood its metropolitan area—the whole country, for that matter—with electronic tellers, and the states couldn't do a thing about it. States, predictably enough, reacted with rage, and the matter has been tied up in the courts ever since.

Having so many regulators is not only confusing, but dangerous as well, since it encourages banks to shop around for the best regulatory deal. Plenty of banks through the years have quit the Federal Reserve System because they found the Fed's rules on reserves burdensome (a way out now closed by the 1980 Act). On the other hand, in the early 1960s, then-Comptroller of the Currency James Saxon deliberately set out to make it more attractive for a bank to have a national charter. A number of banks, including giant Chase Manhattan Bank in New York, made the shift from state-chartered to national. When New York banking regulators balked in 1979 at the takeover of a big U.S. bank by a big foreign bank, the U.S. bank went national and the merger sailed through.

This sort of thing has led Arthur Burns, the former chairman of the Fed, to talk about a "competition in laxity"—regulators shading their rules to keep the banks they regulate from going elsewhere. Henry Kaufman, the very astute managing partner of Salomon Brothers, the giant New York banking house, believes the regulators have too often encouraged bankers to be free-spirited entrepreneurs, while allowing them to slight their fiduciary function of keeping safe the money people have entrusted to them. There's an old adage that bankers are supposed to be prudent rather than clever. In the new banking—and so in the new money —it's cleverness and not prudence that has emerged supreme.

It has been suggested that the Federal Reserve quit regulating and concentrate instead on managing our money. It has also been suggested all the federal agencies—Fed, FDIC, and Comptroller—be merged into a single superagency. Still, we're in the third decade of the new banking and the regulatory mess is as bad as ever.

So far we've talked about commercial banks. There are also savings banks, S&Ls, credit unions, investment banking houses, and a lot more institutions that one way or another operate in the world of money. Many of these institutions have their own regulators quite apart from the agencies that regulate the commercial banks, and their own rules. Illinois commercial banks can have just three offices, all bunched together, but Illinois S&Ls can operate statewide. Further, the lines of demarcation among banks, thrifts, investment banks, and others have so blurred through the years that the rationale for separate institutions with separate regulators and separate rules has mostly vanished. Even a country as big as the U.S. really doesn't need 40,000 depository institutions, ranging from $100 billion banks to $100,000 credit unions, all tripping over each other's feet.

Punishing the Villainous Bankers

There are still more laws governing the banks—those passed during the Depression, when bankers were seen as the villains and so deserving of punishment.

One such law is the Glass-Steagall Act, which severed

commercial banking and investment banking. A commercial bank takes deposits and makes loans. An investment bank serves as a middleman in bringing stock and bond issues to market, buying the stocks and bonds from the issuing corporation and reselling them to the public, which is called underwriting. Investment bankers also give financial advice and counsel to their corporate clients. Some parts of their business are regulated by the Securities and Exchange Commission, and some aren't regulated at all.

Britain has merchant banks that do it all—take deposits, underwrite securities, and the rest. The legendary House of Rothschild is one such merchant bank. U.S. banks used to be able to do it all, too. J. P. Morgan and Company, for instance, was both a commercial and an investment bank, as were most U.S. banks until the early 1930s. The argument for separating the two functions was that it was too easy for a commercial bank to underwrite a new issue of securities and then, rather than bother selling them to the public, simply slip them into the accounts their trust departments managed.

So Congress passed Glass-Steagall, cutting apart commercial and investment banking. J. P. Morgan turned itself into a commercial bank while some partners spun off Morgan Stanley and Company as an investment banking house. Other big banks did much the same sort of thing.

But Congress seldom does anything cleanly. Commercial banks were cut off from underwriting, with a couple of broad exceptions. A commercial bank can market the issues of the U.S. Treasury, and most of the big dealers in government securities are commercial banks. A commercial bank can also market the general-obligation bonds of cities and states —those issues backed by the full faith and credit (for which read the taxing power) of the issuer. A bank cannot underwrite the revenue bonds of a city or state—those issues which go to finance a specific piece of revenue-producing property like a toll road or a sports stadium. Revenue bonds must be underwritten by an investment banking house.

Commercial banks complain that they are barred from underwriting revenue bonds simply because revenue bonds weren't very common in the 1930s and Congress didn't even think of them when it wrote the law. Investment banking houses, in turn, complain that if commercial banks are allowed to underwrite revenue bonds, it will work a great financial hardship on the investment bankers.

The issue is further compounded because such giant investment banking houses as Merrill Lynch operate in so many financial areas that they now resemble commercial banks, but with more freedom and less regulation. Investment bankers, however, grumble that commercial banks are engaged in certain activities—various forms of managing investment funds, for instance—that look suspiciously like those that were supposedly shut off by Glass-Steagall.

That issue, too, has festered for a half-century, and just as bankers have found ways to sidestep the regulatory agencies and the branching rules, so the clever ones have found cracks in Glass-Steagall they can slip through.

If a company wants to sell medium-term bonds to the public, it has to be done by an investment banker. But a company can also borrow medium-term money from a commercial bank, and the banks have made a lot of loans for five and ten years, against the more typical 90-day bank loan.

Finally, there are those limits on what commercial banks and thrift institutions can pay for deposits. The ceilings let thrifts pay a little more than commercial banks, but with no depository institution allowed to pay interest on demand deposits.

The rate ceilings seemed to make sense when they were adopted in the 1930s. If no financial institution could pay more for deposits than another, no institution could outbid its rivals to a point where it dominated a whole market.

. . .

Neither could an institution pay so much for money that this might jeopardize its financial stability. And no institution could pay interest on highly volatile checking-account money.

The negotiable CD was a way to get around the rate ceilings. In time, Regulation Q came to mean there was a ceiling on what banks could pay small depositors. As interest rates shot up in the late 1970s, consumers set up such a howl that the six-month savings certificate was created, permitting banks to ignore Reg Q for anyone with $10,000 to deposit. When people with less than $10,000 to deposit began howling, a 30-month savings certificate was created, and that canceled out Regulation Q for anyone with $100 to deposit.

By 1980, Regulation Q applied only to paupers, and Congress finally tossed it out along with all other rate ceilings when it wrote the Depository Institutions etc., etc., etc. Act of 1980—all the ceilings to be phased out by 1986. Meanwhile, the six-month certificates were such a hit that both commercial banks and thrifts suddenly found themselves swamped with some very expensive money—nearly $400 billion drawn in through six-month savings certificates in the first two years they were offered. Much of the lending boom of 1979 and 1980 was a desperate bid by institutions to get this money—bought at the highest interest rates in history —to work at a profit, and in a hurry.

The prohibition of the payment of interest on checking-account deposits was perverse because there's no such prohibition in other countries. Deposits overseas can earn interest on money left for an instant—and that created both a problem and an opportunity for U.S. banks. A multinational company obviously will hold deposits abroad where they can earn interest rather than funnel them to the U.S. where they will earn no interest. If only to stay competitive, the overseas branches of U.S. banks buy very short-term deposits—often money just left overnight—in that international arena called the Eurodollar market. The other side of that is that if money is tight at home, or if money costs less abroad, a U.S. bank can ship those deposits back home in the time it takes to hit a few keys on a Telex machine. In time the prohibition of demand-deposit interest applied only to banks that couldn't swing a foreign branch.

At home, the prohibition of demand-deposit interest—and a companion prohibition of checking accounts at thrift institutions—cracked wide open in the mid-1970s when thrifts of New England invented the NOW account, which, you'll recall, stands for negotiable order of withdrawal. A NOW account looked like a savings account in that it paid interest, except that you could write what looked very much like checks against the money in the account. Commercial banks countered with their ATS—automatic transfer service—accounts. You kept your money in a savings account, and when you wrote a check, the money was automatically transferred into a checking account. Credit unions, in turn, offered share drafts, which were pretty much like NOW accounts.

In early 1979, a federal court in Washington ruled that financial institutions were playing fast and loose with the law, and it ordered Congress to change the law. Congress did so, of course, by passing the Depository Institutions etc., etc., etc., etc. Act of 1980. On January 1, 1981, NOW and ATS accounts and share drafts—transaction accounts, as they are called—became the law of the land, and soon the demand deposit that pays no interest and the savings account without a check-writing feature will become extinct.

The Slow March into the Future

Piece by piece, the banking system is shaking off the old constraints, but the process has taken far longer than it should have. And it has been done piecemeal and not very logically. Had Congress sat down around 1960 and rewritten the banking laws according to some sensible plan, we might have had a vastly different sort of economy today. Instead we have had two decades of banking by stealth and subterfuge, and the rewards have gone not to the prudent but to those clever enough to see the loopholes and wriggle through them.

When it comes to envisioning the U.S. banking system of the future, everyone points to the great "universal banks" found overseas. Most nations have just a few giant banks— a half-dozen in Germany, five in Switzerland, operating in every corner of the land. These universal banks do everything—acting as commercial bankers, investment bankers, stockbrokers, and with the freedom to buy up companies they lend to. In most countries, a single agency regulates all the banks, to the extent that they're regulated at all.

The contrast with U.S. banks is striking: 14,600 commercial banks of varying size and soundness, regulated by a crazy-quilt mix of state and federal agencies, plus savings banks, S&Ls, credit unions, and a lot of institutions that look like banks but according to law are not. The big U.S. banks have been surprisingly quiet in reacting to the inroads made here by foreign banks. U.S. banks really don't want the foreign banks to go away as much as they want the same freedom the foreign banks enjoy, especially the right to go nationwide.

Obviously things are about to change, and dramatically so. Interest-rate ceilings are fading and soon the biggest and richest banks will be able to outbid their small and poorer rivals for deposits. The weaker fish, because they can't compete with the giants, will fade away—victims of what the Federal Reserve calls "cost shock." The survivors, of course, will become bigger and still more powerful.

In time the limits on branching will disappear—perhaps by act of Congress, perhaps by court order, perhaps because when electronic money finally hits it big, conventional branches will give way to electronic terminals, with one central computer capable of running terminals all over the country. As branching limits fade, banking will fall into the hands of a limited number of financial giants, each operating in every corner of the land. Congress passed the 1980 Act, well aware it would thin the ranks among financial institutions, on grounds that the ranks desperately needed thinning.

It is hard to make any economy work efficiently when that economy must get its capital from a hodgepodge of 40,000 financial institutions—some of them titanic and some minuscule, each institution fighting for its place in the sun, each class of institution operating under a different set of rules. It is like a race in which supercharged automobiles compete with bicycles and joggers. There are other reasons why we are in an age of new money, but this chaos in the financial system is certainly one reason.

How It All Began

All of this is a far cry from how banking looked when it all began in Babylon about 2000 B.C. Our word "bank" comes from the old Italian word for bench—*banca*—the bench in question being the one at which the moneylender plied his trade. When the moneylender ran out of money, his bench was said to be broken, which, from the Latin *ruptus,* comes out "bankrupt."

Banking thrived where civilization and trade thrived—first in the East, then in Greece, and then in Rome. The earliest function of a bank was to safeguard wealth in a world filled with peril. Your caravan arrived safely back in Babylon and you took your gold and silver to the local banker who guarded it for you. In Greece, the temples carried on banking and the vaults were sacred ground.

Having all that money around, it was an obvious next step for the banker to lend some of it out at a nice profit. As coins appeared, the banker also became a dealer in foreign exchange, swapping Lydian staters for Greek owls, and the like. Banking reached a zenith in the Roman Empire, and then Rome fell, the Dark Ages closed in, and for nearly a thousand years banking disappeared from the scene.

Then, as trade revived, banking revived. A bank was established in Venice in 1171 and another in Genoa in 1320. In 1609 Amsterdam got a bank, chartered by the city itself, which served as both commercial and central bank.

English banking got some crucial, if inadvertent, help from King Charles I. Until 1640, merchants commonly kept their valuables in the Tower of London. Then Charles, with a bad case of the shorts, marched off with 130,000 pounds in other people's money. The money was eventually returned, but no one had much faith in the Tower after that, and London's goldsmiths took over the job of guarding the public's wealth. You put your gold into the goldsmith's safe and got a receipt for it. You could later reclaim your gold, or issue instructions to the goldsmith to turn your gold over to someone else, or you could use the goldsmith's receipt to pay bills. In time, both the receipt and the payment request to the goldsmith came to be regarded as legal tender—a currency as good as gold because it was 100 percent backed by gold.

It soon became obvious to the goldsmiths that not everyone wanted to withdraw their gold every day. Some gold could be left in the safe to cover withdrawals and the rest could be loaned out. And so the fractional-reserve system was born—others invented banking but the British perfected it.

Banking was slow to come to America, Britain's unwillingness to permit wealth to flow to the Colonies making it pointless to have banks around. Not until after the Revolution did banks appear in any numbers—the first launched in Philadelphia in 1781, others in Boston and New York in 1784. All were state banks until 1863, each issuing its own currency in that marvelous chaos that marked the American monetary system for most of the first century of independence. Then came the National Bank Act of 1863, and with it national banks, and the first banking regulator, the Comptroller of the Currency. Of the other regulators, the Fed happened along in 1914 and the FDIC in 1933.

How Banking Really Works

As it stands today, 4,600 of the 14,600 U.S. banks are national banks and the rest are state-chartered. All national banks must belong to the Fed, and another 1,100 state banks choose to belong. There are 7,700 banks insured by the FDIC which are not members of the Federal Reserve System. Finally there are some 300 banks that are neither insured by the FDIC nor members of the Fed—all of them presumably believing the just hand of Providence will guard them from harm.

California has Bank of America—the largest in terms of deposits—but New York City has the greatest concentration of banking assets. Of $1½ trillion in U.S. banking assets, about 15 percent is in New York. But the U.S. isn't the giant of world banking it used to be. A decade ago, four of the ten largest banks in the world were U.S. banks. Now the U.S. has only three of the 20 largest—Bank of America, Citibank and Chase Manhattan Bank—and in 1980 a French bank, Crédit Agricole Mutuel, passed all U.S. banks to become the largest in the world.

Of nearly $1 trillion in U.S. bank loans outstanding, some 20 percent are loans to business—called C&I (commercial and industrial) loans. About 15 percent are installment loans to consumers, most to finance cars. Another 20 percent are mortgage and real estate loans, and the rest are a mixed bag: loans to everyone from farmers to stockbrokers. Finally, the banks own about $250 billion in Treasury, government agency, and municipal bonds—held as investments. Banks are in business to make loans, though, and when the demand for money quickens, government and municipal issues are sold to free up money.

The typical bank loan to business is for 90 days. Then it is paid off, or renewed—rolled over in the jargon of banking. If the loan is small enough, a single bank will handle it. A giant corporate customer will have an arrangement with dozens of banks, each bank putting up part of the money. When W. T. Grant, the big retailer, failed in the mid-1970s, it had a $700 million bank loan out, shared by no fewer than 136 banks. If you or I want to borrow, we walk into the bank, apply for our loan, and in time either we get our money or are sent packing. Companies sign up ahead of time, establishing a line of credit with a bank or a string of banks, for as much as $1 billion. When a company needs the money, it begins drawing down the line, writing checks until the line is exhausted. It never draws the full amount, of course, since custom dictates it will leave perhaps 20 percent with the bank as a compensating balance.

The basic interest rate of the banking system is the prime rate, which is what banks charge their biggest and best customers for money. The prime used to change infrequently, and it was a dramatic moment when it did. The age of new money changed that, and in 1980 and early 1981 the prime first went from 15 percent to 20 percent, then plunged to 11 percent, and then climbed to 21½ percent. Lesser borrowers pay more than the prime, and the company that pays "prime plus 1 percent" stands taller in the world than one that pays "prime plus 2 percent."

But corporate business isn't what it used to be for the banks, because many of the biggest corporations have quit the banks to borrow in the market for commercial paper. Commercial paper is an unsecured IOU from a company, promising to repay the borrowed money, plus interest, after a set period of time. The lenders in the market are mostly other corporations with some idle cash. Since it's an unsecured IOU, only the choicest corporate names can sell commercial paper—but those choice corporate names were the very cream of the bank's customers in years gone by.

It usually costs a little less to sell commercial paper than to borrow from a bank, and the borrower gets all the money, there being no such thing as a compensating balance in the commercial paper market. Companies that can sell paper do, and the amount of paper outstanding stood at $50 billion in 1976 and nearly three times that much in 1981—a gain twice as great as the gain in bank loans. As with CDs, there is a trading market in commercial paper and a piece of paper from a blue-chip corporation can be sold to someone else about as quickly as can a CD.

The commercial-paper market had its blackest days in 1970 when the Penn Central collapsed, owing $80 million it had borrowed in the market. The paper market went into a semiswoon, and when it recovered, the list of companies able to borrow in the market was narrowed considerably.

Banks have done a lot of things to offset the loss of some of their best corporate customers. Most have become more aggressive than ever in seeking the business of consumers. Most have also come up with services that can be offered to customers for a fee. If you own a business, your bank will provide economic consulting, help you manage your corporate cash, help with bookkeeping and bill paying, help you through the intricacies of doing business abroad, and generally make itself useful—all for a fee.

Since commercial-paper borrowing is short term—just for a few months—banks have also grown more aggressive in lending money to business for longer terms. Lately, with interest rates shooting to the sky and beyond, and no investor wanting to tie up money for years by buying a bond, companies in search of longer-term money have had almost no place to go but the banks. The corporate bond market revived briefly when interest rates came down in the spring of 1980, but the erratic swings in interest rates and the chaotic market conditions that have marked the age of new money are likely to exist for years. In that climate, bankers expect to take on more of the job of providing long-term financing to business that used to be done mostly by the bond market. Unlike a bond, where the interest rate is fixed for life the day it is issued, the interest on these longer-term bank loans—maybe as long as 15 and 20 years—will change every six months or so according to the prevailing cost of money.

The Chinese Wall, Which Is Made of Swiss Cheese

Finally, besides taking deposits and lending money, banks, through their trust departments, manage the riches of the rich—the richest these days being the giant corporate and government pension funds. In all, the banks today manage about $500 billion—some of it from trusts and estates left to their care, but most of it from pension funds.

In theory the trust departments are the judicious guardians of the pittances of widows and orphans—investing their money only in the safest of safe instruments. In fact, trust departments have as much trouble investing to outrun inflation as everyone else, and in trying to do that, they have made a hash of it in recent years. The worst stock-market break in history came in 1974–5—five times as bad in terms of stock values wiped out as the Crash of 1929—and among the biggest losers in that market were the trust departments of banks (or, more exactly, the customers of the trust departments of banks).

For better or worse, the trust departments are the biggest investors in the stock market in good years and bad. Unfortunately, most banks have tended to do worse in market breaks than the overall stock market, and no better than the overall market when stock prices are gaining, which is hardly the image the banks like to convey.

Stay long enough in a bank trust department and you'll hear someone mention the "Chinese Wall." A bank lending officer will hear a lot of things about companies as he makes his rounds (or as she makes her rounds, since women have gained a considerable place in banking lately). A trust officer with millions invested in International Jelly Bean stock would certainly like to know if International Jelly Bean is on the verge of failure.

It is, however, against the law for a trust officer or anyone else to trade a stock on the basis of information not available to the general investing public. Banks therefore like to say they have a Chinese Wall between lending officers and trust officers—meaning no matter how juicy the gossip, the lending officer can't pass it along to the trust officer.

As might be expected, the Chinese Wall at a great many banks is made of Swiss cheese. There is considerable evidence that the lending officers of some banks involved in the death throes of the Penn Central passed along tidbits to their trust departments, enabling them to sell their Penn Central stock before the roof fell in. Mention the Chinese Wall to a banker and he will first look very stern and then smile like a kid caught with a hand in the cookie jar.

The Skeletons in the Closet

Banking is not all beer and skittles, and about a dozen banks still fail each year. Most do so because someone has embezzled the money, and a few do so because of unwise loans and investments. Most are very small, and because of deposit insurance, depositors are protected against loss.

In fact, few banks really fail these days. If the bank is of any size whatsoever, the regulators will rush in, take control, and quickly work out a merger with a sturdier institution. The buyer takes what good assets are left and the sick bank is absorbed into the healthy one so quickly that most customers don't know what's happened until they see the new name on the door.

Bank regulators have occasionally been known to spot a troubled bank before failure was inevitable. In 1980, federal regulators put together a massive rescue effort, involving more than $1 billion in government money and money from other banks, to support the ailing First Pennsylvania—a giant Philadelphia bank. More often, though, regulators seem to stand around, shuffling from foot to foot, while a giant institution goes down the drain.

The biggest bank failure ever came in 1974. It involved the Franklin National Bank on Long Island, then the nation's 20th-largest bank with some $5 billion in assets—done in finally by staggering losses in trading foreign currencies. The popular villain of the piece is Italian financier Michele Sindona, who took control of the Franklin in 1972 and who had the possibly unique experience of watching financial empires in both the U.S. and Europe come crashing down at the same time.

Franklin might well have tumbled without Sindona's help. It had been badly weakened before he appeared by its attempts to move from peaceful Long Island into the big and brutal New York banking market. Other bank officers besides Sindona went to prison on a variety of counts after the collapse. Sindona got the blockbuster sentence, though—25 years in prison on counts of fraud, conspiracy, and perjury.

Bank regulators are supposed to pass judgment on those who buy America's banks, and why they gave their blessing to Sindona defies rational answer. He'd been involved in enough questionable financial affairs in Europe and the U.S. before he ever turned up at Franklin. Among other things, Sindona is widely believed to have recommended investments that cost the Vatican many millions of dollars. Billions borrowed from the Fed kept what was left of Franklin around until it could be sold off to European-American

Bank, a New York bank owned by a clutch of big foreign banks.

It's even harder to understand why the regulators allowed the U.S. National Bank of San Diego with $1.2 billion in assets to fail in 1973. That bank was run by C. Arnholt Smith, a crony of Richard Nixon's, and possibly the regulators were loath to ruffle the Presidential feathers. In any event, the problems at U.S. National festered until death became the merciful way out. What was left of U.S. National went to Crocker National Bank, and, in time, Smith went to prison.

And then there have been the near-misses. Bankers are only human, and they can't resist a fad any more than the rest of us. The hot thing in the early 1970s was the real estate investment trust, or REIT, which was a mutual fund that invested in real estate. The REITs offered certain tax breaks and the public bought them like hotcakes. Using money from their shareholders, and heaps more borrowed from the banks, the REITs then proceeded to make some of the dumbest investments in the history of American finance. Build a suntan parlor in the middle of the Sahara Desert and a REIT would rush in and build another next door. The roof fell in during the recession of 1974–5 when real estate became a disaster area. At that point the REITs owed the banks more than $10 billion and the banks wrote off at least $1 billion in loans to REITs.

More disturbing was that some big banks started REITs of their own—giant Chase Manhattan Bank being just one. The Chase REIT wound up in a bankruptcy proceeding in 1979, and its losses from 1975 through 1979 came to $254 million. For the record, Chase stands only as the adviser to the REIT, not as its owner. But it was a sad performance for the nation's third-largest bank, whose chairman through the period was David Rockefeller.

Still the grandest scandal in banking involved not a U.S. bank but a giant Swiss bank—Swiss Credit Bank, the third-largest in the land, with $35 billion in assets at the end of 1979.

Guessing wrong on the quality of a loan is understandable. If a bank never lost on a loan it would mean it was being too strict and had probably told a lot of deserving borrowers to take a walk. What happened at the Chiasso branch of Swiss Credit Bank in the mid-1970s involved not a bad guess but outright fraud and deceit. Swiss bankers are supposed to be renowned for their probity, and there are few rages more towering than that of a Swiss banker in full fury against the fiscal laxity of others.

But nearly $900 million in customers' money was siphoned off from the Chiasso branch by the branch managers, to a Liechtenstein company which those managers secretly owned. The scheme, further, went on for years without being spotted either by the bank's management or by Swiss banking authorities. When the case broke open in 1977, the loss to the bank amounted to some $400 million, which even by Swiss banking standards is a pretty fair piece of change. The bank's chairman resigned, the losses have been made up, and Swiss Credit Bank is again one of the shining stars of international money. It would be nice—but probably unreasonable—to think the Chiasso affair made the Swiss more tolerant of the foibles of others.

And yet, those horror stories aside, the remarkable thing isn't how much banks have lost in this age of new money, but how little. U.S. banks have more than $1 trillion at risk in a treacherous, eccentric economy—money bankers have sold to everyone from you and me to the U.S. Treasury—and their losses each year on all that money come to less than a half-cent on each dollar loaned. The risks grow greater the longer the age of new money lingers on, and tomorrow could be a different, sadder story. At the moment, the new banking is surviving the new money a lot better than the new money is surviving the new banking.

Chapter 9
If It Walks Like a Bank and Talks Like a Bank, It May Be Sears, Roebuck

THERE WAS a commercial a few years back featuring a young woman who can't decide where to go for a loan. Suddenly she has a revelation. Commercial banks are for business, while savings banks are for people. "I'm not a business," she trills breathlessly. "I'm a people."

Well, that's true as far as it goes. Historically, commercial banks have basically been for business, their specialty being loans to companies. Savings banks and their companions among the thrift institutions such as savings and loan associations and credit unions have mostly been for people, their specialty being loans to individuals—mortgage loans for the savings banks and S&Ls, and auto loans for credit unions.

Still, that's not the way things are going in this age of new money. Commercial banks have been increasingly aggressive in going after "people business" as their best corporate customers go off to borrow in the commercial-paper market. Meanwhile that wondrous piece of legislation, the Depository Institutions Deregulation and Monetary Control Act of

1980, allows the thrifts to do more lending to business. The same act allows all institutions, banks and thrifts alike, to offer the same kinds of deposits and to pay the same rates for money. And finally, a slew of "near-banks," from Merrill Lynch to American Express to Sears, Roebuck, are big and aggressive enough to compete with both commercial banks and thrifts. Within a decade it will be next to impossible to tell the banks from the thrifts, or the banks and the thrifts from the near-banks.

Even the "people" part is deceptive because it implies "small," and there's nothing small about the financial business people transact in this age of new money, and nothing small at all about the wealth of the thrifts. The combined assets of all thrift institutions is about $875 billion—$635 billion for the S&Ls, $170 billion for the savings banks, and $70 billion for credit unions.

That doesn't match the $1½ trillion of the commercial banks, and no thrift comes close to the $115 billion of Citicorp. The biggest thrift is H. F. Ahmanson and Company, a California S&L holding company with $12 billion in assets, and the biggest savings bank is the Philadelphia Saving Fund Society with $7 billion in assets.

But the thrifts grew more rapidly than the commercial banks in the postwar years—the S&Ls nearly twice as fast as the banks during the 1970s, and the credit unions 2½ times as fast. And in the areas in which the thrifts concentrate, they're very powerful competitors. Savings banks and S&Ls together hold 51 percent of all home mortgages (followed by commercial banks, insurance companies, and agencies of the federal government), and credit unions finance every fifth car bought in the U.S. Of the $1.2 trillion consumers owe to someone, $500 billion is owed to the thrifts.

Why the Future Will Be Different

But things aren't what they used to be for the thrifts, and thanks to ferocious competition, new legislation, and the peculiarities of the age of new money, they'll never be so again.

A salient feature of the age of new money is that everyone is in hock to their eyeballs, consumers most of all. And since lending to consumers is where the action is, that's where everyone wants to be. It's a growth business because, except during recessions, consumers add about $200 billion in new debt a year. It's a profitable business, since consumers tend to pay a high price when they borrow.

Understandably, everyone wants a bigger slice of this business, and the everyone isn't limited to the banks and the thrifts.

Merrill Lynch is, on one hand, America's biggest brokerage house. In recent years, though, it has turned itself into a widely diversified financial conglomerate. A Merrill Lynch customer can now write checks against money left in his brokerage account, and he can also run up charges on a Visa bank credit card provided by Merrill Lynch. And Merrill Lynch is now a major force in the real estate brokerage business.

Or take Sears, Roebuck and Company, which fancies itself a giant retailer but which is a finance company more than anything else. It owns the huge Allstate Insurance complex and, through Allstate, it owns a large California S&L. Sears has some 24 million credit customers, whose debt to the company at the end of 1979 was $7 billion. There have been years when Sears earned more from its financial services than any U.S. bank earned, period. And Sears is subject to few of the regulations that banks and thrifts are subject to.

There is also American Express, with its millions of cardholders, and Diners Club, and other brokerage houses, and other retailers, and life insurance companies, and a few other entities that have staked a claim on the "people" business, and suddenly the battleground is choked with combatants. Unless we suddenly decide to stop borrowing (which is improbable) the battle for the people business can only get hotter through the 1980s.

And if the thrifts have enjoyed a leg up in this battle in the past, they'll enjoy it no longer.

The thrifts must now deal with the loss of their strongest card—their ability to pay more than commercial banks for deposits. That, again, is because the thrifts were seen as more deserving because they financed housing. The Fed had its Regulation Q, the other regulators had their own rate ceilings, and thrifts could pay ¼ of 1 percent more than banks for deposits.

Then came the 1980 Act, and out went the rate ceilings, to be phased out completely by 1986. Soon the thrifts will have to slug it out on even terms with the banks, each paying the same rate for money, and each reduced to offering a superior toaster or electric blanket to win depositors.

The thrifts were the first to offer interest-paying checking accounts—the NOW account. The credit unions followed with their share drafts, and the banks countered with their ATS, or automatic transfer service accounts. But the 1980 Act says all institutions, banks and thrifts alike, can now offer interest-paying checking accounts, and whatever edge the thrifts enjoyed by getting there first is gone. Everyone now offers transaction accounts and everyone pays the same interest on those accounts.

Nor have thrifts done so well lately with their primary business—the making of mortgage loans. A mortgage loan is long term, and if an S&L makes a 6 percent mortgage loan, it's going to keep collecting just 6 percent each year after, no matter what happens to interest rates in the marketplace. Each spasm in the age of new money has seen the rates thrifts pay for deposits go higher, while most of their income still comes from older, lower-yielding mortgages. No one ever got rich by buying dear and selling cheap, which is basically what the thrifts have been doing. So have commercial banks, of course, when they make mortgage loans, but commercial banks have other sources of income, and the thrifts, until now, mostly did not.

The thrifts, in common with other lenders, have switched from the old fixed-rate mortgage to the variable-rate mortgage where the rate goes up in line with inflation. Still, it will be years before the thrifts rid their loan portfolios of the low-yield, fixed-rate mortgages made in years past. The six-month savings certificate was at best a mixed blessing for the thrifts. It appeared to provide lots of new money for lending. In fact, much of it was simply shifted from savings accounts that paid 5½ percent to certificates that have often paid three times that much. The resultant squeeze has put the thrifts in a lot of hot water—savings banks as an industry losing money in 1980, and the S&Ls not much better off.

One result is that the number of thrift institutions has shrunk considerably. There were 6,000 S&Ls in 1960 and only 4,700 in 1980, and there will be far fewer still in 1990.

The 1980 Act, of course, did a lot to narrow the differences between commercial banks and thrifts besides eliminating the interest-rate edge of the thrifts. Recognizing that the thrifts were having trouble getting by in the mortgage business, Congress put them into a lot of new businesses—most of them businesses in which the commercial banks are already well entrenched. Thrifts can now make more kinds of consumer loans, besides mortgage loans. They can now offer credit cards just as commercial banks can. Savings banks have always been able to buy corporate bonds, but now S&Ls can, too, meaning that thrifts can finance business as well as consumers. In short order the only difference between a commercial bank and a thrift will be the name over the door.

One possibility is that a few very large thrifts will become something so close to commercial banks that no one will be able to tell the difference, and the rest of the thrifts will simply fade away. Some of the near-banks will become something nearer still to banks, and instead of 40,000 depository institutions, we'll have just a relative handful of vast financial conglomerates.

The federal agency that regulated S&Ls is the Federal Home Loan Bank Board, and the former chairman of the FHLBB, Jay Janis, has predicted another sort of role for the thrifts. They would become "family financial centers," he said, offering transaction accounts, credit cards, consumer installment lending, trust departments, and financial-consulting services—all aimed at the consumer.

Missing from that list, of course, is the basic business of thrifts today—the making of mortgage loans. One theory is that the thrifts of the future will make far fewer mortgage loans and will instead act as brokers—lining up mortgage borrowers, but with the actual lending done by someone else. The pension funds with their billions are seen as one prime source of mortgage money. Another possibility is that the federal government, which has been providing more and more mortgage money through the years, will ultimately become its largest provider.

They Used to Be Friendly Societies

Yet if the thrifts are fading as a separate class, it's in large part because the special circumstances that led to their creation in the first place haven't existed for years. The change came when commercial banks ceased being for the few and went after the many.

If you were a tradesman or an artisan or a farmer a century ago and you wanted to borrow, you didn't go to the commercial bank, which was a thoroughly intimidating place that didn't much care for the common folk. Instead you joined

with some of your own kind, pooled your financial re-
sources, and borrowed from that pool. The commercial bank
might be alien ground, but the first thrifts ran out of someone's parlor, and decisions on who got money were made by
your friends and neighbors.

The first thrifts appeared in England several hundred years
ago and were known as "friendly societies," being quite
literally groups of friends who each put some money into a
pot to be tapped when one of the group was injured, fell ill,
or lost a job. Next came the building societies, which were
big enough to be able to finance the purchase of a home.

In America, the savings banks came first, with the Philadelphia Saving Fund Society and the Provident Institution
for Savings in the Town of Boston, each established in 1816.
Each is still around today. There are 465 savings banks today
in 17 states—most in the Northeast and with 60 percent of
the industry's assets in New York. The names of even the
largest reflect their humble origins. Among the 100 largest
savings banks are the Dime Savings Bank and the Seamen's
Bank for Savings in New York, the People's Savings Bank
in Bridgeport, Connecticut, and the Farmers and Mechanics
Savings Bank in Minneapolis. There are Dollar Savings
banks in New York and in Pittsburgh, but there's also the
Boston Five Cents Savings Bank (with close to $1 billion in
deposits, which comes to 20 billion five-cent pieces).

Next came the savings and loan associations, the first
being the Oxford Provident Building Association in Philadelphia, founded in 1831. It had 37 members, and each could
borrow once from the common pool to build or buy a house.
When the last member had borrowed, the association was
supposed to go out of business. Instead it was reorganized
with new members, then reorganized again, then reorganized
a third time, and it exists to this day.

There are S&Ls today in every state, plus Puerto Rico and
Guam. As New York is king of the hill among savings banks,
California is the giant among S&Ls, with nearly 20 percent

of all S&L assets in that state—mostly held by giant S&L holding companies.

The credit unions are another kettle of fish altogether, newer than either savings banks or S&Ls, and quite different in both nature and purpose. Most are organized by the employees of a company or the members of an organization. There are some 23,000 credit unions in the U.S. today, with 40 million members, and in 97 percent of them, all the members work for a single company or belong to the same church or labor union. The largest, with nearly 500,000 members, is the Navy Federal Credit Union, based in Washington. As the name implies, all its members are connected with the Navy or the Marines.

The first credit union was started in 1849 by the mayor of Flammersfeld in Germany, one Friedrich Wilhelm Raiffeisen, to keep his townsfolk out of the clutches of the moneylenders. The first credit union in North America was started in Quebec in 1900 and the first in the U.S. was started in New Hampshire in 1907.

While the average S&L has $100 million in deposits, fewer than half the credit unions can boast of $500,000 in deposits (which in credit unions are called share accounts). Because they're smaller, they concentrate on auto and personal loans, with no more than a toe dipped in the mortgage field.

Savings banks and credit unions are all mutual institutions, meaning their depositors are also their shareholders and so, in theory, their owners. Neither is supposed to make a profit, though each is expected to put something aside for a rainy day. Until 1978, all savings banks were state chartered and therefore regulated by the states. Now there's a provision for federally chartered savings banks, and some of the largest have already made the shift. Deposits in savings banks are insured by the Federal Deposit Insurance Corporation. Credit-union accounts are insured either by various state insurance plans, or by the federal government's National Credit Union Administration.

The S&Ls are a more varied lot. Slightly more than half are chartered by the federal government; they operate under the watch of the Federal Home Loan Bank Board (FHLBB) and have their deposits insured by the Federal Savings and Loan Insurance Corporation. The rest are state chartered—though most still are insured by the FSLIC. Most of the 4,700 S&Ls are mutual institutions, but 749—with 20 percent of industry assets—are "stock" companies with publicly traded shares, just as General Motors has. The biggest of these—the California S&L holding companies—all have their shares traded on the New York Stock Exchange.

The Dismal World of Disintermediation

To really understand the nature of the thrift industry, and the reason for much of its woe in recent years, you must know one of the buzzwords of the age of new money—"disintermediation." Years ago, Salomon Brothers, the New York banking house, ran an informal contest to see if someone could do better than disintermediation. No one could and it is still called disintermediation.

An institution that takes deposits is called a "financial intermediary." You hand over your money and the institution, acting as an intermediary, invests the money where it thinks it will do the most good: in mortgages if it's a thrift, and in various things if it's a commercial bank. Your profit on the deal is the interest you get on your deposit.

There are, however, those legal limits on what institutions can pay for money—the theory being that if the institutions paid too much for deposits, they would make high-yield but risky loans to recoup. As it is today, commercial banks can pay 5¼ percent, thrifts 5½ percent, and credit unions even more on savings deposits—and all pay more than that on time deposits. The rate ceilings will vanish before the 1980s end, but they'll be around for some years, and even when they go, prudence still will limit what institutions pay for money.

A 5½ percent return isn't bad when inflation is low and other investments don't yield more. But when yields on such things as Treasury bills soar to levels far beyond what commercial bank or thrift deposits yield—as they have done frequently in the age of new money—some depositors will quit the banks and thrifts and invest directly in the financial markets. Disintermediation, lately, often involves shifting money from a savings account into a money market mutual fund. By investing directly, these people are bypassing the intermediaries, which is why such action is called disintermediation. (That it has taken three rather fat paragraphs to describe disintermediation explains why no one has come up with a less formidable word for it.)

When disintermediation hits the commercial banks, they either cut back lending or they tap their overseas branches to fetch home money from countries where money is still available. But a Citibank among the lenders, or a General Motors among the borrowers, is deemed able to take care of itself come what may, and a bit of disintermediation at the commercial banks is counted as no big thing.

When disintermediation hits the thrifts, however, they must cut back on mortgage lending, and it was long ago deemed both socially desirable and politically wise to keep housing in robust good health as much of the time as possible. First, it's a matter of national interest that everyone be provided with decent housing. Then it's also true that homeowners cast a lot more votes at election time than does either Citibank or General Motors. Finally, when mortgage money dries up, the whole construction industry suffers—and that's our biggest industry in terms of dollars spent.

Yet there are sound economic reasons why it isn't wise to try to keep housing flourishing all the time. Construction consumes close to $250 billion in most years, and that amount is manageable only if there is no vast demand for money from everyone else. If we try to provide money for construction and for everything else, it will take so much new money each year that the result will be (and, indeed, has been) inflation.

Housing was traditionally a countercyclical industry, meaning it was strong when the rest of the economy was weak. When the rest of the economy began to heat up—as evidenced by a rise in interest rates—the thrifts would be hit by disintermediation. Then the flow of mortgage money, and, in turn, the level of construction activity, would slow and much of the steam would go out of the economy. As the demand for money eased and interest rates fell, disintermediation ended, money flowed back to the thrifts, and the resultant pickup in housing helped the whole economy recover.

Then came the credit squeeze of 1966—interest rates pushed sharply higher and the money supply reduced as the Federal Reserve battled against the first flare-up of the Vietnam era inflation. Disintermediation hit with a vengeance and housing took its worst dive since World War Two. There was panic in high places—and the start of a concerted drive to make sure the mortgage market and housing stayed healthy all of the time.

The Federal Home Loan Bank Board started borrowing more to lend to S&Ls that had run short. An individual S&L might get squeezed out, but the FHLBB, as a powerful federal agency, has access to money most of the time. New government agencies were formed to provide mortgage money, and while these agencies held only 8 percent of all home mortgages in 1970, by 1980 that had climbed to 20 percent.

The thrifts, meanwhile, were allowed to offer more high-yield time deposits to keep depositors from straying away. The six-month savings certificate and a companion eight-year certificate came in 1978, and the 30-month certificate came in 1980. These certificates allowed the thrifts (and the commercial banks as well) to compete with almost anything the investment markets had to offer.

But as lenders paid more for money, they obviously had to charge more, and mortgage rates have gone to unbelievable levels. The flood of expensive money into the thrifts, and the need to get the money working at once, helped feed the wild inflation that hit housing in 1979 and early 1980. The need to provide for housing in all seasons is still another reason why the Federal Reserve most of the time creates too much new money.

And for all that, the scheme hasn't worked. The attempt to keep housing healthy all the time has added to inflation, pushed mortgage rates to the skies and beyond, and created still another army of government functionaries, to run the new housing agencies. And yet the scheme hasn't done much to change the cyclical nature of housing. Housing boomed in the late 1970s and then came crashing down in early 1980 as disintermediation hit once again. Even when there was mortgage money available, few of us could afford to borrow it.

Meanwhile, the battle rages on—the banks against the thrifts, the banks and thrifts against Sears, Roebuck and Merrill Lynch. The result will someday be a more rational, more efficient, and less fragmented financial system. But the way to that new financial system figures to be very bloody indeed, and much of that blood will be shed by the thrifts.

Chapter 10
Why Stocks Are No Longer the Only Game in Town

IMAGINE THE mighty Colorado River, strong and swift enough to have carved out the Grand Canyon, cascading against Hoover Dam—the brute force of the river spinning the giant turbines that power the American West. And now imagine the Colorado, split into a dozen tributaries of which only one reaches the great dam. The turbines turn lethargically and lights throughout the West begin to dim.

That's precisely what has happened to the American investment markets in this age of new money. We shy away from paper investments—stocks and bonds—in favor of assets we hope will keep their value as the economy swings violently from inflation to recession. The wealth that once poured into stocks and bonds, powering the growth and ensuring the future of our economy, has been diverted into a dozen markets: some of them new, and most of them having more in common with the gaming tables of Las Vegas than with how we used to invest our money.

We still buy stocks: $300 billion worth in 1979 and more than that in 1980. But too much of our buying nowadays is short-term speculation, not long-term investment, because it's hazardous to keep money in one place for long in the age of new money. We buy bonds (government, corporate, and municipal) when inflation pushes interest rates to the skies, but we do so timorously because price swings in the bond market have been even more violent than those in the stock market. We still buy mutual-fund shares, but we mostly ignore the old-line funds that invest in stocks and bonds in favor of funds that invest in gold or foreign securities, and the money-market funds that invest in very short-term securities for high yields.

Even when the stock market rallies, as it did in 1980 and 1981, the share of our wealth going into stocks and bonds is less than at any time since World War Two.

Many of us have fled the perils of the marketplace for bank accounts insured by the federal government—especially the six-month savings certificate, which offers both safety and high yield. Many of us have fled the marketplace for the investment we perceive to be the safest of all—gold.

Finally, a great—and growing—share of our wealth goes into the back alleys and byways of investment, where, although there are perils, there is also the potential for a return appropriate to the age of new money. And so we buy speculative real estate, precious and semiprecious gems, arts and antiques, and collectibles beyond counting, from vintage wines to vintage cars to Mickey Mouse watches. There's the new and booming market in stock options, where you don't buy the stock but bet on its future price. There's the old but booming market in commodity futures where you bet what 25,000 pounds of copper or 60,000 pounds of soybean oil will cost weeks or months from now. And for every investor who thinks Ronald Reagan will heal our economy, there is another who fears he will not—so the action in these markets continues feverishly.

If none of these should suit, there are stock, bond, and futures markets in nearly every foreign land, and some of those foreign stock markets—Hong Kong, Singapore, Japan, and Canada among them—did very well during the 1970s when the U.S. markets slumbered. While the average U.S. stock stayed flat through the decade, the Hong Kong market was up by 600 percent. Owning London real estate in the 1970s was as good as, or much of the time better than, owning gold; and a timely purchase of German marks or Swiss francs would have doubled your money over the decade.

It's typical of the age of new money that as the 1980s began, some investors were less interested in the stocks and bonds of giant corporations than in the securities of issuers that had long ago failed. London reported brisk sales of the bonds of Czarist Russia and the Chinese Empire, and the bonds of the Confederate States of America—bought by British bankers during the Civil War and kept as curiosities ever since—were a hot item.

How It Used to Be Different, and Why It's Different

This was a monumental change from the days when if your money wasn't in a savings account or a government savings bond, it was in stocks. The financial wealth of all Americans was $470 billion in 1950 and 28 percent was in stocks. By 1965, our wealth had reached $1½ trillion and the share in stocks was 40 percent.

As late as 1970, with inflation and the age of new money nipping at our heels, we still kept 35 percent of our wealth (by then $2 trillion) in stocks. Then inflation came to stay, stocks proved no hedge at all against inflation, and by 1980 our wealth had climbed to $4½ trillion, of which less than 25 percent was in stocks.

The New York Stock Exchange counted 6½ million stock owners in 1952—three times as many as in 1929 just before the great Crash. By 1965, there were 20 million stock owners, and by 1970, 31 million. By 1975, though, the number had fallen to 25 million, and even with the market rally in 1980 there are only 30 million today (of whom more than 12 million aren't investors per se, but savers, being the owners of small amounts of stock acquired through some company's employee stock-purchase plan). In 1975, the average stock-owner owned $10,100 worth of shares. In 1980 the average had fallen to $4,000, meaning that the typical buyer of stock wasn't buying very much.

Even when the stock market rallies, we invest comparatively little in the stocks of our basic industries—steel, automobiles, chemicals, machinery—because we don't see them able to increase earnings faster than inflation or to maintain earnings in a recession. Instead we look for the occasional hot stock we hope will prosper come what may in the economy: the gambling stocks in 1978, the smaller oil companies in 1979, the defense and mining companies in early 1980, and the oils and the high-technology stocks again later in that year. The one thing many of these companies have in common—most notably the gambling and high-technology and the smaller mining and oil companies—is that they provide few jobs to American workers and operate on the margin of the American economy. And sometimes they operate clear outside the American economy, since many of the oil and mining companies are Canadian.

One reason we invest less, of course, is we save less. That's partly because in this age of new money we need more of our income to get by. But it's also because our bizarre tax laws penalize those who save. No matter how great your salary, the maximum tax rate on salary income is 50 percent. If you're wealthy—and the wealthy are most likely to invest—the tax rate on interest and dividends can run as high as 70 percent.

We invest less as individuals today because more of our wealth goes to giant pension funds that invest for us. Pension funds held only 2 percent of our wealth in 1950. Now it is about 10 percent, and total pension-fund assets, mostly managed by the trust departments of banks, are up to $450 billion. Individuals now account for only one trade in three on the New York Stock Exchange. The rest are carried out by institutions—mutual funds, insurance companies, and pension funds.

But even the institutions are less enchanted with stocks much of the time than they used to be. More pension money now goes into real estate, precious metals, commodity futures, and the like, while one big pension fund now puts some of its money into fast-food franchises. Of the money banks invest for the wealthy—some $200 billion today—70 percent was in stocks a decade ago against barely 50 percent today.

Why They Call It the Big Board

Even in their present state, of course, the stock markets are vast, and when the market rallies as it did in 1980 and 1981, it can still generate high drama—and lush profits.

There are 15,000 stocks traded in the U.S. today—one-third of these on a regular stock exchange. The rest trade "over-the-counter"—through a vast amalgamation of dealers who once traded face-to-face but who now mostly trade by telephone and computer. Trading on an exchange remains face-to-face, the broker representing the buyer meeting the broker representing the seller on that part of the exchange floor where the stock in question is traded. Each stock has a "specialist" who matches buy and sell orders and who is supposed to make sure trades are carried out with the smallest possible swing in the price of the stock. If there's a seller and no buyer, the specialist uses his own money to buy—selling out the next time a buyer appears. In time, the specialist will probably be replaced by a computer. Indeed, instead of an array of stock exchanges around the country, where humans trade, all stock trading some day will be both centralized and computerized.

That hasn't happened yet, despite government attempts to make it happen, and the exchanges continue to thrive. Individuals in great number have fled the stock market, but the institutions are there. And while institutions are putting a smaller share of their wealth into stocks, the steady flow of billions each year into pension funds means a steady rise in the amount of trading the institutions do.

The New York Stock Exchange is called the Big Board for good reason. Only one U.S. company in 1,000 has its stock listed there, but those listed companies account for more than 40 percent of the assets of all U.S. companies. The total value of the shares listed on the Big Board is $1 trillion. In 1979, the Big Board traded 8 billion shares of stock worth about $250 billion, handling some 80 percent of all stocks traded anywhere in the country. Next comes the American Stock Exchange (1 billion shares in 1979 worth about $20 billion), and then the various regional exchanges—Chicago, Boston, Philadelphia, and the Pacific Coast Exchange.

Everyone who trades on an exchange has paid for the right to do so by purchasing a "seat," which isn't a seat at all but a license to go on the exchange floor and trade stocks. The cost of a seat fluctuates according to how the market is doing. There are 1,366 seats on the New York Stock Exchange and you can buy one only when someone else will sell. The current price of a Big Board seat is about $200,000.

The stock markets are considered clean today, as opposed to years past when they were very dirty. The exchanges do a tolerable job of policing their own affairs, and all stock markets operate under the watchful eye of the Securities and Exchange Commission, the federal agency created in 1933 to police the securities markets. The first SEC chairman was Joseph Kennedy, father of the late President, and a Wall Street shark in his younger days. Franklin Roosevelt chose

Kennedy on the grounds that, having tried every trick in the books, he would spot trickery by others. If you lose money in the stock market today, it's more likely because you're unlucky or greedy or both than because someone rigged the market.

Still, you can make a good case that the small investor is at a marked disadvantage in a market where trading is dominated by giant institutions—rather like going barehanded up against King Kong. Almost any broker can provide you with reams of material about almost any company whose shares you want to buy. Every big brokerage house has a research department that specializes in preparing such material for customers. But the research offered to small investors is thin stuff compared with what Wall Street provides the big institutions. Further, the big institutions have big research departments of their own. The SEC has ruled that anything significant a company says to one investor must be said to all—meaning a company isn't supposed to leak juicy tidbits to the trust department of a bank without feeding you the same tidbits. In reality, the institutions will hear a lot of things you won't because it makes sense for a company to be nice to anyone that can buy (or sell) 100,000 shares of its stock at a time. That even the institutions don't do all that well in the market these days is confirmation of how treacherous the stock market has become.

Those who run the nation's stock markets mourn the departure of the small investor from the market, on the grounds that he or she brings much-needed "liquidity." That's a polite way of saying the institutions want plenty of innocents around to buy when they want to sell.

There are some exceptions to the above. The big institutions seldom buy the smaller issues on which investors have made a lot of money through the years. Because they must buy in huge lots, the institutions are pretty much obliged to invest only in larger companies. On the other hand, the

smaller stocks are more likely to be out-and-out speculations, and even more investors have lost than made money
on them through the years.

You can go to one of the big, brand-name brokerage
houses and pay a hefty commission in return for the invest-
ment-market research the house will provide. In most cases
the research is of only modest value and you might as well
go to a discount broker who offers no frills, but who also
offers lower commission rates.

Or you might forget about stock-market research and just
use a dart and a page of stock quotes torn from a newspaper.
There's a stock market theory called the "random walk"
that says no one can really pick winning stocks consistently,
and you can do just as well by throwing your dart at the
stock tables and buying whatever the dart hits. Nothing that
has happened in the stock market in most recent years dis-
proves that theory.

On Becoming a Hostage to Fortune

Whether you do lose money or not, this much about the
stock market must be understood, because it explains both
the past strength and the current weakness of the market:
when you buy stock you become a hostage to fortune. The
return on a savings account is fixed by law: you know when
you open the account how much it will pay. The interest on
a bond is fixed when it is sold. If the bonds of U.S. Bedroom
Slipper carry a 10 percent interest rate when they're sold,
they'll still carry a 10 percent interest rate when they mature
in 30 years.

When you buy stock, however, you become an owner of
the company and your return depends entirely on how much
the company earns. If the company prospers and its earnings
increase, your share of those earnings—paid as dividends—
will increase. If the earnings increase, other investors will

pay more for your share of those earnings, and the price of the stock will increase.

The basic measure of the relative attractiveness of a stock is its price-earnings ratio (or P/E): how many dollars per share an investor will pay to buy each dollar of earnings. If investors are optimistic about the ability of a company to increase earnings each year, they'll pay dearly for the stock and its P/E will be high. In early 1980, investors were justifiably pessimistic about the future of Ford, and its P/E was 3. The company earned $10 for each share of stock in 1979 (before losing $1½ billion in 1980) and its stock price in early 1980 was $30 a share. On the same day, investors were more optimistic about the future of Caesars World, an operator of gambling casinos, and its P/E was 26. They were more optimistic still about the prospects for Wilshire Oil, a small Texas oil company, and on that day its P/E was 47.

Some stocks are bought primarily because of the dividends they pay. American Telephone and Telegraph—Ma Bell to its friends—pays each shareholder $5.40 a year in dividends. In early 1981, AT&T shares were trading about $52. Since your $52 would buy a $5.40-a-year dividend, the return (more commonly called the yield) was about 10½ percent. Since AT&T is the richest company in the land, with $125 billion in assets, money invested in AT&T is considered nearly as safe as money put into a savings account—and, as AT&T earnings go up, the dividend—and the price of the stock—figure to go up as well.

One type of stock—preferred stock—is almost always bought for its dividend. What we buy mostly is common stock. That makes you an owner of the company with the right to vote at annual meetings, but it doesn't guarantee a dividend. If the company earns money it probably will pay a dividend, and the more it earns, the more it can pay out as dividend. With preferred stock, you're also an owner of the company. You may or may not vote at annual meetings, depending on the company and the terms of the preferred stock. But preferred stock pays a set dividend, year after year, no matter how much or how little the company earns. You're "preferred" because you get your dividend before the owners of the common stock see a penny.

Not everyone invests in the hopes of a higher stock price. You can "go short" and bet the price will go down. You borrow the stock from a broker at an agreed-upon rate of interest, and then you sell the shares. If the price goes down you buy the shares back at a lower price, return the shares to your broker, and pocket the profit.

Say Amalgamated Cough Drop is selling for $100 a share, which you regard as a ridiculously high price given the current malaise in the cough-drop market. You tell your broker to short 100 shares of Amalgamated. The broker lends you the shares at 10 percent annual rate of interest. In a twinkling the 100 shares have been sold for you at $100 a share, or $10,000 in all. Soon your faith (or lack thereof) in Amalgamated Cough Drop is rewarded and within a week the stock is at $50. At that point you instruct your broker to buy back 100 shares, which he does at $50 a share, or $5,000—half of what you sold the shares for. The broker has the stock back and you've made $5,000—less interest on the borrowed shares—which isn't bad for one week.

What's bad is if the price of Amalgamated Cough Drop shares goes up while you're short. You must eventually buy the shares back no matter what the market price is, and you're paying a hefty amount of interest each day you are short. When the market takes a big jump, the sound you hear in the background is the moaning of investors who are short and must cover at current—and higher—market prices. And cover you must, no matter what, since you have contracted to do so. A classic bit of Wall Street doggerel came from Daniel Drew, a nineteenth-century speculator, who observed: "He who sells what isn't his'n, buys it back or goes to prison."

A favorite Wall Street practice in days gone by was to buy

so much stock that those short couldn't find enough shares to cover. That was called a "corner"—someone having cornered a vast amount of the stock. At that point the shorts went cringing to whomever had the corner and settled as best they could, handing over the wife, the children, even the dog if that's what the "cornerer" wanted. There are laws against corners today and there hasn't been one in at least two decades. But they were common enough back in the 1920s and before, rigged by the grandest banking houses of the day.

Also gone are "pools," in which a band of investors would pool their money and begin bidding up the price of a stock —say Amalgamated Cough Drop—through timely purchases and a lot of glowing predictions about the golden future of Amalgamated. In time, the public would swallow the bait and bid the price still higher. At that point the pool operators would sell out at the inflated price and let the public watch the stock go crashing back down.

There is margin buying, which still goes on today but not as it did before the Crash of 1929. You can pay cash for your stock, or you can buy on margin, which involves borrowing part of the purchase price from the broker. The Federal Reserve sets margin rules, and the present rule says you can put up 50 percent cash and borrow the other 50 percent, with the stock serving as collateral for the loan.

The scary part comes when the price of the stock drops and your broker starts issuing margin calls—demanding you put up more cash to offset the drop in the value of the shares he's holding as collateral. You either put up the cash or the broker sells the shares—dumping more stock into a market that's already falling. The 1929 market was built on margin, investors often putting up only 10 percent of the purchase price, against the 50 percent required today. As the market broke in 1929, it touched off margin calls, followed by massive selling by brokers to save at least part of their loans. There's relatively less margin in the market today, of course.

Still, each market break produces margin calls and, in turn, anguish for investors.

The Golden Age of Wall Street

If the stock market is treacherous ground for investors now, it was the original perpetual-motion machine through most of the 1950s and 1960s. Because no one bought much stock in the 1930s or 1940s, by the early 1950s stocks were dirt cheap. Corporate earnings had been throttled, first by the Depression and then by wartime controls, and when the war ended and the postwar boom began, those earnings simply exploded. U.S. businesses earned $19 billion after taxes in 1945 and $73 billion in 1965. Stock prices advanced apace and one could hardly go wrong in the market. If you were smart enough or lucky enough to have bought one of the postwar wonder stocks—IBM, for instance, or Xerox or Polaroid—your fortune was made.

And if stocks were considered the best thing to buy at any time, they were considered the only thing to buy in times of inflation. The return on savings was set by law. The return on a bond was set when it was issued. But common stocks were another matter. In a time of inflation, earnings could still go up. So, in turn, could dividends, and so could stock prices—and the value of your shares would increase as fast as, or faster than, inflation.

That was true enough when there was just a little inflation, which is what we had for two decades after World War Two. The most widely followed stock-market index is the Dow Jones industrial average. It includes only 30 of the 1,500 stocks listed on the New York Stock Exchange—mostly such good gray giants of U.S. industry as GM, DuPont, Bethlehem Steel, and International Harvester. Not until 1979 did IBM make the list. Still, it's the most widely reported index, and when people talk about "the market" they usually mean the Dow. The Dow stood at 216 in 1950 and nearly 1000 at the end of 1965—a gain of 363 percent.

A far broader index is the one that measures the performance of all common stocks listed on the New York Stock Exchange. It stood at 12 in 1950 and 50 at the end of 1965—an increase of 317 percent. Between 1950 and 1965, consumer prices increased by just 31 percent.

If you bought a stock hoping for an increase in price, it probably did increase in price, and by far more than the rate of inflation. If you bought a stock for its dividend, you were also richly rewarded. The companies listed on the Big Board paid $5 billion in dividends in 1950 and $15 billion in 1965—an increase that again was well ahead of inflation.

With the average stock selling at 17 times earnings in 1965 —with a P/E of 17, in other words—people were paying dearly for those shares and putting a lot of faith in the ability of companies to keep boosting earnings year after year. Because stock prices were so high, the dividend yield on common shares—the annual payback for each $1 invested—had fallen from 7 percent in 1950 to 3.2 percent in 1965. Still, that was in line with what savings accounts and bonds were paying then, and neither savings accounts nor bonds offered the potential for price gains that stocks offered. There were market breaks now and again, including a grim one in 1962. Mostly, though, the market kept going up.

Big, established companies seldom sell much new stock, since each new shareholder is one more person who must be cut in on the profits. Adding new shareholders means "diluting earnings"—dividing the pie more ways—and existing shareholders don't like it much. Of all the money raised by business each year, the stock market seldom provides as much as 5 percent; the rest comes from banks and the bond market. Concern about diluting earnings is one factor. Another is that the interest on borrowed money is a tax deduction while the dividends paid to shareholders are not, making it more advantageous for companies to borrow than to sell stock.

Still, at that time any company that wanted to sell stock could do so, and the bull market of the 1950s and 1960s did permit hundreds of new companies to raise money. A banker might have qualms about an untested venture. The pension funds and insurance companies that buy most of the bonds might be similarly leery. But a company could usually find enough investors in the stock market willing to take a gamble. The investor might lose on three of every four new issues—but the fourth might be a Polaroid.

Inflation Rears Its Ugly Head

And then came the day of reckoning—which is hyperbole, of course, since what happened to the stock market took over a decade to unfold. What did happen was the arrival of the age of new money—and the gradual realization that while stocks might be a hedge against a little inflation, they weren't much of a hedge against a lot of inflation. And what we've had since 1965 has been a lot of inflation.

Inflation produces one sort of pressure on business, and the worse the inflation the more intense the pressure. The cost of doing business goes up, and while companies try to offset this by raising prices, not all succeed and the growth of earnings slows. What gains in profits there are become suspect because more and more of the gain is inflation-induced. Widgets that used to sell for a nickel now sell for a dime, and that fattens earnings. But the profit will evaporate as soon as you buy the materials to make new widgets because the cost of materials has also gone up.

And then comes the government's inevitable reaction to inflation—tighter and more costly money and, in time, a recession—and that produces pressure of another sort. During a recession profits don't grow at all, so companies can't increase dividends, and the incentive to buy stocks evaporates. The first inflationary outbreak associated with the Vietnam war came in 1965. The first major countermove by the Federal Reserve came in 1966. Dividends paid by companies listed on the New York Stock Exchange rose by 13 percent in 1965, but by only 5 percent in 1966. Between February and October 1966, the New York Stock Exchange index fell by 23 percent.

Inflation produces other reasons for avoiding stocks. A 3 percent return on common stocks was fine as long as other investments didn't yield more, and as long as stock prices kept moving up. As interest rates went up in response to inflation—as they inevitably do—the yield on common stocks began to look tepid compared with the returns now available on other forms of investment—bonds, Treasury bills, time deposits, etc. If the potential for a gain in the price of the stock is gone, these other investments look all the more attractive.

Finally, the worst enemy of the stock market is uncertainty. You buy stock because you believe the future holds the promise of higher earnings, higher dividends, and higher stock prices. In the age of new money, all the future holds is uncertainty.

The stock market recovered from the 1966 slump with the short-lived "peace rally" of 1968 when it seemed the war might end any day. Yet it was less a rally than an exercise in mass self-delusion. It was the go-go era—a frantic search for the relatively few hot stocks that could outrun the overall market, and outrun inflation as well. The heroes of the day were the "gunslingers"—young, publicity-hungry investment advisers and mutual-fund managers who were supposedly shrewd and quick enough to spot the hot stocks before anyone else did. It was also the golden age of the conglomerates—corporations hastily slapped together through the acquisition of wildly disparate companies that had nothing in common except they could be bought cheap. The gunslingers and the conglomerates were both born in the mid-60s and 1968 was the high-water mark for each.

The conglomerate typically made its acquisitions by issuing bizarre securities that came to be known as "Chinese paper." The gunslingers bought deeply of the conglomerates, and it was the rare conglomerate that didn't sell for at least 50 times earnings—and for earnings that were wildly inflated by some of the most ingenious accounting tricks known to man.

It was an age of wonderful nonsense and it lasted until inflation roared back worse than ever, and the Federal Reserve countered with more tight money until in 1970 the economy fell into recession. There was another market break in 1969–70 and this time the New York Stock Exchange index fell by 38 percent. That killed off the go-go market and banished the gunslingers and a good many of the conglomerates back into the night.

Then came the day of the "Nifty Fifty." The institutions —particularly the banks with the billions in pension-fund assets to invest—decided that while inflation was bad for stocks in general, and while inflation seemed here to stay, there were some stocks that (A) were big enough to absorb the sort of money the banks had to invest, and (B) were likely to increase earnings faster than the rate of inflation. The institutions identified approximately 50 of these stocks —hence the Nifty Fifty—including such companies as IBM, Citicorp, Avon, McDonald's, Xerox, Johnson & Johnson, and so on. The institutions concentrated their investing in those issues, and to hell with the rest of the stock market.

Paced by the Nifty Fifty, the market rallied once again. This one lasted from the spring of 1970 until early in 1973 when Armageddon arrived. In successive waves the market was pummeled by inflation, Watergate, tight money, the oil-price explosion, and the worst economic downturn since the Great Depression. The market peaked early in 1973 and then fell into what was not only the worst market break in history, but—counting all that was lost in all the investment markets —the worst financial disaster of all time.

The New York Stock Exchange index fell 50 percent in 18 months. The Dow Jones industrial average hit a record high of 1052 in January 1973 and then fell to 577 in December 1974. In the three years after the 1929 Crash, the total value of all stocks listed on the Big Board dropped by about $70 billion. During the 1973–74 market break, the value of Big Board shares dropped by $400 billion.

That was just on the Big Board. There are other exchanges, and the over-the-counter market, and in every market fortunes were lost. The market value of all stocks was $1.2 trillion at the end of 1972 and $675 billion two years later—a loss of $525 billion. When John F. Kennedy became President in 1961, the gross national product of the U.S. was less than $525 billion.

Individual investors lost some $400 billion—15 cents of every dollar in financial wealth they owned. Foreign investors in the U.S. market, including the supposedly shrewd Swiss, lost another $15 billion. Banks lost about $100 billion —half of it money belonging to pension funds, and the rest money it managed for wealthy individuals. In early 1981 the market value of all stocks was just back to where it had been at the end of 1972. Even then, investors were getting back 1981 dollars, which were worth barely half the 1972 dollars they lost. Given inflation, the Dow Jones industrial average would have to top 1500 to match a Dow average of 1000 in 1973.

The market has had its moments since, and the sages of Wall Street have been freely predicting that the 1980s will be the "decade of common stocks"—and they may well be if President Reagan can do what he says he can do. The average stock sells for barely 10 times earnings, meaning bargains galore for those who think the U.S. economy will stabilize in the 1980s.

Even so, most investors are still ignoring most stocks to ride the fads. Basic industry stocks are as unloved and unwanted as ever while almost anything labeled "energy" or "high technology" has soared to the heavens. On an October day in 1980 a genetic engineering company named Genentech sold its first shares to the public at $35 a share. On the first trade after that initial offering, the stock topped $80. But while these high-technology companies may represent America's future, they aren't America's present, and it's the present we're worried about.

As things stand, the stock market still is missing at least 1 million of the 31 million investors who were around a decade ago. And those who remain are putting very little of their wealth into stocks. Some stocks have outrun inflation, but most haven't. Virtually no stock has been able to outrun both inflation and recession, and the combination of inflation and recession is our portion in the age of new money.

A few companies can raise money in the stock market today, but most—including some of the biggest—cannot. And while the stock market may regain favor with investors, it will never again be *the* investment market as it was in the 1950s and 1960s. There has been too much water under the bridge—too many market breaks, too much money lost by too many people, and just too many alluring alternatives to stocks, with new ones popping up every day.

Chapter 11

What to Do When Stocks Don't Suit—and Why It'll Probably Cost You a Bundle

YOU SAY that stocks and bonds have done you wrong. You say the cure for what ails you is a plunge into pork bellies, a dive into Deutschmarks, a sortie into soybeans. If that's what you say, you've been bitten by the alternative-investment bug, and the only known cure is to rush out and buy a piece of real estate, a diamond or two, a futures contract in sugar, or a slapdash of color by a young artist waiting to be discovered.

If you've been bitten by the alternative-investment bug, you aren't alone in this age of new money, but you could be in big trouble. While the alternatives to stocks are numberless, most aren't for Everyman (or Everywoman, for that matter). The potential for gain is considerable, but so's the potential for losing your shirt.

You invest to preserve capital while building up more—gains in capital now being taxed at no more than 20 percent while the maximum tax rate on income is 50 percent. The aim of investing in the age of new money is to build capital faster than inflation can take it away and to protect capital when the inevitable recession hits. But the basic truth about investing is that the higher the potential return, the greater the risk. There are no known exceptions to this rule—there being, once again, no free lunch.

You could bet $100 at a million to one that the Empire State Building will collapse at high noon on St. Patrick's Day. Should it actually collapse at high noon on St. Patrick's Day, you'd be in clover. But the Empire State Building has stood for half a century and the chances it will collapse any time soon are pretty remote. More likely, you'd simply lose $100.

At various times in the past few years there appeared to be two exceptions to the rule that the higher the potential gain the greater the risk: six-month savings certificates and money-market mutual funds. Each has offered record yields as inflation pushes interest rates to the skies, and each has pulled in torrents of new money. Yet each has drawbacks that make them something less than perfect.

A six-month savings certificate offers a return indexed to inflation, the yield being tied to the rate on six-month Treasury bills. As inflation pushes interest rates higher, the return on the certificates goes higher—to 16 percent in 1980 and again in 1981, against 5½ percent on an ordinary savings account. And your money is insured up to $100,000 by the Federal Deposit Insurance Corporation.

Still, your money is tied up for six months, and in the age of new money, six months can be an eternity. An investor who counted himself lucky to get a certificate yielding 10 percent in late 1979 could only writhe when his neighbor got a certificate yielding 16 percent a few months later. And while a six-month certificate is fine when inflation is pushing interest rates to the skies, other investments look better when rates begin to fall—if only your money weren't tied up for six months.

A certificate seemed the perfect investment in March 1980.

Had an investor only known, a better investment was the stock market, which was beginning a rally that would soon carry stock prices to heights not seen in more than three years. By the time the certificate matured in September, much of the initial fury of the rally had been spent.

Money-market mutual funds tend to yield approximately what savings certificates yield; and the return on the funds also went to the skies in 1980, and again in 1981. And unlike a savings certificate that locks you in for six months, you can get out of a money fund any time by writing a check against your investment. Finally, most money funds are owned by organizations that own other kinds of mutual funds, and most permit you to move your money from one fund to another—say, from a money fund to a common stock fund—merely by placing a telephone call.

But the money funds do invest in some securities—certificates of deposit in U.S. and foreign banks, and those unsecured IOU's of corporations called commercial paper—that could conceivably turn bad in a severe recession. Money-market funds don't carry government insurance, and while the risk of failure because of bad investments is remote, it does exist.

Finally, those high yields on both savings certificates and money funds are before the tax collector shows up. Once the Internal Revenue Service takes its cut—up to 50 percent on interest and dividends as well as on salary—your actual return is almost certainly going to be less than the rate of inflation. Your money is safe, and it earns among the highest returns available when you buy a savings certificate or shares in a money market mutual fund. But it is money you might otherwise have invested in something—stocks, real estate, anything—that can produce capital gains. And again, the maximum tax rate on capital gains is 20 percent after the 1981 tax cut (reduced from 28 percent), and for most people the capital gains rate is even lower than that.

And that's the bind in this age of new money. If you play

it safe, your after-tax return probably won't match the inflation rate. If you try to outrun the tax man and inflation, you're taking risks that could eat you alive.

The 1981 tax law created the All-Savers Certificate with up to $1,000 a year in tax-free interest income ($2,000 on a joint return). But it's a one-year certificate, meaning you're locked in for the whole year. And the top yield—70 percent of the yield on a one-year Treasury bill—makes sense only if you're in a high enough tax bracket (30 percent and up) to make use of the tax-saving feature.

Whatever anyone tells you, stock options, commodity futures, real estate (except for home ownership), arts and antiques, gems, and high-priced collectibles are for those with money to lose, and with attorneys and accountants schooled in the byways of money. If the age of new money cries out for alternative investments, common sense begs for caution.

Buy an antique, a work of art, a diamond, or a piece of real estate, and you pay what the seller demands. Unless you're a serious student of the market, you have no idea whether you got a bargain or got taken. One diamond will be worth three times as much as another because of differences you couldn't spot in a million years. Buy the right apartment building in the right neighborhood at the right time and you gain income, tax breaks, and the potential for a juicy capital gain. Buy the wrong building in the wrong neighborhood at the wrong time and it could be a financial disaster.

When you sell, you take whatever the buyer offers and most of the time you won't know whether you got a good deal or got taken. Further, you can't sell until a buyer shows up and if you guessed wrong on the trends and fads of a market, that can be forever.

For all the negatives, the stock market offers some indisputable advantages. You know, any hour, day or night, exactly what a stock is worth. You can buy or sell in minutes, and your broker will tell you in advance how much commission you'll pay on the trade. Every publicly held company

—meaning every company whose shares are traded in any market—must make available to you all relevant information about itself. Most of what the company doesn't tell you you can learn from your broker or from any number of research works available at the nearest public library.

Rules for Survival

If you don't want the stock market, and you hanker for something beyond a six-month savings certificate or shares in a money fund, at least follow these rules:

1. Invest only money you don't need. You won't lose on every play in the alternative markets, but you may lose on most of them.

2. Before you invest, learn the rules of the market. If you want to try the futures market, at least understand why even veteran plungers lose on nine tries out of ten.

3. Before you buy in, know how you're going to get out. You can buy and sell stock options and commodity futures as quickly as you can stocks, but without a strategy for getting out you could be stuck in a real-estate play or in arts or antiques for a long time.

4. Except for home buying, be leery of investing long term. Time is compressed in the age of new money, and accurate economic forecasting is nearly impossible. If you invest short term you can jump from one investment to another as circumstances dictate. When you invest long term, you give up that flexibility.

5. Learn all you can about how the economy works. Become, as much as possible, your own economic forecaster, at least for those sectors of the economy in which you're investing. Plowing through economic reports and financial publications may be a dull alternative to watching Monday-night football, but the wealth you save will be your own.

The Big, Bad Bond Market

Of all the alternatives to stocks, the largest, most diverse, and least intimidating market is in fixed-income securities. That takes in everything from a 90-day Treasury bill to a 30-year AT&T bond. It encompasses Treasury bills, notes, and bonds; federal agency issues; corporate issues; state and local government issues; and issues from a variety of foreign borrowers who choose to borrow in the U.S.

The market involves at least $1½ trillion worth of securities, which makes it larger than the stock market. Some corporate bonds and a few municipal bonds are traded on the New York and other stock exchanges. Most trade over-the-counter—the "counter" these days being telephone, Telex, and computer. The common point of all such securities—whatever they're called, wherever they're traded, and whoever issued them—is that the rate of interest is fixed when the security is first brought to market and, except for a few of the newer "floating rate" issues, won't change until the securities mature. In time, most new issues will probably have rates that change in line with inflation, but such variable-rate issues are still few and far between. If you bought the 2¾ percent bond of AT&T when it appeared in 1952, it will continue to pay 2¾ percent each year until it matures in 1982. Why you would want a security yielding 2¾ percent is something else again. Unless you've been marooned on a desert island, or an inmate in a maximum-security prison, you probably sold it long ago.

And that introduces the other side of the equation: price. When a bond is issued, it's sold at par or close to it: par being $1,000 for most bonds. A 2¾ percent bond, bought at par, will yield 2¾ percent (or $27.50 per $1,000 bond) each year to maturity. Once a bond is issued, though, it trades in the marketplace, and, as with stocks, its price will fluctuate according to supply and demand. If 2¾ percent is a good yield, given inflation and what other bonds are yielding, the price will stay close to par. If inflation soars and newer issues return a lot more than 2¾ percent, investors will pay less for it and the price of the bond will drop. The yield would be 2¾ percent if you paid $1,000 for the bond. But if you could buy it for $500, the yield, based on what you paid, would be closer to 6 percent.

Say that in 1965 Amalgamated Cough Drop sold 30-year bonds to buy automated cough-drop-making machinery. To make sure the bonds sold, it offered what in 1965 was a handsome return—6 percent a year until the bonds matured in 1995. Each investor paid $1,000 for each bond and each bond returned $60 a year in interest. But now it's years later, inflation is higher, and bonds being sold today must yield not 6 percent but 12 percent and more if investors are to buy them. Were each Amalgamated Cough Drop bond still selling for $1,000, no one would buy them—not even the president of Amalgamated Cough Drop.

In fact, as new bonds with higher returns came to market, the original buyers of Amalgamated Cough Drop bonds sold out at lower and lower prices to buy new securities that paid more. Bonds are usually tagged with a nickname and these bonds would be called the "Cough Drop 6's of '95," indicating that the issue carries a 6 percent rate and matures in 1995. In time you could buy a Cough Drop 6 of '95 not for $1,000 but for $500. The interest rate on the bonds is 6 percent and will remain 6 percent until 1995. But you paid only $500 for each bond, and your return on that $500 investment is 12 percent. If you hold the bond until 1995, you'll get the full $1,000 back from Amalgamated. So you've done nicely for yourself, getting both a handsome return through the years and a capital gain. The closer a bond gets to maturity, the closer the price will move toward par—unless there's reason to believe Amalgamated won't be able to pay the bonds off at maturity.

Bonds used to be the province of the wealthy and of big institutions—insurance companies and pension funds. One reason was that bonds cost a minimum of $1,000 each and stock could be bought for a few dollars a share. Another was that until the mid-1960s, it was the rare bond that yielded more than 4 percent a year. Since rates didn't go up by much, prices didn't fall by much, and older bonds seldom sold at much of a discount from par, meaning the potential for capital gain wasn't very great. By contrast, the potential for gain in stocks was seen as unlimited.

Finally, there's something mysterious about the way bonds are quoted. You look at a newspaper on a day in 1980 and find AT&T common stock at 51¾—meaning $51.75 a share. That's easy enough to understand. Now you turn to the bond quotes and find 13 different AT&T bonds listed, each followed by a string of digits and letters. There is one listed as ATT 7s01, which apparently goes for $67 a bond. First off, the 7s01 means an AT&T bond with a 7 percent interest rate, maturing in 2001. The closing price doesn't mean $67 a bond, which would be a real bargain—but $670 per bond. By custom, and to save space in listings and in dealing, the final digit is always dropped. A quote of 95½ would be $955, while 97¾ would be $977.50. Meanwhile the Telephone 7s of '01, priced at $670 per bond, will return 10.4 percent (or a shade more than $70 a year) to a buyer each and every year until 2001, at which point AT&T will hand over $1,000 in cash.

There are painfully few stocks returning 10.4 percent these days and none with guaranteed capital gains built in, which is why more people are paying more attention to the bond market.

Companies, too, have a fondness for issuing bonds over stock, and in any given year, U.S. business will borrow $4 in the bond market for each $1 it takes from the stock market. There's that dilution factor: The owner of common stock is an owner of the company with the right to a share of profits. The bond owner is just a nice soul who loaned you some money. The interest paid on bonds is, in common with any interest expense, a tax deduction. The dividend to shareholders comes out of net profit.

The danger in selling debt is that the company has taken on a fixed expense for years to come. In a bad year, Amalgamated Cough Drop tells its shareholders things are tough and it won't be paying a dividend that year. The shareholders will mutter, and some will sell their stock, but that's the extent of it. Bad year or not, Amalgamated has to pay the interest on its debt even if that takes the last penny it has, and the higher the interest rate it took to sell the bonds, the more the company has to pay.

Bonds come in two varieties: mortgage bonds, which are secured by some piece of real property, and debentures, which are backed simply by the credit standing of the issuer. A company will have to pay more to sell a debenture than a mortgage bond since the mortgage bond is secured and the debenture isn't. There are also convertible bonds, which after a time can be converted into a certain number of common shares. The investor takes a lower return because of the potential for conversion into common stock, and a chance to share in the earnings of the company. The company, in turn, hopes it can shake off the fixed costs of a bond down the road by converting bondholders into stockholders.

A company can sell bonds to the public by registering them with the Securities and Exchange Commission and finding a banking house willing to buy the bonds and resell them to the public. It can also sidestep that and find one or more institutions willing to buy the bonds in a private sale. Life insurance companies are big buyers of these private bonds—known in industry jargon as "private placements."

Once a company decides to borrow, there are obvious advantages in borrowing long-term, since it doesn't have to pay back the money for a good many years. The drawback, of course, is that it's stuck with that interest expense for a like number of years. Most bonds contain a "call" provision, meaning the company can call the bonds in early and pay off investors before the bonds are scheduled to mature. Seldom, though, can a bond be called in less than ten years, so the interest expense goes on at least that long.

Investors obviously want the highest possible yield for the longest possible time. If they think rates will be higher a month from now, they'll hold off buying bonds until next month. A company that needs money in that kind of situation has little choice but to borrow short term from a bank until it can find buyers in the bond market. Through most of 1980 and into 1981, when no one knew where rates were going, buyers simply boycotted bonds, and companies that needed money could whistle for it. As a rule of thumb, investors want a bond that will yield the rate of anticipated inflation, plus 3 percent. If you think inflation will average 10 percent over the years, you'll want a bond to yield at least 13 percent. The problem in this age of new money is that no one knows what the inflation rate is going to be next year, let alone 30 years from now.

While long-term money isn't always available, it's also dangerous for companies to borrow too much for the short term, since short-term loans must constantly be renewed, or rolled over. If the need to renew a loan coincides with a bout of tight money, the company can find itself in trouble, with bills piling up and no money available.

Still another handicap to a company's ability to sell bonds is the way the age of new money has whittled away at the financial health of a big slice of American business. Many of the companies that need money the most are least able to borrow it. And that gets into another sad fact of financial life: all bonds aren't created equal.

Amalgamated Cough Drop is a nice enough company as companies go, but it doesn't have the financial might of an AT&T. On the other hand, it is in far better shape than Consolidated Cough Drop, which lost a fortune when its rum-flavored cough drop bombed in the marketplace. And Consolidated Cough Drop is a veritable pillar of financial strength compared with International Cough Drop, which is said to be on the verge of bankruptcy.

With world enough and time, you could learn about the relative financial strengths and weaknesses of all the companies that have sold bonds. Happily enough, there are organizations that will do it for you. They're called rating agencies, the giants of the business being Standard & Poor's Corporation (owned by McGraw-Hill) and Moody's Investor Service (owned by Dun and Bradstreet). Almost every issue that comes to market carries a rating by one or both agencies, the issuing company having paid the agency a handsome fee to rate its bonds because it knows that unless a bond carries a rating, no one will buy it.

To the very bluest of blue chips go the very highest of ratings—AAA at S&P, Aaa at Moody's. The assumption here is that the company is in such superb financial shape that hell would have to have been frozen over for 24 hours before the company would fail to make good on its obligations.

Below AAA comes AA, then A, and then into the Bs, then down through the Cs (things are looking very dark), and then down to D (it's all over but the sale of the office furniture). The higher the rating, the less a company has to pay to borrow—peace of mind being worth a lot to investors. A triple A issue might carry an 11 percent rate, an A issue a 12 percent rate, and a BBB issue a 13 percent rate. (BBB is the S&P rating. The equivalent rating at Moody's is Baa). Seldom will an issue ever come to market with less than a B rating. C and D belong to companies that have truly fallen on hard times—D meaning the company has already defaulted on the bonds in question.

A bank, tending the estate of a widow with eleven children, will choose among the highest-rated companies, safety here being paramount. Rarely will an institution buying for itself or for a customer go much below BBB. Below that you get into speculations pure and simple. The bonds are priced cheap and the gamble is that the company will somehow be able to pay the issue off.

Our Trillion-Dollar Debt

There's one borrower whose securities carry no rating, and that is the U.S. Treasury. Since Treasury issues are backed by the taxing power of the government, they're deemed so secure no rating is necessary. It's possible, in the dark of the night, to marvel at how the Treasury can run up $1 trillion in debt with not a prayer of being able to pay it off, and still find willing takers for every new issue it brings to market. A Treasury security, regardless of maturity, is nothing more than an IOU from the government—a piece of paper on which is written the government's promise to pay back a certain amount of money on a certain date. That the Treasury will do—by printing new securities to replace those maturing (plus more new securities to finance the current year's deficit). It's inconceivable that the national debt will ever shrink by any great amount, all of President Reagan's hopes and dreams notwithstanding—and quite conceivable that it will amount to $2 trillion by the time the twenty-first century dawns.

The Treasury borrows (whether refinancing old debt or financing new debt) by auctioning off its securities to the highest bidders—the bidders being the three dozen banks and brokerage houses that trade in Treasury issues. The winning dealers will then resell the issues to the ultimate investors—banks, corporations, insurance companies, pension funds, foreign governments, and wealthy individuals—at prices slightly higher than they paid. But an individual can also buy direct by placing an order with the local Federal Reserve Bank—actually going to the Fed bank and placing a bid for one or two bills or notes or bonds. The Treasury announces new offerings about a week before securities are actually sold.

Every Monday, just after lunch, the Treasury auctions about $7 billion in three- and six-month bills. Bills are sold in units of $10,000 and more, and most buyers take them $100,000 and more at a clip. This is one market that isn't for the common folk, and it was to keep the common folk content that the six-month certificate was created. But it takes $10,000 to buy a six-month certificate, so in 1980 the government created the 30-month certificate (tied to the rate the government pays for 30-month money), and the entry fee there is just $100.

Periodically the Treasury will sell one-year bills (anything maturing in one year or less being a bill). It will more infrequently sell notes (maturing in one to ten years), and still more infrequently bonds (ten years and out). Other things being equal, the Treasury would like to sell longer-term issues, because it won't have to refinance them for a good while. But the Treasury has the same problem corporations have, that of people not wanting to commit money for long periods; so it mostly borrows for short terms.

The Treasury had some $930 billion in interest-bearing debt outstanding at the end of 1980. Of that $623 billion was counted as "marketable debt," meaning that you or I or Citibank could own it: $216 billion of that in bills, $322 billion in notes, and $85 billion in bonds. There was also $300 billion in nonmarketable debt, including $75 billion in U.S. savings bonds, $25 billion in special issues held by foreign governments, and the rest owned by the Federal Reserve and by various government trust funds. The American public isn't asked to finance the whole national debt—just most of it.

When the Treasury borrows, it does so to make up the difference between government revenues and government spending. There are other units of the government, called federal agencies, that borrow for more specific purposes, and their debt amounts to about $250 billion. The Federal Home Loan Bank Board and a clutch of other agencies borrow to support the mortgage market. The Export-Import Bank borrows to finance the sale of U.S. goods abroad. In this age of new money there are agencies around to support virtually every human endeavor.

These agencies can't match the Treasury for sheer classiness. Every Treasury issue carries the explicit backing of the government—the pledge that, whatever it does to our tax bills, all the debt could be paid off if worse came to worst. The agency issues carry only an implicit backing from the government—the understanding being that the Treasury will never let any security of any unit of government go bad. In return for the slightly higher risk, agencies pay a little more to borrow than does the Treasury. If a one-year Treasury bill carries a 10 percent rate, a one-year agency issue will bring about 10¼ percent.

From Schoolhouses to Sports Stadiums

Cities and states are vast borrowers, with a combined debt of $325 billion in 1980. The entire market for these issues is called the municipal bond market. Some municipal issues are general-obligation bonds, backed by the taxing authority of the issuer just as Treasury securities are backed by the taxing power of the U.S. government. Other municipal issues are revenue bonds, those sold to pay for some income-producing facility such as a toll road or a sports stadium, the bonds to be paid off from the income from that facility.

General-obligation bonds were once considered less risky than revenue bonds, and investors got a higher return on a revenue bond. The financial plight of such cities as New York and Cleveland has raised doubts about the safety of general-obligation bonds, while some facilities financed by revenue bonds have become fantastic moneymakers.

The nifty feature of all municipal bonds is that the federal government can't collect a penny in taxes on the interest paid on those bonds. The idea at one time was that municipal bonds would finance such vital services as schools and sewers and street lights, and the tax-exempt feature was to ensure that investors would put up the money to finance those services. It's another time now, and a municipal bond is as likely to finance a domed sports stadium as a schoolhouse, but the tax-exempt feature endures.

What the age of new money has done to the whole bond market is to turn it wildly erratic. Inflation sends interest rates up and—in order to bring yields of older issues into line with new issues—bond prices go down. Recession slams interest rates down and so sends bond prices up. When inflation raged in early 1980, interest rates soared, and bond prices fell as never before. When the 1980 recession hit, interest rates fell and bond prices soared as never before. When the recession ended, interest rates again shot up and bond prices plunged—and what was once the most stable of markets has become the most erratic. For every shell-shocked investor in stocks, there's a shell-shocked investor in bonds.

So, what plenty of investors have done is quit both stocks and bonds and gone elsewhere. One big "elsewhere" is real estate—everything from the family home to sprawling shopping centers to towering skyscrapers. The value of all real estate in America is measured in the many trillions of dollars —making it by far the biggest investment market of all—and much of that real estate changes hands each year.

Real Estate: A Hedge with Thorns

Real estate has always been considered a fine inflation hedge—the idea being there's just so much land, while the demand for land must inevitably increase over the long haul.

And, in fact, over the long haul, land and real-estate prices have climbed higher. On the other hand, there have been some bleak periods—the past two years being such a period —when mortgage money got scarce and mortgage rates soared. Lots of people want to sell real estate but few people can afford to buy at today's prices and at today's mortgage rates.

There's also a herd mentality in real estate, and too many people tend to do too much of the same thing in the same place at the same time. Too many condominium apartment houses were built in Florida in the mid-1970s, and some of those buildings stood empty for years, eating up tax and mortgage payments and returning nothing but grief. The past few years have seen a madcap real-estate boom in California, with speculators bidding prices higher and higher until the average California home sells for twice the national average price for a home.

Still, time heals all wounds. Most of the Florida condominiums are now occupied, and most of today's unsold property will in time be sold. Since no market ever goes straight up indefinitely, the California real-estate boom will cool and some speculators will lose their shirts. Then, for a time, California real-estate prices will go up more slowly than they have, and some of the buyers closed out of the market will be able to come back in.

What keeps the real estate humming is the expectation that while prices are high compared with past years, they are low compared with what they someday will be. In this age of new money, not only have real-estate prices gone up in most years—they've advanced faster than the rate of inflation. Consumer prices climbed by 13.3 percent in 1979—the biggest one-year gain in 33 years. The price of the average one-family home increased by about 20 percent, and prices of cooperative and condominium apartments in the better locations did even better. Prices of better-quality commercial property—office buildings, shopping centers, and the like—

did better still. Finally, there's the tax deduction on interest paid on borrowed money, and real estate is invariably financed with lots of borrowed money.

You can't bank on 20 percent gains in home prices year after year, and mortgage rates will remain high for as far ahead as anyone can see—12 percent being the likely floor, with frequent leaps above that. You'll almost certainly have to settle for a mortgage where the interest rate moves up in line with inflation. To get a lower mortgage rate you'll probably have to cut the lender in for a share of the profit when you sell.

Yet the demand for homes and cooperative and condominium apartments also promises to remain strong enough to keep prices moving up. For one thing, the huge crop of post-World War Two babies is now moving into the peak home-buying age. For another, owning a home has been the best investment for most people in recent years, and that should continue to hold true in the future.

Home buying is a big thing in our economy, involving more than $200 billion in most years. Still, it's far from all there is in real estate. There are in addition small apartment houses, big apartment houses, small office buildings, big office buildings, very big office buildings, small shopping centers, big shopping centers, raw land, farmland, resort land, and on and on until the mind reels.

You can buy on your own. You can assemble a group of partners and buy. You can buy into a tax shelter—a partnership put together by a packager of such deals to buy something, in which primary consideration is given to the tax breaks available in real-estate investment.

What's true about all real-estate investment, except for home buying, is that it takes a lot of money (most of which can be borrowed if the interest rate doesn't scare you away), often involves considerable risk, and shouldn't be undertaken by anyone who doesn't have experience, or access to someone with experience. There have been books written by the hundreds on every facet of real-estate investment, and there are lawyers and accountants schooled in the intricacies of the market. Look very hard before you leap.

Along with investments in real estate, there are now a lot of investments in real-estate-related securities. The cost of buying in is high—$25,000 and up usually—but the risks are far less.

There is, for instance, the Ginnie Mae passthrough. Ginnie Mae is the nickname for the Government National Mortgage Association, which is a federal agency created to provide money to mortgage lenders. Ginnie Mae takes pools of home mortgages, and sells slices of those pools to investors. They're called passthroughs because the interest and principal payments on the mortgages in the pool are passed through to the investors in the pool. The pool lasts until the last mortgage in it is paid off—in about 12 years on average. Then you look for someplace else to put your money. Other government agencies, and a growing number of private mortgage lenders, now offer securities comparable to the Ginnie Mae passthrough, and with mortgage rates sky-high, the return on these securities has been pretty impressive. The mortgages that go into a pool have been screened by professionals, so the quality of these mortgage-backed securities tends to be pretty high. If you have the purchase price, they're worth looking into.

Or, if you're feeling especially daring, you may want to look at the two markets that are most clearly the offspring of the age of new money: listed stock options and commodity futures. Each has existed for years, but each has been enlarged and refurbished in keeping with the times. You invest in stocks and bonds, and in most forms of real estate. In options, and even more so in futures, you gamble, pure and simple. Most players lose on most trades. When they do win, however, they can win very big compared with the money they've put up.

Consider Your Options

The market in listed stock options dates only back to 1973, and its creator was not a stock exchange but an offshoot of the Chicago Board of Trade—the largest of the futures markets—called the Chicago Board Options Exchange. Brokers had made over-the-counter markets in options for years, but the CBOE turned it into an organized trading market with ground rules, with each transaction reported publicly as soon as it happened, and with the daily closing prices on all listed options published by major newspapers. Since then, other exchanges have gone into options trading, including the American Stock Exchange, and volume in the options market now approaches trading volume in the stock market.

When you buy a stock, you own it—to have and to hold until you make enough to sell at a profit or until you lose so much you quit in disgust. If you bought 100 shares of Western Bubble Gum at $100 a share, you have $10,000 on the line. You could turn a nice profit, but you could also lose most of your $10,000. Meanwhile your $10,000 is tied up—maybe for years—waiting for something to happen.

In the options market, you don't own the shares of Western Bubble Gum. Instead you gamble on what those who do own Western Bubble Gum will do to the stock. If you buy an option and the price goes up you can win big. If the price goes down, you lose—but seldom as much as if you owned the Western Bubble Gum shares outright. In the stock market, as stated, $10,000 will buy 100 shares of Western Bubble Gum; in the options market, $10,000 will buy an interest in many hundreds of shares, with a chance to profit accordingly.

When you buy an option, you're paying a fee for the privilege of doing something at a future date at a price agreed upon now: that something, in a stock option, being the purchase or sale of stock in the future at a price set now.

In explaining the options market, professionals cite a situation in which you're offered some real estate for $100,000. You're interested but you want to think it over. So you take an option on the property—paying $1,000 now for the right to buy it within a month at $100,000. There might be news during the month—say an oil strike on the land—that would make it worth more than $100,000. Because you hold that option you still get the land for $100,000 no matter what its market value is from now till it expires. If you decide against the deal, you're still out only the $1,000 you paid for the option, and not the $100,000 the property would have cost.

There are two different kinds of stock options:

1. The call option. For a price—called the premium—you buy the right to buy 100 shares of a stock at a predetermined price (called the striking or exercise price) during a given period of time (the end of that period being the expiration date of the option). The bet here is that the stock price will go up and you can buy the option stock for less than the market price of the shares.

2. The put option. It's just like a call option, except that you buy the right to sell 100 shares of a stock at a predetermined price during a given period of time. You buy a put because you fear the stock price will fall. If it does you can sell the option stock for more than the market price of the shares.

The exchange sets the exercise price for each option—puts and calls—there usually being several different prices available for each stock for which there is an option. The exchange further sets the expiration date for each option, the options expiring at three-month intervals up to nine months.

There were options available in some 400 stocks in early 1981, with more coming up all the time, and with enough different options available in each stock to make several thousand combinations in all. For each stock, there are both puts and calls, several different exercise prices, and three different expiration dates available.

In mid-1980, for instance, Exxon appeared 19 ways on the Chicago Board Options Exchange. There were call options with exercise prices of $50, $55, $60, and $70 a share—most of them available to expire in July, October, and January—plus an equally broad array of put options. Mobil was available 35 different ways. Each way represents a different option, and there is a separate price quote for each; each represents a different sort of gamble and is priced accordingly.

Say, for instance, that it is June 1980 and you are interested in the Exxon $60 option that will expire in January 1981. On this day the option sells for a premium of $9.50. Since the option is for 100 shares, you actually pay $950 ($9.50 times 100). Your $950—plus maybe a $50 broker's commission—has bought you the right to buy 100 shares of Exxon at $60 a share between the time you buy the option and its expiration date in January 1981. On the other side of the deal is the owner of the Exxon shares, who must sell you those 100 shares at $60 a share if you decide to exercise the option.

On this day, Exxon shares closed at $67.50 on the New York Stock Exchange, meaning you could buy 100 Exxon shares for $6,750, plus a broker's commission of about $100 —$6,850 in all. If you owned Exxon shares, you could sell them for $6,750, less the $100 commission, or $6,650 in all.

Obviously you wouldn't exercise the option this day. You paid $950 for the option and another $50 in commission, or $1,000 in all. Were you to exercise the option at once, you'd pay $6,000 for the optioned Exxon shares, plus another $100 in commissions to actually buy the shares. Your total cost —option, stock, and commissions—would be $7,100. You'd do better buying Exxon shares in the market, where the cost, including commissions, would be $6,850.

The point, of course, is that you don't have to exercise the option immediately. You have seven months before it expires in January 1981. You bought the option because you believe Exxon shares will go up during those seven months, the outlook being bright for the oil stocks and Exxon being the world's largest oil company.

In fact, you hit the jackpot because before 1980 ended, Exxon shares climbed from $67.50 to $88 on the New York Stock Exchange. Now you're in business because while Exxon is selling for $88 on the Big Board, you have that option on Exxon at $60.

As the price of Exxon shares moved up, the price of the option moved up as well, and most likely you would have sold the option to someone else along the way, taking a moderate profit and moving your money elsewhere. Let's say, though, that the gods whispered in your ear and you held on to the option until Exxon hit $88. Now you decide to exercise.

You buy the 100 Exxon shares for the option price of $60 —$6,000 plus a $100 commission. Between the cost of the option, the cost of the shares, and commissions, you've paid out $7,100. But now you own 100 Exxon shares, which can be sold in the market immediately for $8,800. Deduct a $100 broker's commission and you stll get $8,700 for your shares, which is $1,600 more than you paid for them. Your real investment was the cost of the option—$1,000, counting the commission—and a profit of $1,600 in a few months on a $1,000 investment isn't bad.

It could have gone the other way. Exxon shares might never have gone above $67.50 during the life of the option. In that case you wouldn't exercise the option and you'd be out $1,000. That, of course, is what the person who sold you the option—known as the "writer" of the option—hoped would happen. He owns the stock, and since it pays a nice dividend, he's none too eager to sell. A good many big institutions have taken to writing options to wring a little extra profit from the stocks they hold in their portfolio, and they do this because experience has shown that few options are ever exercised.

Still, you knew in advance you couldn't lose more than $1,000 on the option. You could have bought the stock, but then you'd have tied up $6,750, plus commission. This way you committed only $1,000 and the other $5,750 could have been invested elsewhere.

For instance, you might have tried a more daring play. Let's say it is still June 1980, and you notice there's a $15 Zenith option on the American Stock Exchange and the price of that option, expiring in February 1981, is 50 cents a share, or $50 for the whole 100-share option. On that, you'd probably pay about $3 in commission. Your bet is that Zenith shares, which this day sell for $11, will go above $15 a share before the option expires.

Plainly the odds are against Zenith topping $15 a share, which is why the option cost only $50. Again, however, you get lucky, because late in 1980 Zenith shares hit $21. And there you sit with an option to buy Zenith at $15. You have paid $53 for the option, including commission, and you can buy the Zenith shares for $1,500 plus a $50 commission. Your total outlay is $1,603 for the option and the stock, plus commission. You pocket about $500 on a cash investment of $53. The return on $53 in a money-market fund for eight months would have been around $4.

Turn it around by buying a put option, and the profit potential is the same. Instead of hoping the price of a stock will go up, you hope it will go down. If you have the Zenith $15 option as a put and the price of Zenith shares in the market breaks wildly before the option expires, you have made some money. Say Zenith shares now sell for $5, meaning you can buy 100 of them for $500. Sitting there on the other side of the put is some poor sap who must pay you $1,500 for those shares.

It's this promise of big gains on a minimum investment that makes options so alluring. If you hit on only a few of the

options you try, you're still nicely ahead of the game—and
of inflation. The trouble is that when markets turn as erratic
as they have in this age of new money, it's quite possible to
lose on every trade. One veteran trader in options said he
found the markets so frantic early in 1980 that he woke at 3
A.M. each day, and trembled violently for three hours.

Market professionals say more people could make more
money from options if they settled for lots of smaller gains
instead of holding on for the big killing. If you see a small
gain, grab it before it gets away rather than gamble on a
bigger killing down the road. That most people don't is what
keeps the sellers of options rich and most buyers poor.

From Gold to Pork Bellies

It's the same potential for big gain on a small investment
that makes the market in commodity futures so attractive. In
options you bet on the future price of a stock. In commodities you bet on the future price of such things as soybeans,
cotton, cocoa, and pork bellies (from which bacon is made).
Gold, silver, copper, and sugar were hot commodities in
1979 and 1980. At other times, pork bellies, coffee, frozen
orange-juice concentrate, wool, and soybeans have been
hot. What makes for profits in commodities is the price volatility, and the age of new money has had that in abundance.
There's no point in betting on the future price of sugar if you
believe the future price will be very close to the present
price. If you think the price will double or triple, the gamble
makes a certain amount of sense.

There have been futures markets for centuries, and the
Chicago Board of Trade was founded in 1848. In recent
years, though, the exchanges have created markets in new
commodities, new exchanges have come into being; and the
enormous price volatility in the world and the disenchant-

ment with stocks and bonds have combined to bring lots of new players into the game.

The markets used to trade only the staples: the grains, industrial metals, wool, sugar, cotton, eggs, and livestock. Then came new markets in such things as lumber and orange-juice concentrate. When it became legal in 1975 for Americans to own gold, gold contracts appeared on the Commodity Exchange in New York and on the International Monetary Market, an offshoot of the Chicago Mercantile Exchange. The IMM also introduced futures trading in foreign currencies, allowing you to gamble on the future price of the British pound, the Canadian dollar, the German mark, the Swiss franc, and the Japanese yen.

When interest rates began churning in the age of new money, exchanges began offering an opportunity to gamble on the future cost of money—or, more specifically, on the future price of a Treasury issue or a Ginnie Mae passthrough certificate. In the summer of 1980, even the New York Stock Exchange joined in, opening the New York Futures Exchange to trade in Treasury issues and foreign currencies. There are now under consideration by various exchanges gambles on the future price of various forms of energy, including electricity, and even on the future price of common stocks.

Before you understand how the markets work, you must understand this about the commodities markets (and the stock-options market as well). All are what are called "zero sum" markets. For someone to make a buck, someone must lose a buck.

I can buy a stock for $5 and sell it to you for $10. You can sell it to someone else for $20 and they can sell it for $50. Each of us has made a profit on the stock. In time the price of the stock may fall and the owner at that time might lose it all. It's possible, however, for a stock to trade at progressively higher and higher prices indefinitely, with everyone making a profit. The same is true with arts and antiques and collectibles and almost everything else.

But think of commodities (and again of options) as a two-person, winner-take-all bet. I think the Chicago Cubs will win tomorrow and you think the New York Mets will win. So we bet $100. If the Cubs win, I get the $100 and you lose. If the Mets win, you win the $100 and I lose. What you bet on in commodities (and, once again, in options) is the future price of something, as opposed to the current price, which in commodities is called the "spot" or the "cash" price.

Putting Your Money Where Your Sweet Tooth Is

Say it is December 28, 1979, and you want to bet on the future price of sugar—a reasonable thing to do since most experts expected (correctly, as it turned out) the price of sugar to go up in the months ahead.

Sugar is traded on the New York Coffee, Sugar and Cocoa Exchange, one of the four exchanges that now share very modern facilities on the eighth floor of the World Trade Center in lower Manhattan. Exchanges set the size of each trading contract, and the life of the contract (each one running for 18 months, with a separate 18-month contract expiring every month or two).

The quantities of a commodity that make up a futures contract vary widely. Sugar is 112,000 pounds, while gold is 100 troy ounces. There are contracts for 5,000 bushels of wheat, 38,000 pounds of pork bellies, 100,000 board feet of lumber, 125,000 German marks and $1 million in Treasury bills. These never vary. What does vary is the price someone will pay at any moment for a contract. Once the contract is established—112,000 pounds of sugar to run for 18 months —traders in the market move the price of that contract all over the place.

On this day you decide the price of sugar is going up, and

that—stocks and bonds and French impressionist paintings having failed you—you will make your pile by putting your money where your sweet tooth is. You call your broker (who more than likely these days trades commodities as well as stocks and bonds) and ask him to buy a contract in sugar. You have eight different expiration dates open to you—contracts expiring in January, March, May, July, September, and October of 1980 (all of this happening in December of 1979), and in March and May of 1981. Because you think the price of sugar will be pretty high by late spring, you pick the May 1980 contract.

On this day, the price of a May 1980 sugar contract on the Coffee, Sugar and Cocoa Exchange is 16.91 cents per pound, or $18,939.20 for the 112,000 pounds of sugar in the contract. (Count yourself lucky. On the same day a contract for 100 ounces of gold on the New York Commodity Exchange cost $51,780.) Your broker is an understanding chap who doesn't expect you to come up with $18,939.20 in cash. All commodity contracts are bought on margin, and he'll certainly ask for no more than 20 percent of the money—about $3,800—and if you're an old and valued customer, he may ask for only 10 percent. He'll also charge you a commission of about $60.

And now you have a bet running. Specifically, you're betting that the price of sugar will be higher in May than it is in December. You really don't want the sugar, since 112,000 pounds of sugar fills a lot of sugar bowls. You want the profit.

Nonetheless you have now contracted to buy 112,000 pounds of sugar at 16.91 cents a pound, to be delivered to you in May. On the other side of the contract is someone who must sell you 112,000 pounds of sugar at 16.91 cents a pound in May. In the parlance of the trade, you have gone long May sugar and the other person has gone short. This being a zero sum game, one of you will win and the other will lose.

As it happens, you won—sugar sells for 24.10 cents a pound when the contract expires. The person you contracted with must sell you sugar at 16.91 cents which you can immediately sell in the cash or spot market at 24.10 cents. That's a profit of 7.19 cents a pound, or $8,052.80 in all, less commissions. Since you only put up $3,800 in cash, and probably less, to buy the contract, you've nearly tripled your money in five months. The seller, of course, had to buy sugar in the spot market at 24.10 cents a pound to sell it to you at 16.91 cents a pound—your gain being his loss.

More likely, you didn't hold the contract until May. You don't want the bother of selling 112,000 pounds of sugar on your own (you wouldn't actually have gotten the sugar, but rather a warehouse receipt giving you ownership of it), and fewer than 1 percent of all commodity contracts involve someone's actually taking physical possession of the commodity. You probably sold your contract as soon as you rang up enough profit to make it worthwhile and moved on to something else. Indeed, at one point the May contract sold for 28.14 cents a pound, and you'd have been better off selling out before the contract expired. You'd have been still better off buying a September 1980 contract, since by the summer of 1980 sugar was up to 39 cents a pound. Any way you played it, though, you almost certainly made money.

Had you bought any number of other contracts, however, something much direr would have happened. Instead of going up as sugar did, prices of most commodities went down as the economy slipped into recession. And when commodity prices fall, the markets turn ugly.

Say you have put up $2,000 in cash to buy a grape-jelly contract that is worth $20,000. If the contract price falls so the 1,000 gallons of grape jelly that make up the contract are now worth only $19,000, your broker will ask you to put up another $1,000 in cash. If it falls to $18,000, you come up with still another $1,000. It's called "marking to the market," and if you're not careful, it can devour you. Most speculators in commodities bail out as quickly as possible when the margin calls start, electing to lose their stake rather than throw good money after bad.

And that's the trap of the futures markets. The same price volatility that makes for big gains can also produce wild price swings that can wipe you out in an instant. Even if you guess right on the overall direction of a commodity, day-to-day swings can kill you. And while in stock options you know to the penny how much you can lose on any play, there's almost no limit to how much you can lose on a plunge into commodity futures.

Between early 1979 and early 1980, the price of silver went from $6 to $50 an ounce. There were times during that span when silver climbed by 10 percent a day, producing enormous gains for anyone with a contract to buy silver. On the other side of each contract was someone who had to deliver silver at those incredible prices.

Mother Nature and the Hunts

Markets are volatile enough in the age of new money. The volatility in commodities is something else again. A storm or a frost somewhere, a rumor of a coup in a distant land, a misunderstood word from a government official: any or all can send a commodity, and sometimes the whole market, off on a tear. And sometimes it's just you against Mother Nature —winner take all. Who, for instance, could doubt that, between the recession and the prospects for bumper crops, grain prices would fall in 1980? And who could be blamed for betting accordingly? Anyone who did bet that way got clobbered, of course, when the heat wave and the drought wrecked the harvest and sent grain prices shooting up.

In early 1980 the silver market came as close to not working as any future ever has, and behind that lies the strange tale of the Hunt brothers of Texas—Nelson Bunker Hunt and William Herbert Hunt. People almost never take possession of the commodities in which they trade, but the Hunts aren't your ordinary family, being worth many billions of dollars. Nor, in this age of new money, is silver just any old commodity.

As the price of silver soared in 1979, the Hunt brothers began taking possession. By one account, the Hunts by early 1980 owned or controlled more than $5 billion worth of silver, which represented a considerable part of the available supply. Suddenly and ominously there were a lot of people who had contracted to deliver silver with not nearly enough silver to go around. Faced with a potential corner—meaning that people who had contracted to deliver silver might be unable to find enough to deliver—the Commodity Exchange, on which silver trades, blew the whistle. No new contracts could be purchased and the only trading allowed was to close out existing contracts. That was later modified to limit the number of silver contracts a speculator could buy. Both the Commodity Exchange and the Chicago Board of Trade, which also trades silver, also raised the cash margin that speculators had to put up.

All that, plus the onset of recession, ended the surge in silver, and the price in short order dropped from $50 back to around $10 an ounce. And there, as the price plunged, sat the Hunt brothers with all their silver, losing fortunes—on paper at least—every time prices fell a little more. And since the Hunts, in common with all those who speculate in commodities, did it with borrowed money, those who made the loans were faced with the equally staggering losses. For a few days in March 1980, it looked as though some major brokerage houses might fail, and the nation's financial markets quivered. In the end, with some behind-the-scenes prodding from the Federal Reserve, a billion-dollar loan package was arranged for the Hunts, the brothers themselves pledging much of their personal wealth as collateral. In time things got unwound in a reasonably orderly way.

How much the Hunt brothers actually lost is sheer conjecture, since no one knows for sure how much silver they owned or how much they paid for it. Much of it was bought at very low prices, and it's possible that for all the storm and fury the Hunt brothers lost not a penny. If you're squeamish, it pays not to think about the small investors who got caught up in the maelstrom in silver.

The trading of commodities is a colorful spectacle. When stocks are traded on the floor of the New York Stock Exchange, it's gentleman to gentleman—mostly conversational tones and controlled gestures. Commodities are traded at a "pit"—actually a wooden ring that everyone mobs around. The mob includes traders for the big brokerage houses that trade commodities as well as stocks and bonds, traders for the houses that trade only commodities, and lots of people (mostly quite young) who have scraped together enough money to purchase a seat on a commodity exchange to trade for themselves.

You trade by shouting a little louder than anyone else. One trader shouts out a price on one side of the contract, another bellows back his acceptance. The faster the trading, the louder the din, and veteran traders have raspy voices and hearing problems. Lowell Mintz, the forty-two-year-old chairman of the Commodity Exchange in New York, says there are certain sounds he no longer can hear and that he'll never be asked to sing in anyone's choir.

The mob around each pit is a blaze of color, each brokerage house outfitting its people in jackets of a specific color. The aim is not to be stylish but to help traders know who they're dealing with in the frenzy of a hot session. It costs about $150,000 to buy a seat on the Commodity Exchange —a hot exchange since it trades both gold and silver, but a suspect one, too, since the fiasco in silver. A would-be trader must prove his or her financial standing to the exchange. Once in, and assuming the trader has the right feel for the markets, the potential for making heaps of money quickly is considerable. "It's a young person's game," Mintz agrees. Most traders either make it so big they retire young or they quickly lose their stake and move on to a more suitable line of work.

While the commodity markets are gambling dens for speculators, they do serve a critical function for companies that use lots of commodities, and that function is hedging against price fluctuations in those commodities.

Amalgamated Cough Drop uses a lot of sugar in making cough drops, and it has contracted to buy 100,000 pounds of sugar for cash when the crop comes in, at whatever the price is at that time. It fears, however, that the price of sugar will be higher when the crop does come in than it is now. To hedge, it buys sugar contracts that will expire about the time it must pay for its sugar. If the cash price of sugar goes up, Amalgamated will have to pay more than it hoped to for its 100,000 pounds. But the higher sugar price will have also pushed up the price of sugar futures. By selling those contracts at the higher price, it makes enough in the futures market to offset the higher cost of sugar in the cash market.

Or say Amalgamated holds a lot of sugar in its inventory and fears the price—and therefore the value of its inventory —will go down before it can turn the sugar into cough drops. Then it would sell a sugar contract, agreeing to deliver sugar when the contract expires. Should the cash price fall, the value of the sugar in its inventory would fall, but so would the price of futures contracts in sugar. Amalgamated would then buy back its contracts at the lower price, and the profit on that transaction would offset the loss on its inventory.

With interest rates gyrating all over the place, it's not surprising that the fastest-growing side of the market has been in the futures tied to interest rates of Treasury and Ginnie Mae issues. If the price of money moves one way, that can be offset by the right hedging move in these "financial futures."

Things are looking up for the amateurs who want to play

in futures. Mutual funds that invest your money in futures are coming on the scene. The idea is, while you might drown in the futures markets, the professionals who run the commodity funds know how to survive in those markets. These still aren't risk-free investments—nothing in the futures market is. But they do offer you a better run for your money, if not the enormous potential for profit that a solo plunge into these markets can produce.

And All the Rest

Finally, there's everything else: arts, antiques, collectibles, precious gems, semiprecious gems, books, stamps, coins, and all the other things people invest in today. Books have been written about each market, and each market has its code of conduct and its rules for survival.

If there's a common thread running through it all, it is *Caveat emptor.* Stocks and bonds and options and commodities can be hair-raising, costly markets in which to play. Yet each is traded on an established exchange, with posted rules, posted prices, and a considerable degree of regulation. With all that, you can lose your shirt.

In these other markets you're on your own, armed only with what you know about the items being traded and your own instinct for survival.

The price appreciation in these markets has been staggering. A diamond that sold for $10,000 five years ago would fetch $50,000 today. Prices of some U.S. coins have trebled or better in just a year. A dealer in gems says there are no semiprecious gems today. Prices have gone up so rapidly that all gems are precious. Robert S. Salomon, Jr., partner at Salomon Brothers, the New York investment banking house, notes that while common stocks appreciated by only 3 percent a year from 1968 to 1979, the value of stamps appreciated by close to 20 percent a year. While recessions can hit these markets, through the years they have offered gains that have outrun inflation by miles.

The danger is that it is you against the connoisseurs and the professionals, with neither the formal structure of an exchange nor government regulators to protect you. If you can't tell a D-flawless diamond (the top grade) from a rhinestone, stay out of the diamond market. If you don't have the knowledge and experience to know why one young painter shows promise and another doesn't, stay out of that market.

You're better off in markets where things are precisely identified and catalogued, with published price lists. There are books that list almost every collectible stamp in the world. There are books that will tell you the latest price for a 1907 Saint-Gaudens $20 gold piece in mint condition (more than $15,000). You and the coin dealer might quibble over whether the coin is fine or extra fine, but you'll have a pretty good idea of what to pay, and what to expect when you sell. There are comparable books for a lot of things people invest in, from Oriental carpets to vintage cars. Once you get away from those "catalogued" markets, you're on your own. And if you haven't taken the trouble to learn about the market, you're just another lamb waiting to be fleeced.

Chapter 12
Gold, Which Needs No Further Introduction

I'M PEEVISH at times, but you're good as gold. I get by, but you have the golden touch. You're mean sometimes, but I live by the golden rule. I live in a pleasant residential neighborhood, but you live on the Gold Coast. And so it goes.

We haven't used gold as money in America since 1933 and we may not ever again—Ronald Reagan's apparent fancy for the gold standard notwithstanding. The gold standard, in which all money was gold or backed by gold, is offered as a cure for all that ails our economy—but only by those who forget that the gold standard never worked well for most countries most of the time, and that it failed utterly when it was needed the most: during World War One, the inflation that followed the war, and the Great Depression that followed the inflation.

But no matter that gold isn't money any more. The romance and the mystique linger on—woven deep into our language and into our souls. The government gives us unbacked paper money and coins made of cheap alloy. We accept and make use of them—most of the time. But let an invader march upon our gates or an inflation threaten to turn hyper, and then the demand for gold becomes enormous.

Spies go behind enemy lines carrying gold to bribe their way out if they are discovered. When Vietnam fell to the Communists in the mid-1970s, those with gold bought their way to freedom and those with none became slaves. When inflation tore the world, and events in Iran and Afghanistan turned ugly, sellers disappeared from the world's gold markets and buyers pushed the price up by $300 an ounce in a few weeks until a single ounce of gold, no bigger than a poker chip, cost $850. That's astonishing, considering that the U.S., thanks to our vast gold hoard, was able to hold the price nearly everywhere in the world at a rock-steady $35 an ounce from 1933 until 1968.

Gold first sold above $100 an ounce in 1973. Not until 1978 did it top $200 and not until well into 1979 did it pass $300. For an investor who bought gold in 1970 and held it until early 1980, the profit was 2,000 percent, while prices in the U.S. climbed by 150 percent during that period, and the Dow Jones industrial average was up by 4 percent.

Other things did even better than gold: silver, for a time, and various works of art. But silver's vogue was short-lived and art is for the connoisseur and faddy to boot. Gold is for everyone—available in coins and trinkets weighing an ounce or less, or in bars about the size of a small building brick that were worth $340,000 each on the day gold hit $850 an ounce, and still worth $200,000 each when gold retreated to $500 an ounce in early 1981.

And then there is the safety factor. Even when the price isn't going up, there's comfort in knowing gold will keep its value long after our paper money and our coins of base alloys have turned to dust. Gold is a superb store of value—more likely than anything else known to keep its intrinsic value tomorrow and next month and next year.

You can further argue that gold is the only thing of absolutely fixed value there is. On that basis, it isn't the price of gold that is going up, but the value of the paper money going down. The rapid advance in the price of gold in dollars, therefore, is the result of an enormous, and accelerating, decline in the value of the dollar. A proof offered to support this view is that an ounce of gold will buy about as many barrels of oil today as it did ten years ago—the price of gold and the price of oil only appearing to go up because the value of the dollar has gone down.

In Which We Discover Gold

Americans couldn't own gold from 1933 until 1975, and not only the big gold markets but also the big gold buyers were in Europe and Asia. One of the world's best-beaten trails was the smuggling route that led from London and Zurich through the Middle East to India, the Indians selling silver to buy gold. That Indians legally could neither export silver nor import gold didn't slow the trade one whit.

Americans reentered the gold market in 1975—timorously at first and then as the age of new money swallowed us up, with a madcap rush. By mid-1980, according to Merrill Lynch, U.S. citizens had become the sixth-largest holders of gold—paced only by the U.S. government, French citizens, the International Monetary Fund, Indian citizens, and the German government.

We're heavy buyers of the South African Krugerrand—a popular coin because it contains precisely one ounce of gold. We have also bought large numbers of Canadian Maple Leafs, another one-ounce coin, introduced in 1979, and of the Mexican 50-peso piece. In the summer of 1980, the U.S. offered its own gold pieces—not coins that could be used as money, but specially struck gold medallions available in ounce and half-ounce weights. The medallions carry the portraits of famous Americans, new faces to appear each year. None of the coins and medallions are of interest to collectors, being common as dirt. They are bought solely because they are made of gold.

Today, New York is the world's biggest gold market, having moved ahead of London and Zurich. Gold is also traded in Hong Kong and at various spots in the Middle East (where it has also become a favorite investment in recent years—a nice place to park some oil money). By the time one gold market closes for the night, another is opening, and there isn't an instant when someone isn't trading gold in some corner of the world.

One thing that gives gold its allure is there isn't much of it. All the gold mined since the beginning of time—roughly 100,000 tons—would fit into a high school gymnasium with room enough for a couple of cheerleaders. All of the mines in the world together produce about 40 million ounces of gold a year, which at current prices is worth about $20 billion. Americans spend three times that much each year on restaurant meals.

About 60 percent of the world's gold comes from the deep mines of South Africa and about 2½ percent comes from U.S. mines, with South Dakota the biggest gold-mining state, followed by Nevada and Utah. Russia is second to South Africa among gold producers, followed by Canada and the U.S.

How much gold Russia does produce in a year is a mystery because the Russians don't tell. The U.S. government's best guess is 8 million ounces a year—about $4 billions' worth at current prices. Having gold is critically important to Russia's economic well-being. The dollar is accepted in virtually every country in the world; the Russian ruble is accepted only by its East Bloc neighbors. If Russia wants to buy from the West, it must either work out a barter deal or sell off some gold to buy dollars in the world money markets.

What adds to gold's allure is that it's not merely scarce—and therefore valuable—but also that it's a very useful metal. It is widely used in jewelry, and if you are an adult you probably have gold fillings in your teeth. But it's also an industrial metal that doesn't rust or corrode, and it is impervious to nearly all acids. You could bury gold for a thousand years, dig it up, brush it clean, and it would look as good as new. Gold is a superb conductor of electricity, and even at current prices, it is used in electrical appliances because a little gold replaces a lot of something else.

Finally, you can fit a lot of gold into a very small space because it's a very dense element. It's commonly cast into bars (rectangular if cast in the U.S. and trapezoidal if cast elsewhere), and each bar (again about the size of a small building brick) will weigh 400 troy ounces, or approximately 27 pounds. You could carry a few thousand dollars' worth of gold in your watch pocket and a half-million's worth will fit easily into a middling-sized safety-deposit box.

According to International Monetary Fund figures, all the governments of the world together held some 1 billion ounces of gold in mid-1980—worth, at current prices, about $500 billion. America's share was 265 million ounces, worth about $135 billion. Next came Germany with $50 billions' worth, followed by Switzerland with $40 billion. The OPEC countries together held about $20 billions' worth.

Only half our gold is buried in the bullion depository at Fort Knox. Another quarter is either in the New York Assay Office or the bullion depository at West Point, New York. About 10 percent is at the mint in Denver and there are small amounts at the mint in Philadelphia and the assay office in San Francisco.

Beneath the Streets of New York

The greatest hoard of gold in the world—indeed the greatest hoard of treasure in the world—is in New York City, 85 feet below Nassau Street in the vaults of the Federal Reserve Bank of New York. At the start of 1980, those vaults held about 361 million ounces of gold, worth at current prices about $180 billion—all of it stored in an area about half the size of a football field. Unfortunately, not an ounce of it belongs to us. The Federal Reserve acts as guardian for gold bought by other countries from the U.S. and left for safekeeping in New York. There's no charge for the service, although the Fed does collect a small handling fee when gold comes in, goes out, or is moved around in the vault.

At the end of World War Two, the U.S. owned much of the world's gold. The postwar international monetary system, created at Bretton Woods, New Hampshire, in 1944, called for all currencies to be valued in terms of the dollar and the dollar to be valued in terms of gold. The dollar would officially be worth ⅓₅th of an ounce of gold. To make that value stick we promised that any foreign government appearing with 35 U.S. dollars could buy one ounce of U.S. gold. Many dollars went overseas through the years, and lots of those dollars were then used by governments to buy U.S. gold.

We officially broke our promise to sell gold for dollars in 1971—at which time there were $5 in the hands of foreign governments for every dollar's worth of U.S. gold. It was to free gold for possible sale to foreign governments that we finally removed the gold backing from the dollar in 1968—although if all those governments had presented their dollars, there still wouldn't have been nearly enough gold here to satisfy them.

Meanwhile, most foreign governments that did buy our gold left it with the Fed, and that's where it is today, resting atop the bedrock of Manhattan and protected by some of the most elaborate security methods ever devised. If you're hankering to get rich, don't expect to do it by knocking off the gold vault at the Fed. In fact, if you incline just the littlest bit toward paranoia, it's a good building to stay away from. Writers, would-be filmmakers, and assorted cranks turn up periodically at the New York Fed with theories on how the vault might be cracked. The Fed isn't amused, and suggests to each they get lost.

You can tour the gold vaults, though, and some 10,000 visitors do that each year. There's even a little booklet called "Key to the Gold Vault" that is handed out to tourists.

Enter the New York Fed and you're instantly picked up by an armed guard who asks your business. You must sign in, get a name tag, and then pass through a massive set of barred doors that admit you to the interior of the building. There are similar sets of doors throughout the building, and should an alarm go off, all doors are locked until the all clear sounds. Beyond the gold, the New York Fed also holds billions in currency and government securities.

You go by elevator to the basement, and even there you're still four doors away from the gold—three sets of barred doors that open with a key, and the world's largest vault door, which operates on a time lock. The vault door weighs 90 tons and rotates within a 140-ton frame. The door is really a cylinder, and when it swings open, it creates a passageway into the vault. When it swings shut there are 90 tons of steel between you and the gold, and no one person knows the whole combination that will open it. When the door shuts it also drops ⅜ inch, creating an airtight, watertight seal. The vault opened in 1924, and perhaps a quarter-trillion dollars in gold has passed through it since then.

The interior of the vault is in blue, yellow, and cream, set off, of course, by the gleam of the gold. There are stacks of 400-ounce gold bars on wood and metal pallets—on this day, gold belonging to the International Monetary Fund, which is to be sold at auction. But most of the gold is still one more remove away from the visitor—locked inside one of the 122 cages within the vault. Each cage belongs to a foreign government or international institution that stores its gold at the Fed. There are no names on the cages, only numbers, so you don't know whose gold is in which cage. When gold is transferred from country to country, it's simply moved from one cage to another.

The largest cage holds some 107,000 bars of gold, worth about $21 billion at current prices. The Fed won't say whose cage it is.

A visitor who bends to pick up one of the bars in the vault instantly finds an official arm clutching his. The Fed isn't afraid that someone will filch a bar. But each bar does weigh 27 pounds and the Fed doesn't want mashed toes among its visitors. Workers in the vault wear special magnesium toe protectors when they move gold, in case a bar is dropped.

Each bar that comes in is weighed on a huge scale so sensitive it can measure in $\frac{1}{100}$th of a troy ounce. That, the Fed likes to point out, is equal to the weight of one-third of a dollar bill. Each bar carries a stamp to show its fineness—how much is pure gold—and where it was cast. To be used in international trade, the bar must be 99.5 percent pure gold, the rest being silver, copper, and other impurities that would be too expensive to remove during refining. If the bar is badly nicked, it's melted down and recast.

The gold is suprisingly dull in tone, and slightly cold and greasy to the touch. It doesn't glitter as you'd expect it to. And in truth the gold vault is a disappointment because there's too much gold around for the mind to handle. A single gold bar set on black velvet would be impressive. That five bars of gold, each about the size of a hero sandwich, could be worth close to $1 million is equally impressive. But there's no way to comprehend $180 billion in gold in a single room: each bar now equal to 10 years' salary for the average person, 122 cages around the vault, and a king's ransom in each. It is wealth beyond measure, a profusion that dulls the senses.

And then there's this point: it's wealth but for Americans it's not money. If you wanted to make a phone call, you'd be better off with a dime made of copper and nickel than with all the gold in the Fed's vault.

A few dozen countries around the world still make gold coins today and a few provide some gold backing for their money. But even where there are gold coins, they aren't widely used. It's hard to think about using gold as money or about a money supply backed by gold when the price can change by $50 an ounce, and more, in a day.

The Substandard and Gold Standard

Those who quake at the rate at which the Federal Reserve has created money in recent years suggest a return to the gold standard, which is dandy except it's hard to imagine its happening. If the evil of paper money is inflation, the evil of the gold standard was there never was enough gold to go around. For most people, most of the time, the gold standard meant a life of perpetual recession. For the luckless souls and the luckless nations that had no gold, it was fullblown depression.

As things go, the gold standard had a short life. It was born early in the nineteenth century as gold from California, South Africa, Russia, and Australia poured into world markets; it was worldwide by the 1870s, limped through the years after World War One, and was dead by the early 1930s.

In theory, the gold standard was so perfect, so beautifully symmetrical, as to have been ordained by heaven. In theory, being on the gold standard meant that every inflation, every depression, every imbalance in trade with other lands carried within it the seeds of its own cure.

To understand the gold standard, look at my country, Fantasia. The gold vaults of Fantasia are empty and we're all as poor as church mice. Because we're so poor, we toil for 20 hours a day without a whimper, and for pauper's wages. What we make are anvils, and because we work so hard for so little, we produce anvils for less than anyone else in the world. In time our work pays off and our anvils conquer the world market. Since the world is on a gold standard, we're paid for our anvils in gold. And since Fantasia is on the gold standard, all the gold flowing in swells our money supply. We can mint more gold coins and issue paper money backed by gold.

Soon prosperity sweeps the land and we can now buy all the goods the world produces—the choicest of foods, the rarest of wines, the finest of garments. And so we do until our ports are filled with ships bringing the products of other lands to our doors. Unfortunately, because we're so rich, we will no longer work 20 hours a day, or even 10 hours a day, and those who do work demand high wages. Instead of making cheap anvils, we now make expensive anvils, and our grip on the world anvil market loosens.

Our true passion is for potato peelers, and that's where your country—Dyspepsia—enters the picture. You're poor as church mice because you spent your gold buying our anvils. Your people now work 21 hours a day for virtually no wages at all making your principal product, potato peelers. You can now charge so little for your potato peelers that in short order they dominate the world. Now gold pours into Dyspepsia—much of it to pay for the potato peelers we've bought from you—and you become rich.

We, of course, have spent our gold on the good things of life, and because our anvils are so expensive, little new gold flows in. We can mint fewer gold coins and there is less gold to use in backing paper money. Depression again sweeps the land and again we must work 20 hours a day for modest wages. In time our anvils again begin to dominate the world market—and so the cycle runs, on and on and on.

It was this automaticity—this theoretically perfect discipline—that made the gold standard so appealing and makes it so appealing today. Work hard enough for low enough wages and your exports will come to dominate world markets. Gold will then flow in and there will be prosperity for all. Squander all your gold on high living and it will flow right back out again. The gold standard will automatically cure depression and halt inflations and governments can devote themselves to more important things, like minding their own business.

The trouble was that, like almost everything else in life, the gold standard sounded better in theory than it worked in practice. Even with all the new gold from the new mines of America, Australia, South Africa, and Russia, there never was enough to go around, and most of the world had to scrimp and save to get by. Prices in the industrial countries fell by 40 percent between 1873 and 1896, and wages fell apace.

A nation with raw materials, or with a colonial empire that could provide them, obviously did better than a nation that had to spend its precious gold buying raw materials from others. For many countries it was a hopeless struggle to generate the exports that would bring in gold.

Nor did gold spread out evenly within a country. In America it flowed to the commercial-industrial East, but not to the agricultural West, and the resultant rise of Populism threatened the nation with a second civil war in a generation. Not only in America, but worldwide, the rich got richer and the poor got poorer. Never has the line between rich and poor —rich and poor nations, rich and poor within nations—been so clearly or so harshly drawn as during the years of the gold standard.

The ultimate failure of the gold standard was that it couldn't work at all when it was needed the most—to control the inflation that wars breed. If there wasn't enough gold to finance the world economy in peacetime, there certainly wasn't enough to finance it in wartime. World War One was financed, as wars inevitably are, by printing money in whatever quantities were needed. There would be time enough to pay the bills, and to pay the piper, when peace returned. When peace did return, no one wanted the deflation that returning to the gold standard would bring, and to all intents and purposes the gold standard was a casualty of the war.

The U.S. pretty much stayed with gold until the end. Most countries, however, talked gold into the 1930s but played a different game altogether, piling up as much gold as possible and then making sure not an ounce of it ever left home again. The perfect discipline, the beautiful symmetry of gold became a joke, if gold could come in but never could leave. Each nation was free to follow whatever economic policies it chose, with little regard for the longer-term consequences for itself or for other nations. It was inevitable that the world economy would get into trouble—and so it did.

Each step the world took closer to depression, the more aggressive nations became in acquiring and keeping gold, until the pursuit of gold became a frenzy. These policies were called "beggar thy neighbor," and that they surely did, turning the depression into the Great Depression. Even the dimmest of governments saw the light, and by the mid-1930s the Golden Age of Gold was over. In the United States it was Franklin Roosevelt who took us off gold in 1933, and we've been off gold ever since.

Today, nations hold gold for reasons of national prestige. They hold it because in recent years it has become a rewarding investment. If a nation needs to purchase the currency of another country, it can always sell gold to do so. Finally, nations hold gold because, like the rest of us, they're deeply afraid of the future and there is nothing more secure than gold.

The New Market in Gold

If gold was money for eons, it has become an investment only recently, and a profitable investment only in the past few years. We've had a "free" gold market—one in which market forces and not government intervention sets the price —for just a decade.

There was no point in investing in gold for a profit back when gold was money, any more than you'd invest in a dollar bill in hopes it would appreciate in value. A $20 gold piece was a $20 gold piece and would presumably always be worth $20. There were modest flutterings in the price of gold from year to year and from country to country—but they were very modest. Gold stayed at $20 an ounce from 1834 until 1934, when Franklin Roosevelt devalued the dollar by pricing gold at $35 an ounce. It stayed at $35 an ounce until 1968 and close to $35 an ounce until 1972. Had you bought gold in 1933 and held it for 35 years, your net appreciation would have been zero, and you would have paid to store the gold and insure it.

People did buy gold, but as a hedge against uncertainty rather than to turn a profit. A sophisticated European investor might have 90 percent of his wealth in stocks and bonds and land, and—for safety's sake—10 percent of it in gold. The other things were to keep the wolf from the door. The gold was in case the wolf broke in.

There were gold markets in London and Zurich, but with the U.S. pledged to keep gold at $35 an ounce, these were hardly free markets. Seldom did the price stray more than a few pennies on either side of $35.

But the 1960s were years of tension and turmoil in the international financial markets. The two great currencies of the postwar years—the dollar and the British pound—each came to look more than a little peaked, and instead of holding dollars and pounds, more people decided they'd like to hold a little more gold. By March 1968 the demand for gold had reached such proportions that the cost of maintaining the $35 price simply became prohibitive. It was decided that governments would continue swapping gold back and forth at $35. The public's demand for gold would henceforth be satisfied in free markets where supply and demand set the price.

The "official" price of gold went to $38 an ounce in late

1971 when the U.S. devalued the dollar and to $42.22 in 1973 when we devalued again. The U.S. still carries its gold on its books at $42.22 an ounce, even though the world price is more than 10 times that much. It's all for show, though, since in August 1971 the U.S. broke the gold-dollar link by breaking its quarter-century pledge to sell gold to any foreign government with the dollars to buy it. Once that pledge was broken, the official price no longer had any meaning and the gold markets have been totally free ever since.

Gold quadrupled in price between 1971 and 1974, then broke sharply, and then began advancing again in 1978. All was prelude to 1979–80, when the price quadrupled in barely a year, approaching $900 an ounce in early 1980. Then the price broke again, and gold settled at around $500 an ounce, but with plenty of day-to-day movement.

In today's markets, London and Zurich mostly trade gold bullion, the standard unit of trade being the 400-ounce bar, which again works out to about $200,000 per bar. The customers are mostly giant banks—and mostly giant Swiss and German banks—buying for themselves or, more often, for a client. Many of those clients are in the Middle East, where the oil boom has created a lot of rich people who, by tradition, like neither banks nor paper money. The banks may trade in 400-ounce bars, but you can buy gold in almost any market in the world, any way you want, from a full bar down to a wafer of gold no bigger than a postage stamp.

The U.S. gold market is another sort of market altogether: not in bullion, but in gold futures traded on the Commodity Exchange in New York and on the International Monetary Market in Chicago. The U.S. markets were launched in 1975, when it again became lawful for Americans to own gold, and they've grown very vast, very fast—contracts involving 650 million ounces of gold were traded on the Commodity Exchange in 1979, which is ten times the amount traded in 1976.

When the Flags Go Down at Rothschild's

But if the U.S. has the biggest market today, London remains the heart of the market, and the home of the most hallowed tradition of all—the gold "fixing." The price is fixed twice a day, at 10 A.M. and again at 2:30 P.M., and the fixing always takes place in the London offices of N. M. Rothschild and Sons in St. Swithin's Lane. Besides being bankers to the high and mighty, Rothschild's is also one of the five premier bullion dealers of London.

The original idea was to fix a price from which the market could then begin trading. Nowadays the fixing doesn't mean what it used to, since London dealers have been trading for at least an hour before the fixing and the big Hong Kong market has already shut down for the night.

Still, by bringing all dealers together face-to-face, some very big blocks can be traded at the fixing. And the fixing is one of those things that makes the City of London (which is its financial center) such a charming place. Take the flags, for instance. Each dealer has a small British flag at hand, which is kept upright as long as the dealer has orders to feed into the market. As a dealer finishes dealing, he tips the flag on its side. When all the flags have been tipped, the price has been fixed and the fixing price is flashed to a waiting world. It matters little that by the time that most people learn of the fixing price there have been more trades and the price is now something else.

If you're attracted by neither the opporunity to buy 400 ounces of gold at a whack in London or to gamble on the future price of gold in the U.S., there are still plenty of ways to invest in gold.

Those are those gold coins mentioned earlier—the Krugerrand, the Maple Leaf, and now the U.S. gold medallions.

Having no value beyond their gold content, all sell at the current price for gold plus a sales charge of $6 for the half-ounce U.S. medallion and $12 for the one-ounce piece, and a little more for the foreign coins.

There are also numismatic coins which are of value beyond their gold content because they are rare. The actual value depends on the rarity of the coin, its condition, and, of course, how much someone else will pay for it. Prices of U.S. gold coins in top conditions have gone through the roof in the past couple of years—perhaps to unrealistic levels. Still, should the market price of gold break, you would have a coin with value beyond its gold content, and with the potential for future appreciation.

There are smaller bars available than the standard 400-ounce bar. There are mutual funds that invest in gold-related stocks, and there are the shares of the gold-mining companies: U.S., Canadian, and South African. All trade in U.S. markets, and as the price of gold moves up and down (mostly up), the shares of the mining stocks move as well.

Finally, you can buy a gold certificate in which you own the gold but someone else stores it for you. What you get is a certificate proving your ownership of gold stored in someone else's vault. Citibank in New York offers a gold certificate for as little as $1,000, with the gold itself stored in vaults in Delaware or in Europe. In mid-1980, Merrill Lynch offered a program in which customers could buy gold for as little as $100 to start.

However you buy gold, it just isn't the gold market of old. Speculators rule the market now, and as long as that's so, it's hard to see how the old gold standard could be revived —meaning the restraints on how much money a government can create must come from someplace else. Governments hold gold, but the all-powerful role gold once played in international affairs was long ago usurped by the dollar, and by the dollar's strapping, precocious offspring, the Eurodollar.

Chapter 13

Eurodollars, Petrodollars, and the Gnomes of Zurich

THERE ARE Eurodollars and petrodollars, both of which sound deep and dark and mysterious. And then there are New Jersey dollars and Tabasco Sauce dollars, which don't sound mysterious at all. Yet there are more similarities than differences between Eurodollars and New Jersey dollars, and between petrodollars and Tabasco Sauce dollars.

A Eurodollar is a dollar on deposit in a bank outside the U.S. Maybe you spent it on your last trip to London, or maybe it paid the Japanese manufacturer for the Toyota sedan you bought last year. No matter how or why the dollar left the country, once it did and was deposited in a bank abroad, it became a Eurodollar. A New Jersey dollar, of course, is a dollar on deposit in a bank in New Jersey. Maybe it got left behind when you paid a toll on the New Jersey Turnpike.

A petrodollar is simply a dollar paid to one of the OPEC countries for oil (the payment for nearly all OPEC oil is still being made in dollars). And a Tabasco Sauce dollar? Obviously it's a dollar paid to the manufacturers of Tabasco Sauce.

There's a gigantic banking system abroad in which Eurodollars are deposited and loaned. There are also foreign-exchange markets all over the world in which dollars and other currencies are bought and sold, but they come later in the story. And then there are the Gnomes of Zurich, and they turn up later still.

A dollar is a dollar, one being quite like another no matter where in the world it happens to be. A dollar can be a Eurodollar one minute, a petrodollar the next, and a New Jersey dollar the next. When the makers of Tabasco Sauce travel abroad, the dollars they spend become Eurodollars. Should an oil sheik develop a zest for Tabasco Sauce, Petrodollars would become Tabasco Sauce dollars (and Louisiana dollars as well, Tabasco Sauce being made in Louisiana).

Obviously there are differences between New Jersey dollars and Eurodollars, and between Tabasco Sauce dollars and petrodollars, and it's the nature of those differences that makes the age of new money so perilous.

There are $30 billion New Jersey dollars—the total of deposits in all the banks of New Jersey. That's three times as many New Jersey dollars as there were 20 years ago. All those banks operate under the watch of regulators, including the Federal Reserve, the Comptroller of the Currency, the Federal Deposit Insurance Corporation, and the state of New Jersey. Each New Jersey dollar must be backed by some fraction of that dollar held in reserve. There are limits on how much each bank can lend to one borrower, and if the financial standing of that borrower isn't up to snuff, the bank can expect harsh words from the next bank examiner who happens along. Should a New Jersey bank run into trouble, it can get help from the discount window of the Federal Reserve.

There are $1½ trillion Eurodollars, compared with almost none 20 years ago, the market already as big as the whole

U.S. banking system and growing faster. While the U.S. banking system is rigorously policed, the Eurodollar banking system is not policed at all. There are no flinty-eyed regulators, no reserve requirements, no restrictions on who banks can lend to or how much they can lend, no rules on what they can pay for deposits, and no Federal Reserve discount window to turn to in times of need.

Eurodollar banks (mostly the titans of international finance) and Eurodollar borrowers (mostly giant corporations and foreign governments) like it that way, and it's this lack of regulation that has allowed the market to grow as it has. Still, there have been some close calls in that market. There was the 1974 collapse of Germany's Bankhaus Herstatt, which threw the international financial markets into a blue funk for weeks. And a lot of Eurodollars have been loaned to some very seedy borrowers: developing nations a whisker away from insolvency, and Communist Bloc nations (including Russia) that would have few qualms about defaulting if the world political climate turned ugly.

A little Tabasco Sauce goes a long way and its annual sales can be counted in the millions of dollars, and not so many millions, either. On the other hand, the world will pay OPEC $300 billion for oil in 1981—25 percent of it paid by the U.S. and more than 25 percent of it paid to Saudi Arabia alone.

Each of those $300 billion will become a petrodollar. Some will pay for new industry and new roads and housing in the country that earned it. Some will buy armaments. Some will buy U.S. government securities. Some will buy companies in the U.S. and in other industrial countries as the oil states flex their economic muscles. Most, though, will go into a bank and petrodollars will become Eurodollars. The Eurodollars, in turn, will probably be borrowed by some needy nation to pay its oil bills, thus becoming petrodollars again.

This marriage of Eurodollars and petrodollars is absolutely central to the age of new money. Only the giant banks that dominate the Eurodollar market are big enough to absorb the torrents of petrodollars and to channel them to those who need dollars: the developing countries to pay their oil bills, but also to the giants of international business who need the money to grow. No government agency, fettered by rules and red tape, could have done it. Because it is both vast and unfettered, the Eurodollar banking system has been able to handle with dispatch the greatest shift of wealth the world has ever seen.

The question now is whether all who have borrowed Eurodollars can pay them back. The industrial countries are modest borrowers of Eurodollars—less than $30 billion a year for all of them put together. The OPEC countries themselves borrow a little and the Communist lands take about $5 billion a year. But the developing countries take $50 billion and more a year, and some of those developing countries are barely a half-step from the poorhouse. The interest alone on the foreign debts of these less-developed countries—LDCs —is now $50 billion a year, and that will soar as the cost of oil goes higher.

In fact, it's doubtful that many of the LDCs can ever earn enough from what they sell to pay off their loans. On the other hand, it would be devastating to the international banking system if many of the LDCs defaulted on their loans. It's assumed that the Federal Reserve would help a U.S. bank, and U.S. banks are among the giants of the business. But no one wants to test that assumption and so the banks go along, renewing loans for ever-growing amounts, while praying for salvation from some quarter not yet seen. When a loan isn't paid off and is instead rolled over and over, it's known, in the jargon of bankers, as an "evergreen" loan. There are enough evergreens in the Eurodollar banking system to make a forest.

There's a further dark side to OPEC besides its ability to supply or withhold oil at will, and that is its ability to channel its vast wealth for maximum political advantage. So entwined are Eurodollars and petrodollars that the one couldn't exist without the other. A decision by OPEC could turn off the flow of petrodollars to one or another of the giant banks, leaving that bank in sorry shape. By threatening to withhold deposits, OPEC could force a big bank to lend to some borrowers and not to others.

This hasn't happened so far, although Jewish banking houses have been left out of some big international financial deals because other bankers were afraid of antagonizing OPEC. But neither has the West made any serious effort to challenge OPEC. Should there be such a challenge, OPEC holds the power to retaliate to the point of driving some big banks to the wall.

OPEC is already building some big banks of its own—banks that could grow into titans of international finance some day, with the power to lend or withhold money as suits their fancy. And OPEC countries are buying directly into the giant corporations of the industrial world, and some day they could control the policy decisions of these corporations. Libya owns 10 percent of Fiat, the Italian auto company, and Kuwait owns pieces of some big U.S. banks and of such oil companies as Texaco, Getty, Mobil, and Exxon. At the rate OPEC's wealth is growing, its ability to buy is almost without limit.

What Makes a Eurodollar

And so there's the Eurodollar market—huge already and growing bigger every time a dollar is taken from the land of its birth and carried off to some distant shore.

Some of these dollars went to pay for OPEC oil. Some were carried abroad by servicemen and tourists. Some were borrowed in America and taken home by a foreign corporation or government. Some were sent abroad to finance the overseas expansion of a U.S. company. The U.S. imported more than $200 billion of goods from abroad in 1980—cars and cameras and TV sets, in addition to oil—and the payment for nearly all that was in dollars.

Further, Eurodollar banks can do the same sort of multiple-expansion magic with money that U.S. banks can at home—all the more so since Eurodollar banks need freeze little or no money as reserves against deposits. Couple that with an enormous—and growing—demand for dollars to pay oil bills and to finance many other things, and it isn't surprising the market has grown as it has.

There are other currencies in the market besides dollars: Euromarks, Eurosterling, and Euroyen, and so on. The name for the whole vast market is the Eurocurrency market. Still, 75 percent of all Eurocurrencies are Eurodollars. The dollar has taken its licks through the years, and the postwar international monetary system built on the dollar has been dead for a decade. But the dollar still is the nearest thing to a universal currency the world has.

It isn't a one-way street. Some Eurodollars come home in time—ceasing to be Eurodollars the instant they reenter the country. When U.S. companies sell goods abroad they are paid in dollars. Plenty of U.S. companies have been bought by foreign interests besides the OPEC countries, using dollars made cheap by the drop in the value in the 1970s of the dollar against such currencies as the German mark, the Swiss franc, and the Japanese yen. More and more petrodollars are sent to the U.S. and invested not only in U.S. businesses but also in Treasury issues. And a lot of investment dollars from Switzerland and elsewhere flow into the U.S. stock and bond markets.

A U.S. corporation in need of money can borrow here, but it can also borrow in the Eurodollar market and bring the money home—the decision on where to borrow being based on where money is the cheapest. When the Federal Reserve makes money tight at home, U.S. banks can usually tap their foreign branches for funds. One major criticism of the Eurodollar market is that it serves to thwart the aims of national governments by providing banks and businesses access to money when a country's domestic interests would be better served if the money were not available.

There are outposts of the Eurodollar market in every corner of the globe—in New York, Bahrain, Hong Kong, Singapore, the Bahamas, and the Netherlands Antilles, and there isn't an hour, day or night, when you can't borrow or lend Eurodollars somewhere. Some are Eurodollar centers because they're strategically located, some because they were world financial centers before Eurodollars happened along, and some because the local authorities don't ask too many awkward questions.

Still, the market was born in London, and London remains its heart. The grand old British merchant banking houses— Rothschild's and the others—no longer dominate international finance as they once did. Nowadays the Eurodollar market is ruled by a relatively small number of giant banks with offices in London and all the other centers where Eurodollars are traded. The biggest U.S. banks in the Eurodollar market are also the biggest banks at home: Bank of America, Citibank, Chase Manhattan, Manufacturers Hanover, and Morgan Guaranty. The British, German, Japanese, and now the OPEC banks, are in it, and while the Swiss banks were slow to move into that market, they are out in force now.

In all, some 50 giant banks from around the world compete for deposits in the market, and what sets the Eurodollar system apart from the U.S. banking system is that banks overseas can pay interest on demand deposits and U.S. banks cannot. A dollar left with a U.S. bank for less than 14 days (until 1980, it was 30 days) earns no interest, while a dollar put into the Eurodollar market for as little as a single night does earn interest, which is why so many dollars stay overseas instead of being sent home. And while there now are interest-bearing checking accounts (NOW accounts) for consumers, there is nothing comparable for business. There are other reasons why the Eurodollar market has thrived, but the ability of depositors to earn interest on very short-term deposits is certainly a key factor.

You can borrow just about any way you like in the Eurodollar market, taking the money for a day or for 30 years.

There's a Eurobond market just as there's a U.S. bond market, and it thrives because of a fact of international financial life. Most countries (including the U.S. at times) don't like foreign borrowers coming in and muscling out local customers. The Eurobond market, by contrast, is open to all borrowers all of the time and a borrower can have the money in whatever currency it chooses. Most issues have been in dollars, however. One reason is that U.S. corporations are among the biggest borrowers. Another is the long plunge in the value of the dollar—for years, a borrower could reasonably expect to repay in dollars that were cheaper than when they were borrowed.

The big banks underwrite these issues, and here the Swiss banks play a key role, since they can invest a lot of the $150 billion in funds they manage for other people in Eurobonds. One reason investors like Eurobonds is that most are bearer securities, meaning they belong to whoever holds them at the moment. Nowhere on the bond does the investor's name appear. A German businessman buying a Eurobond through a Swiss bank probably has no intention of paying taxes on the income from that bond. And since the bond will stay in the bank in Switzerland, the German tax collector won't be the wiser.

More recently, the Eurobond market has also seen the rise of the gigantic syndicated loan. A borrower will approach one bank and that bank will line up other banks until there is enough money to make the loan. Eurobond issues are seldom for more than $100 million but some syndicated bank loans have been for $500 million. Iran was a big borrower in the market, and the instant the U.S. froze Iranian bank deposits in this country after the hostage seizure, U.S. banks grabbed those deposits to cover loans they assumed would never be repaid. Part of the hostage-release agreement involved the unfreezing of the deposits.

It All Began with the Russians

The Russians are borrowers in the Eurodollar market, which should be no surprise: this most capitalistic of markets owed its start, in the 1950s, to the Communists.

The Russians held some dollars after World War Two, and, fearing the U.S. might someday freeze Soviet bank deposits in this country, they held the dollars overseas. Indeed, the Russians even have their own banks in Western Europe: the Moscow Narodny Bank in London and the Banque Commerciale pour l'Europe du Nord in Paris. Since there weren't nearly enough dollars to go around back in the 1950s—the world then being in the grip of what was called the "dollar gap"—the Russians found they could turn a nice profit by lending those dollars out. A Japanese importer might borrow dollars to pay for goods bought from the U.S. Once the goods were sold in Japan, the importer would take his yen, convert them into dollars, and pay off the loan. Because the currency involved was the dollar, and because the trade was based in Europe, they became known as Eurodollars.

Still, the market remained a modest affair until the early 1960s—no more than $5 billion or $10 billion in the market at any one time. What pushed the market into the big time was the chaos and carnage that accompanied the collapse of the postwar international monetary system in the 1960s and early 1970s. As the formal monetary structure broke apart, the Eurodollar market rose to take its place—government bankers, battered and bruised, more than willing to hand the ball to the Euromarket bankers. When the postwar monetary system finally breathed its last in the early 1970s after a deathbed scene that went on for a decade, the Eurodollar market was already a vast affair. When world oil prices quadrupled in the mid-1970s, the market grew bigger still.

Ironies abound in the rise of the Eurodollar market. It did provide some order in a world where the established financial order was breaking down. But one reason the established order was breaking down was that it wasn't designed to cope with the ocean of unregulated wealth to be found in the Eurodollar market. It was as though a bank guard, trained to tackle the lone bandit, was suddenly confronted with a platoon of bank robbers, all armed with automatic weapons. Each step that nations, especially the U.S., took to save the old international monetary system simply made the Eurodollar market that much bigger, for reasons we'll come to later in this chapter. And, in the end, the Eurodollar market did the old system in.

Bretton Woods—and What Came After

That the postwar international monetary system finally breathed its last in the early 1970s was shocking, and yet utterly predictable. Economists, like generals, invariably prepare to fight the last war. The international monetary system built at the end of the World War Two was designed to prevent a recurrence of the economic anarchy of the 1920s and 1930s. It failed because the world refused to relive the 1920s and 1930s and instead developed problems unique to the 1960s and 1970s.

The world was still at war when the leading bankers and economists on the Allied side met at Bretton Woods, New Hampshire, in the summer of 1944. All at Bretton Woods could remember the 1930s when the lack of international monetary rules cast the world into the Great Depression— the gold standard gone and each nation free to set the value of its currency to gain the maximum trade advantage for itself, and to do maximum damage to its trading rivals. After the Depression came the war, and by 1944 there was no world economy: only the U.S., with nearly all the world's wealth, and the Allies, mooching off Uncle Sam.

So at Bretton Woods, the keenest financial minds of the day tried to write some new international monetary rules. Starring for Britain was John Maynard Keynes, who was in failing health and would be dead within two years. Starring for the U.S. was Harry Dexter White, who would later be accused of being a Communist agent. Had Keynes been in his prime, the outcome might have been different. Had there been a more even balance between the financial might of the U.S. and that of the rest of the world, the outcome might have been different. But America owned all the gold and it had the only currency in the world worth having. (The Swiss franc, too, was definitely worth having, but the Swiss aren't much for monetary alliances. Every island in the ocean belongs to the International Monetary Fund and the World Bank, but the Swiss belong to neither. They were too busy being neutral in 1944 to cast more than a glance at Bretton Woods.)

Keynes wanted a new international currency, called a Bancor, which would be managed by a world central bank with muscle. America wanted—and got—a system in which the dollar was central. The International Monetary Fund, created at Bretton Woods, was made to look like a central bank with muscle. In reality its only central bank function is to be lender of last resort to impecunious nations. The World Bank, also born at Bretton Woods, makes long-term loans to the world's neediest nations.

At the heart of the Bretton Woods system was the dollar. All currencies would be valued in terms of the dollar, and the wealth of nations would be measured in how many dollars each could accumulate. The dollar, as befitted its special role, would be valued in terms of gold, one dollar being equal to $\frac{1}{35}$th of an ounce of gold. To give other nations a chance to win back some of their gold, every time a country accumulated $35 it could hand the dollars back to the U.S. and receive one ounce of gold.

To make sure nations didn't replay the 1920s and 1930s when each was free to manipulate its currency to gain an edge in world trade, the Bretton Woods nations agreed to keep their currencies fixed within 1 percent on either side of par—par being the value of each currency, stated in terms of the dollar.

Take the Republic of Hysteria. Its currency is the Wail—one Wail being worth one U.S. dollar. Each dollar will buy one Wail's worth of Hysteria's principal export, which is pipe cleaners. Were Hysteria to reduce the value of the Wail so it was worth only 50 cents, its position in world trade would improve considerably. One dollar would now buy two Wails' worth of pipe cleaners, and unless other nations also reduced the value of their currencies accordingly, Hysteria would soon own the world pipe cleaner market.

On the other hand, it would now cost two Wails to buy U.S. goods that used to cost one Wail—and Hysterians would buy little from abroad because imports cost so much. Dollars from the sale of pipe cleaners would pour into Hysteria, and with every 35th dollar Hysteria could buy an ounce of U.S. gold. And because Hysteria bought almost nothing from abroad, the ounces of gold would simply pile up in its vaults.

A policy aimed at piling up gold and letting none of it leave again is called mercantilism. Mercantilism waxed until the nineteenth century, waned during the great boom in trade and industry of the nineteenth and early twentieth centuries, and waxed again during the late 1920s and 1930s. Mercantilism and free trade are incompatible, and the aim of Bretton Woods was to make sure mercantilism didn't wax in the postwar years.

Under the Bretton Woods rules, Hysteria couldn't arbitrarily cut the value of the Wail in half to gain a trade advantage. Instead it had to pledge to keep the value of the Wail

within 1 percent of par—never letting its value go above
$1.01 or below 99 cents.

There are trading markets in the Wail and in other currencies, called foreign exchange markets, just as there are trading markets in stocks and bonds. People are always selling
one currency and buying another. Say you're off to Europe
and your plane has just landed in Frankfurt. You're carrying
dollars, probably in the form of traveler's checks. But German cab drivers and shopkeepers expect to be paid in marks,
so the first thing you do is cash a $100 traveler's check and
pocket $100 worth of marks. You've just sold dollars and
bought marks, as Exxon might do—though Exxon, of
course, would do it on a far grander scale.

Or say you're the German importer of Jack Daniel's whiskey and you're about to import $1 million worth of Jack
Daniel's. The maker of Jack Daniel's can't spend German
marks in rural Tennessee and wants to be paid in dollars.
You deposit $1 million worth of marks in your German bank
account. The bank sells the marks to another bank with dollars for sale and you use the dollars to buy the whiskey.

Or say you think the value of the Swiss franc is about to
take a big leap. You sell dollars, buy Swiss francs, and hang
on. If the value of the franc increases, you sell the francs for
more dollars than you paid, taking a nice profit. Giant multinational corporations and international banks aren't above
taking fliers in the foreign-currency markets with whatever
idle cash they have around.

Between currencies traded by tourists, currencies traded
for use in world commerce, and currencies traded in hopes
of turning a fast profit, a lot of currencies get traded in the
course of a year. The trading is done by giant banks around
the world, linked together by telephone and Telex, and it is
a dull day when they don't move a few billion from one
currency to another.

The banks are supposed to act as middlemen in the market, buying and selling currencies when instructed to do so

by customers. Most, though, lured by the profits to be made by jumping into a currency whose value is moving up, have also taken speculative positions in the market, and some banks have lost fortunes by doing so.

Early in 1974, for instance, Germany's Bankhaus I.D. Herstatt was sitting on some $700 million in foreign currencies—an amount that exceeded its deposits and capital. Specifically, it was betting on a rise in the value of the dollar against the German mark—a bet that, through the 1970s, was like betting on Donald Duck against Godzilla. The dollar fell by 15 percent against the mark in early 1974, and by March Herstatt had lost $150 million in the market. Instead of quitting, the bank began doubling up—plunging in ever deeper in hopes of a big win that would make up for all the losses. That, as any horseplayer will tell you, is a sure way of losing everything—which is what happened to Herstatt.

On June 26, 1974, the German banking authorities stepped in and shut the bank—the biggest bank failure in postwar German history. What turned it into more than just a German bank failure was that the closing caught a lot of transactions in midair. Banks had sold dollars to Herstatt but had not received in return the marks owed them. For weeks after the Herstatt failure, the foreign exchange markets around the world operated at half-speed. But that was in 1974—and now the trading in foreign currencies is bigger and faster than ever.

When The Dollar Was Still Almighty

The dollar is central to currency trading for two reasons. First, it's the currency in which most international trade is carried out, and so it's the most widely traded currency. A Japanese refiner buying Kuwait oil will pay for it in dollars. An Ecuadorian importer of German Volkswagens will pay for them in dollars. Someone is always selling some currency to buy dollars, or selling dollars to buy some currency.

Second, the dollar is the standard international reserve currency—the currency governments keep on hand for use in maintaining the value of their own currencies. Sterling used to play this role—for the world until World War Two, and for the Commonwealth countries into the 1960s. But the dollar was made the reserve currency at Bretton Woods and it remains so to this day—battered and bruised, but still the only game in town.

As in any market, the interplay of supply and demand determines the value, or the price, of a currency. If people want lots of German marks—to pay for vacations there, or to buy German goods, or because they think the price of the mark is going up—they'll buy more marks, and that will push the price of the mark up. If the supply of a currency is greater than the demand, the price will go down. The game under the Bretton Woods rules was to maintain such a balance between supply and demand that the price of every nation's currency would stay within 1 percent of par.

Take the Hysterian Wail again. If there were more people selling the Wail than wanted to buy it, the price would soon go down unless some kindly soul appeared to buy the Wails no one else wanted to buy. That someone would likely be the government of Hysteria, using whatever dollars it had in its reserves to buy those unwanted Wails. If it ran out of dollars, it would have to sell gold out of its hoard to buy more dollars to keep the value of the Wail from falling. Conversely, if more people wanted to buy Wails than wanted to sell them, Hysteria would have to print more Wails to fill the demand.

The theory back in 1944 was that the Bretton Woods system had been made nearly as marvelously self-correcting as the gold standard, except that it was built on the dollar and not on gold. But since the dollar was backed by gold, and since accumulated dollars could be turned in for U.S. gold, it was called a gold-exchange standard.

If there are always too many sellers and not enough buyers of a country's currency, its government will soon run out of dollars, and then of gold, and then it must take more drastic action, taking steps to build exports and cut imports until its dollar pile builds up again. If there are always too many buyers and not enough sellers of a currency, the result is inflation—the result of constantly printing new money to meet the demand for the currency. And then the government must take corrective action of another sort—allowing in more imports and cutting back on exports until the demand for the currency eases.

If the supply-demand situation stayed out of balance for long enough, the country would have to take the next step: permanently changing the price of its currency. It would officially raise the price to damp down demand ("revaluing" in the jargon of the trade), or officially reduce the price to increase demand ("devaluing" in the jargon of the trade). Unlike the bad old days when nations could change the value of their currencies by whim, Bretton Woods required nations to go before the International Monetary Fund and seek permission before revaluing or devaluing.

To give the IMF more clout, and to enable it to act as lender of last resort to nations, each member country put up a certain amount of its currency and a certain amount of its gold. A nation that had exhausted its stock of reserves could borrow from the IMF until things got better.

And so, armed with the Bretton Woods system, the world marched bravely into the postwar years. And for the better part of two decades the system worked as its creators hoped it would. The only real problem at first was that the system was built on the dollar, and in the postwar world we owned most of the dollars. There was that dollar gap, and wise economists predicted it would go on forever.

We not only had the dollars, we also had the goods the

rest of the world wanted, while the rest of the world didn't have very much the U.S. wanted. Other countries could buy from us to the extent that they had dollars. But most countries didn't have dollars, and most had little enough to sell us to gain more dollars.

Still, it wasn't in the best interests of America—on grounds both humanitarian and commercial—to permit the dollar gap to last. Our factories had things to sell which no one overseas could buy unless they got some dollars. And that gave America a fine chance to do well by doing good. By sending dollars abroad, we could help rebuild foreign economies. The dollars would then come back to us as payment for U.S. goods.

There were direct loans to the needy, including a $4 billion loan in 1946 to Britain. There were the Marshall Plan and other forms of foreign aid. American troops quartered abroad spent dollars by the truckload, and by the early 1950s American tourists were again flocking overseas, spending like drunken sailors in economies where prices were dirt-cheap by U.S. standards. The International Monetary Fund and the World Bank did their part by lending dollars to needy nations. And finally, as foreign economies revived, U.S. industry began investing overseas and U.S. consumers began buying foreign goods that were still cheap by our standards.

And so the postwar economic miracle was born. World trade boomed and the economies of Europe and Japan thrived. Britain had a rough time of it, with its empire gone. The U.S. limped through some years of slow growth in the late 1950s. For most of the industrial world, however, it was economic paradise.

In fact it was a fool's paradise. In 1960 the Bretton Woods system seemed to be functioning to perfection. By 1965 it was clearly in deep trouble, and by 1971 it was dead—done in by the unwillingness of governments to recognize that a system designed for the world of 1944 needed drastic revision to cope with the world of 1964.

Dollars, Pounds, and—Finally—the Gnomes of Zurich

The world suffered when there was a dollar gap and the postwar economic miracle began when the dollar gap ended. But when the dollar gap ended, we kept sending more and more dollars overseas, and suddenly there was a dollar glut that proved to be as bad as the dollar gap.

Other nations had to collect dollars, slowly and laboriously, by developing the skills necessary to build exports. When we needed more dollars, we simply ran the printing presses a little longer and we had more dollars. The first U.S. companies to go abroad after the war were greeted enthusiastically by countries struggling to rebuild. But the Americans kept on coming, wave after wave of them, buying up great chunks of the world with our dollars. And since we could keep printing new dollars until the presses melted down, it seemed as though in time we would own everything.

Countries less profligate than the U.S.—Germany and Japan among them—found themselves swamped by dollars offered for sale against marks and yen. The dollars had to be bought up even if it meant printing new marks and yen because the Bretton Woods rules required it. Since all the newly printed marks and yen threatened domestic inflation for Germany and Japan, neither liked the situation very much.

We argued that these dollars were being spent to provide a military defense for the rest of the world and to carry U.S. management and technology to nations that needed both. We further argued that where it really counted—in international trade—we were still a net taker of dollars, since we still sold more to foreign nations than they sold to us. The U.S. was running a substantial suplus in its trade with other nations, as it had in every year of this century, and as long as that was true, we argued, the dollar could hardly be counted a sick currency. If you think the dollar is sick, we said, look at the British pound. There, we said, is one sick currency. Sick the British pound was—and that introduces the Gnomes of Zurich to the story.

The loss of its empire was a devastating economic blow to Britain. There was also the matter of Britain's having to make do with aging, increasingly inefficient factories in contrast to Germany and Japan, which, of necessity, got brand-new factories after the war. British trade suffered, and the obvious answer was to devalue the pound from its postwar value of $2.80. That, unfortunately, was the one answer Britain wouldn't accept.

One reason was that the pound was still a reserve currency —not on a level with the dollar, but a reserve currency at least to the Commonwealth. And the rules said that while other currencies might change their value against a reserve currency, reserve currencies couldn't change their value at all. Finally, there was the matter of national pride. The empire was gone, but the Union Jack still floated aloft and the pound still stood at $2.80.

The players in the international currency markets aren't dumb, and while Britain may have thought the pound was still worth $2.80, no one else did. People kept selling the pound, and it took every penny Britain had, plus lots of money borrowed from other nations and from the IMF, to hold the pound at $2.80.

It also took a lot of sacrifice on the part of the British people—the economy kept in a state of perpetual recession to keep imports out and to keep prices of British goods competitive in world markets. To explain it to the British people it was necessary to find a scapegoat, and the scapegoat chosen was the Gnomes of Zurich—Zurich being the banking capital of Switzerland, and the Gnomes being the bankers of Zurich. People were selling the pound not because it was a sick currency, said British Foreign Secretary George Brown in the mid-1960s. The pound, he said, was being wickedly manipulated by those Gnomes of Zurich for reasons Brown said he couldn't fathom.

Swiss bankers aren't the sort of folks you'd invite to your next sex orgy. As a breed they exude a moral rectitude that soon begins to grate. If you've just heroically saved your home from a raging forest fire, using only your garden hose, your average Swiss banker will chide you for having wasted water.

But the Gnomes of Zurich line was a gross distortion—evidence, if any is needed, that governments will take all the credit when things are going well, and will always blame someone else when things are going poorly. People were selling the pound because it wasn't worth $2.80. Britain finally devalued in 1967, about five years after it should have. By then, the Bretton Woods system was well on its way to disintegration, and the massive selling of pounds through the years was at least one reason.

More to the point, Britain's refusal to devalue the pound showed a major weakness of the Bretton Woods system: It had no mechanism to force nations to change the values of their currencies. In fact, that point hadn't even come up at Bretton Woods. Before the war, nations were constantly changing the value of their currencies to gain a trade advantage. It never dawned on anyone at Bretton Woods that for reasons of national pride nations might someday forgo a possible trade advantage by refusing to devalue. That's just what Britain did, and what France did a few years later. When a nation did devalue, the action invariably came too late—not at the 11th hour, but at the 13th hour.

Also, Bretton Woods did not contain any mechanism to force a nation to revalue—to increase the value of a currency. Currency values assigned at Bretton Woods were mostly still in place two decades later, even though the world of 1964 was as remote from the world of 1944 as the age of new money is from the stone age. Germany and Japan, for instance, had emerged from the ruins to become rich and powerful nations. But the values of the mark and the yen still were pretty much where they had been set right after the war, each now as blatantly underpriced in the markets as the pound was overpriced.

The Coming Collapse

The first signs of crisis showed up in the London gold market. The market reopened in 1954 and did a reasonable amount of business, considering that the price of gold was fixed at $35 an ounce and wasn't allowed to move more than a few pennies on either side of that price. In October 1960, however, it looked as though John F. Kennedy would be the next President of the U.S., and Europeans feared Kennedy would do nothing to reduce the dollar glut. In a market where a price change of a penny a day was considerable, gold suddenly jumped to $40 an ounce.

This selling of currencies to buy gold would become commonplace, but in 1960 it was shocking. In hindsight it was a clear warning to governments in general, and to the U.S. in particular, that the Bretton Woods system was in trouble and someone ought to do something about it.

Typically enough, governments looked at the smoke and ignored the fire. Instead of trying to revise the monetary system, they tried to stabilize the price of gold. The industrial powers, including the U.S., pooled their gold, selling into the market when the price started to move up, and buying in the market when the price started to move down. And that held the gold price steady for eight more years. Meanwhile, President Kennedy came into office promising to do something about the dollar glut, and that bought a few years of peace in the international money markets.

Things began to heat up again in the mid-1960s. First came those massive sales of the British pound. The U.S., meanwhile, was now fighting in Vietnam, and that sent a lot more dollars overseas, making the dollar glut worse than ever.

And once Britain devalued the pound in 1967, speculators were free to attack the dollar—and so they did, with mounting frenzy. They sold dollars, buying German marks, Swiss francs, Japanese yen—and gold.

By March 1968, the demand for gold overwhelmed the ability of governments to hold the price at $35, and the $35 price was abandoned. Governments would still trade gold at $35 but henceforth the public could trade gold in the big London and Zurich markets at whatever price suited their fancy.

The Germans tried to deal with the demand for marks by revaluing the mark slightly. The Swiss answer to the flood of money into francs was to quit paying interest on bank accounts from abroad, instead charging depositors a fee for putting money into Swiss banks. All of this was too little, too late.

All that was really left of Bretton Woods was the U.S. pledge to keep the dollar as good as gold by selling our gold to any government that had the dollars to buy it. But so many countries had taken so much U.S. gold through the years that even that pledge wasn't worth much. Thanks to the unending flow of dollars abroad, foreign governments held many more dollars than we held gold. In 1968, the last gold backing was removed from the dollar to make all our gold available to foreign governments that wanted it. Even then there wasn't enough gold in our vaults to cover the dollars held by other governments. Those governments were wise enough not to press their claims on our gold, since we couldn't satisfy them, and that permitted what was left of Bretton Woods to go on a little longer.

America Adds Fuel to the Fire

The U.S. tried to prop up the dollar, but everything we tried made the situation worse.

The first step—and in many ways the most disastrous—came in 1963, when we put an "interest-equalization tax" on foreign borrowing in the U.S. Because interest rates were generally lower in the U.S. than abroad, and because most foreign markets were closed to all but their domestic borrowers, many foreign companies and governments turned to the U.S. market, borrowing in the U.S. and taking the dollars home. But now that interest-equalization tax would be put on all foreign borrowing here, raising the cost of borrowing in the U.S. and forcing borrowers to look elsewhere.

Actually, foreign borrowers never took more than a few billion in dollars out of the country, and whatever they borrowed would be repaid with interest, so that we'd ultimately gain more dollars than we lost. The idea of the interest-equalization tax was to show foreign governments that we were at least doing something about the dollar glut, and it helped a little.

What the tax really did, though, was take the Eurodollar market and make it a lot bigger. Since they could no longer borrow in the U.S., more borrowers turned to the Eurodollar market, and as the demand for Eurodollars increased, so did the supply. That seemed benign at the time, but there was more to come.

The U.S. next imposed controls on foreign investment by U.S. companies—voluntary controls in 1965 and mandatory controls in 1968. Companies had to limit the amount of dollars they invested abroad, to ship more dollars back home, and to finance their foreign business as much as possible with dollars borrowed abroad.

Again we traded a long-term advantage for a cheap short-term gain. Assuming that U.S. companies invested wisely abroad, they'd eventually earn more than they invested and more dollars would come home than had gone abroad. By limiting U.S. investment abroad, we sacrificed a big dollar inflow in the future to check a moderate dollar outflow now. Again, this was done to convince people we were serious about controlling the dollar glut—and to allay fears that in time U.S. companies would own the world.

What the controls really did was further to enlarge the Eurodollar market. Now U.S. borrowers, as well as foreign, thronged to that market, and again, as demand increased, so did the supply. As U.S. business turned to the Eurodollar market, U.S. banks jumped in, opening branches abroad to help their customers find money. In 1960 the Eurodollar market amounted to less than $10 billion. By 1970 it was reckoned at $100 billion or more, and growing by leaps and bounds. Each move the U.S. made to help the dollar simply enlarged the Eurodollar markets, and that was a blunder we would pay dearly for.

Access to the Eurodollar market gave U.S. banks another source of dollars when the Federal Reserve made money tight at home, as it did in 1966 to counter the first signs of the Vietnam war inflation. Since 1966 the Fed has tried a number of measures to isolate the domestic market from the Eurodollar market and none have worked very well for very long. No matter how tight the Fed makes money, there's that avenue of escape for U.S. banks and corporations.

The much enlarged Eurodollar market also provided nearly limitless dollars to be sold to buy marks and yen and Swiss francs. There were days in which $5 billion moved into the German mark in a morning, with Germany bound by the Bretton Woods rules to buy all those dollars with newly printed marks to keep the mark at par. Speculators moved in, hoping for a fast profit. Multinational business moved to protect itself against the inevitable day when the dollar would be formally devalued.

Aspirins and Chicken Soup

Governments patched as best they could, and there were endless crisis meetings, government bankers rushing from place to place in search of remedies. All they could do, though, was to offer aspirin and chicken soup to a patient who was terminally ill. There were too many dollars in the world and not enough U.S. gold, with the Eurodollar market creating more dollars without limit. It was a quarter-century after Bretton Woods and the value of most currencies bore not the slightest relationship to economic reality: the dollar overpriced and the mark and the yen wildly underpriced.

In May 1971, Germany gave up altogether. Instead of the mark being held within 1 percent of par, it would now "float" in the foreign exchange markets—its value henceforth being whatever people would pay for it.

With Germany out of the system, it was dead anyway, and on August 15, 1971, Richard Nixon made it official. To fight domestic inflation there would be a freeze on wages and prices. To help the U.S. in international trade, he set a 10 percent surcharge on foreign goods coming into the country. No longer would the U.S. sell gold to foreign governments that held dollars, and the dollar was set afloat in the markets. With the dollar floating, and all other currencies pegged to the dollar, that meant all currencies were now afloat.

The float lasted until December 1971, when finance ministers and central bankers from the industrial powers met at the Smithsonian Institution in Washington to create a Son of Bretton Woods. The dollar was devalued by 8½ percent and the price of gold went to $38 an ounce. The mark and the yen were revalued and the value of all other currencies was adjusted. The 10 percent surcharge was dropped. Finally, instead of the 1 percent band around par, currencies could now trade within a 2¼ percent band. When all that was done, President Nixon turned up at the Smithsonian and proclaimed it "The most significant monetary agreement in the history of the world." That simply proved that Nixon, who once said he "didn't give a shit about the Italian lire," didn't know much about money generally.

The new currency values weren't enough changed from the old ones to make any difference. The dollar was still overpriced and the mark and the yen were still dirt cheap. With the Eurodollar market still able to supply dollars without limit, the 2¼ percent band was no more realistic than the 1 percent band. The dollar was devalued by another 10 percent in early 1973 and the price of gold raised to $42.22. That still didn't help, and by 1974 all currencies were again set afloat, and essentially they have been floating ever since.

There have been attempts to create a new fixed-rate monetary system and the Common Market nations run a sort of fixed-rate system tied to the mark. But if fixed rates were impossible a decade ago, they are unthinkable now, with the Eurodollar market as vast as it is and with those torrents of money flowing in and out of OPEC. It would be like trying to hold back the tides with a wall of beach sand.

Yet neither have floating rates worked as they were supposed to. The monetarist economists—again with Professor Milton Friedman in the vanguard—had always argued that fixed rates represented nothing more than government intervention in markets that should be allowed to operate freely. In this view, fixed rates are always artificial and must ultimately give way to the more realistic rate assigned by the markets. Set rates afloat, the argument runs, and they will soon settle at appropriate levels. Then the speculators will go away and the markets will be at peace.

Again, theory is theory and fact is fact, and the currency markets have been more tumultuous and currency values more erratic since floating than before. Because there are no longer any limits on how much a currency can move, the potential for profit when a currency does move has become enormous—as have the amounts bet on such moves. And because governments still have a keen interest in the prices of their currencies, they spend as much today to keep currencies at favorable levels as they did under Bretton Woods when they were required to keep currencies at par.

The U.S. would like the dollar cheap to keep down prices on goods we sell abroad. Other countries want their currencies cheap enough so their trade doesn't suffer—yet dear enough that the currency will buy a lot of dollars to use in paying for OPEC oil. OPEC wants the dollar kept dear to preserve the value of the dollars they have taken in for their oil.

The Filthy Float

With all this pulling and hauling, the movements of currencies have been wild in recent years. The dollar first lost half its value against the German mark and the Japanese yen, and more than half its value against the Swiss franc. It has since rallied a few times, usually when high U.S. interest rates made an investment in the dollar irresistible. It has also sunk a few times, usually when U.S. interest rates fell. In early 1981, with dollar investments paying a record high return, European economies in a slump, and Russia poised on the borders of Poland, the U.S. looked very stable and very secure, and the dollar was again a strong currency. How long that might last was sheerest conjecture. And even a rallying dollar still bought barely half as many marks and Swiss francs as it did a decade before—the dollar's newfound strength being very relative, indeed.

Friedman and the monetarist economists can offer some persuasive arguments for why their theory didn't work. One is that the floods of petrodollars are simply greater than even a floating rate system can handle. More to the point is that governments aren't keeping hands off but are trying harder than ever to control the price of their currencies in the market. There are "clean" floats, in which governments leave it all to the marketplace, and "dirty" floats, in which governments do try to hold currencies at optimum prices. On that scale, floating most of the time has been filthy.

There's plenty of evidence of governments in this age of new money again doing what they did in the 1930s—trying to rig the value of their currencies to gain the maximum trade advantage and to do maximum damage to trading rivals. Among the villains here is the U.S.

When the Carter Administration took over in 1977 the once-vast U.S. international trade surplus was a thing of the past. U.S. goods had become less competitive in foreign markets and our hunger for foreign goods had become insatiable. Instead of running a trade surplus, as we had every year for the first two-thirds of the century, the U.S. was now running gigantic trade deficits.

The Carter Administration's answer was to "talk down" the dollar, telling anyone who would listen that the dollar still was wildly overpriced and wasn't worth nearly what people were paying for it. The aim was to make the dollar cheap enough that prices of our goods would fall in world markets, while prices of goods made by countries with strong currencies would rise in the U.S. market. We would sell more abroad, buy less from abroad, and our trade problem would disappear. And indeed, upon being told by the U.S. that they were paying too much for the dollar, all those who had reason to sell the dollar did so with great relish.

The assumption, of course, was that as the dollar fell and such currencies as the yen rose, we would stop buying Datsun cars and Nikon cameras because they were too expensive and would start buying homemade goods. But the U.S. offered almost nothing comparable to foreign-built compact cars, and it still offers nothing at all comparable to Japanese-made cameras. So, to the dismay of the Carter people, we kept on buying from abroad, paying higher and higher prices, and thus feeding an inflation that was bad enough already.

The drop in the dollar enraged OPEC since they were paid for oil in dollars and those dollars were losing value at an alarming rate. The plunge in the value of the dollar helps explain why OPEC suddenly began raising its oil prices in 1979 after five years in which the price went up by very little.

Because the world was now awash in very cheap dollars, anyone who wanted dollars to invest in the U.S. could find plenty available, and at bargain-basement prices. Suddenly big chunks of U.S. business passed to foreign ownership, including Howard Johnson, A&P, Alka-Seltzer, and the former Liggett and Myers tobacco company, now known as the Liggett Group. Vast quantities of U.S. farmland went to foreign investors, and foreigners became the highest bidders at U.S. art auctions. The fear in the 1950s and 1960s was that U.S. business would rule the world. The fear in the age of new money is that foreign business will rule the United States.

In time, the Carter Administration stopped talking down the dollar, and the dollar has recovered a bit in the foreign exchange markets. Still, the price of propping up the dollar has been high. To keep foreigners willing to hold dollars, U.S. interest rates must be kept higher than the investor could find if he sold dollars and invested in some other currency. That helps explain why U.S. interest rates went to such incredible levels in 1980 and again in 1981—and why the Federal Reserve kept rates unduly high during the 1980 recession. Your contribution to supporting the dollar is to pay more for money when you finance a car or buy a home. Smile when you do so because you are making an oil sheik or some Gnome of Zurich happy.

And so the world limps along in this age of new money—currency rates leaping and bounding all over the place, the Eurodollar market bigger than ever and still totally unregulated, and an unwholesome amount of money loaned by some of America's biggest banks to nations that most of the time couldn't spring for an airmail stamp. Finally, there is now far too much of the world's financial future tied to the whims of OPEC for anyone's peace of mind.

Chapter 14
Electronic Money: Tomorrow Is Already Here

IF YOU were in Massachusetts early in 1981 and had a mind to, you could telephone a computer that both talked and understood 22 banking words, including "balance" and "postdate," if spoken slowly and distinctly.

That was hardly sophisticated banter in the manner of Oscar Wilde. It was, however, an intriguing test of banking by telephone in which the computer, rather than a human teller, handled the bank's side of the conversation. As such, it was just one more sign of how close to reality nowadays is the longtime dream of electronic money, in which some of our cash and most of our checks (70 percent of them by the year 2000) will be replaced by blips in a vast computer system. Sponsors of the test—a group of mutural savings banks —hope to have the talking, listening computer in permanent operation by the end of 1981.

The idea of electronic money may unnerve you, since there are vast and troublesome questions about security and privacy still to be resolved, and for most of us, talking one on one with a computer is going to take some getting used to. Indeed, the idea of electronic money still unnerves a good many bankers, since they must deal with those issues of security and privacy, and they must also foot the bill for costly machines, supersophisticated computers, and other things before this age of new new money arrives for real.

Yet we're already far deeper into electronic money than you may realize. And matters of economics may push us the rest of the way in less time than you'd expect—the cost of our present system, with all the paper and all the human hands it involves, soaring out of sight while technological breakthroughs bring down the cost of going electronic.

We're going electronic if only because each check you write now costs 50 cents to process, and will soon cost a lot more, while you and the other billpayers of America now write some 40 billion checks a year. The postage alone involved in mailing all your canceled checks now comes to at least $2 billion a year. And since even the cost of mailing a letter is now indexed to inflation, that, too, will keep costing a lot more.

In fact, most of the technology needed to make money electronic has already been invented and much of it is already in place.

There are at least 20,000 automated teller machines (ATMs) around the country, already handling several billion transactions a year: machines that take deposits, dispense cash, transfer funds from one bank account to another, and handle other routine banking chores. An ATM costs $20,000 and up, but a brick-and-mortar bank branch costs many times that, needs human beings to run it, can't stay open 24 hours a day, and can't pay for itself when tucked away in the corner of an airport or a shopping center, which is where many ATMs have found homes.

There are 120 million bank cards in use today, and while most are the familiar credit card, used only to charge things, more and more are access (or debit) cards which serve as keys to such electronic banking devices as ATMs. In time the debit card will also be your key to remote banking terminals, or "electronic cash registers," which will be spotted in shops and other places around the country. You'll make your purchase, pop your card into the terminal, and in a twinkling your bank account will be charged and the merchant's account credited with the amount of the transaction.

At least 500 banks around the country now offer bill paying by telephone, and after a slow beginning, that idea seems to be catching hold. You dial the bank, list the bills you want paid ($89.40 to the local electric utility . . . $49.50 to Dr. Phibbs . . . $75.25 to Snaffles' Department Store . . . $109.70 to the body shop that repaired your mangled left, front fender) and you're spared the bother of writing checks. The bank's computers then move the money electronically from account to account, sparing the bank the bother of clearing checks.

Mostly there are human tellers on the other end of the line —each getting paid a salary and various fringe benefits, and each going home when day's work is done. That computer up in Massachusetts is a step toward replacing the human teller with a machine that works around the clock, demanding no more than a steady flow of electricity to keep it happy.

Into Your TV Set I'll Creep

And present-day banking by phone is merely a step toward how it is going to be. Tucked away in your home—in the living room or the game room or wherever you keep your TV set—is the bank branch of the future. The link between your television set and your bank will be the same cable that brings cable TV into your home—that cable already being capable of providing communications channels for a lot more than the late night movie.

Maybe you'll talk directly to your TV set and it to you—two-way, interactive cable is being tested right now. Maybe you'll use a home computer terminal (which no home of the future will be without) that is tied to your TV set. Either way, you'll call up your bank's channel on the TV monitor, provide your personal identification number (everyone with a debit card already has a personal identification number, or PIN), and ask to see your unpaid bills (which have been flashed electronically to your bank instead of being mailed to you).

In short order, the bills appear on the screen. Talking to the TV set, or strumming out signals on your home computer terminal, you instruct your bank to pay each bill. As you do, the word "paid" appears after each bill and your balance at the bank is reduced as each bill is paid. When you're done, your TV screen shows a balance in your account of $57.30. And then, having wished you good health and long life, your TV screen goes dark and your bills for the month have been paid.

Already a tremendous share of our money moves around the country electronically. There used to be a $100,000 bill (more precisely the $100,000 gold certificate of 1934, bearing the likeness of Woodrow Wilson) which the Federal Reserve used to transfer money from one branch to another. That's done electronically now over what is known as "Fed wire" —a sophisticated computer network with its heart at Culpeper, Virginia, that heart known as the Culpeper Switch—and there hasn't been a $100,000 bill (or any bill larger than $100) made since 1945. When a New York bank buys federal funds —extra bank reserves—from a bank in Peoria, the transfer is handled by Fed wire. Banks transfer money among themselves over a computer network called "bank wire." Bank wire and Fed wire together move about $200 billion around the country each day.

More than half the banks around the country now belong

to automated clearing houses (ACHs), which are located in most big cities and which shift money electronically among the banks that belong to the ACH, eliminating some 5 billion checks Americans might otherwise write each year. More companies pay salaries today by transferring the money to the employee's bank account. Instead of mailing out such checks as Social Security, the government would rather transfer the money to the recipient's bank account. In some places you can tell your bank to tap your account each month to pay recurring bills—your utility bill or the mortgage payment. The bank is told how much you owe and it pays the bill electronically and charges your account.

Granted, not all of this works as well as it might, and not nearly as well as it will once the bugs are taken out. Electronic money today is about where television was in the late 1940s—intriguing, potentially very exciting, but still primitive and still only a shadow of what it someday will become.

For instance, no system of banking by telephone has yet satisfied either customers or bankers. Bankers, of course, will be happy when there are nothing but computers handling their end of the call.

Making customers happy with banking by phone is something else. As things stand now, you tell the bank who to pay and how much. Since there's no visual record of the transaction, you must wait anxiously until your next bank statement shows up to confirm payment of the bills as you instructed. Since the transaction is electronic, there's no canceled check, and if there's an error, it can be a mess to clear up. And since there's no check, how do you stop payment, if necessary? How do you soothe an anxious creditor with those immortal words, "The check is in the mail"? In time, of course, you'll watch each transaction on your TV screen, or maybe you'll get a printed record of it through your home computer terminal. And that will eliminate some —though not all—of the drawbacks.

The Costs of Going Electronic

The truth is, there are profound disadvantages for consumers in every aspect of electronic money. And while the banks stand to gain mightily from it, the costs of going electronic are so great that banks have been very slow in deciding to pay them. People have been talking about electronic money for more than a decade, and only now is it beginning to catch hold.

For one thing, most of us are pretty satisfied with the system we have now. Nobody much likes paying bills, but our system of paying by check has worked well enough for a century and we're in no great hurry to change it.

Now, when we pay by check, there's time enough to think about the transaction and to stop payment if we change our minds. If we pay electronically, the money will be gone just like that, and if we want our money back, we can whistle for it. The stop-payment order is a powerful weapon and consumers won't give it up without a fight.

Most of us like our present system because most of us at one time or another practice what bankers call "living on the float." We write a check on Monday and deposit the money to cover it on Wednesday because we know the check won't come back to our bank until Thursday.

When the Federal Reserve some years ago installed electronic gear that speeded up the processing of checks, business retaliated with the "extended disbursement float." A business based in New York would use a bank account in Alaska to pay a supplier in Florida—gaining the use of the money for the extra days it took the money to go from Alaska to Florida and back. When money goes electronic, the float will go out the window, and for some of us it's going to hurt.

It will take getting used to for the Federal Reserve to manage money when it goes electronic, since that will greatly increase the speed with which money moves around our economy. It will pass faster from hand to hand, and each new dollar the Fed creates will add that much more to economic activity. Since the Fed has trouble enough managing money today, it can be expected to have still more trouble tomorrow.

There is, further, the normal hesitancy people feel in dealing with a machine—particularly one that can talk, and especially one that has control over our money. Experience has taught us that computers make mistakes, and unsnarling those mistakes can be unnerving. My public library has a computer which insists I borrowed a book on vegetable dyes in 1978 and never returned it. I am unable to convince the computer that I have never borrowed a book on vegetable dyes, my interest in the subject being nil. There's another computer that keeps sending letters to *Business Week*, addressed to Mr. B.W. Mag and assuring us the Mag family of New York City will want some product or another. Haggling over an overdue library book is one thing. It's the image of an errant computer adding General Motors' electric bill to our own that gives us the cold shivers.

The Electronic Criminal

Finally, no one yet knows how to make an electronic system truly secure, and until it's made secure, electronic money will prove a hard sell.

Criminals have been known to lurk in the shadows near an automated teller machine, cosh in hand, waiting for some luckless soul to withdraw some cash. That can happen outside a bank in broad daylight, but it's more likely to happen at night at an ATM in a deserted shopping center.

And that's just old-fashioned smash-and-grab stuff. The potential for electronic crime is awesome.

In the old days, banks had stacks of blank deposit slips around. You filled in the amount of the deposit, wrote down your account number, and handed the slip to a teller. When checks and deposit slips acquired machine-readable numbers, crooks would start mixing their numbered deposit slips among the blanks. An unsuspecting customer would grab an encoded slip, write his own account number, and make a deposit. The bank's computer would read only the encoded number and credit the deposit to the crook's account.

Electronics technicians will tell you there isn't a computer system that can't be broken into or a telephone line that can't be tapped—and electronic money will make goodly use of both computers and phone lines.

The danger from within is that a crooked employee will work a program into the bank's computer that would siphon off money by the truckload. Some bank employees have done just that, and presumably more will try—banks already losing $3 to embezzlers for every $1 they lose to bank robbers. What about a terrorist group seizing control of an electronic-banking computer and threatening to wipe out the financial records of thousands of people unless a fat ransom is paid?

If I can reach into your account, I can clean it out faster than you can say Jack Robinson. The debit cards contain a secret personal identification number (PIN) that's supposed to give you, and you alone, access to your account. If anyone cracks your PIN, they also gain access to your account. The more money goes electronic, the more computers and phone lines there will be—and the greater the opportunity for some electronic wizard to break in. Bank officials are, for obvious reasons, reluctant to talk about how vulnerable they are to electronic thievery, but it's clear they are very vulnerable indeed.

And there's the whole matter of privacy.

We regard our financial dealings as private, and there are those among us who would go to jail if anyone had an inkling of what we were up to. When money goes electronic, all our dealings, all our financial records will be an open book to anyone with the ability to eavesdrop. And since all our banking records will be stored in some vast computer, a lot of people will be trying to gain access to them. The Internal Revenue Service would obviously like to peek inside the computer. So, at times, would the police and the FBI and the CIA and who knows how many other government agencies. There are hundreds of court-ordered wiretaps today and thousands of illegal taps. Is it reasonable to assume there won't be taps, legal and illegal, on the lines that carry the data when electronic money comes?

When everyone has a personal identification record, it will be nearly impossible for anyone to hide. Your number will follow you everywhere, recording every financial transaction you make. Skip out on a loan in Atlanta, and the instant you draw some cash in Walla Walla, the authorities will know where you are.

The potential for abuse is awesome in electronic money. You buy a TV set that proves defective and you stop making payments until the store repairs the set. But what if the agreement you signed when you bought the set gave the store the right to tap your account for $37.50 each month until the set was paid for? In the March–April 1979 issue of *Bankers Magazine,* writer Steven Pastore imagines a computerized traffic-control system, "linked . . . to photographic sentinels, which, in turn, could debit the offender at a fraction of the cost of maintaining a state trooper."

Think of it: You pass a radar trap that marks you as going 45 in a 30-mile zone. The unit notes your license number, asks a computer who you are, and instructs your bank to hit your account for $50, which is the amount of the fine. You've been judged, found guilty, and fined before you hit the next stoplight. Granted, this is an extreme example which takes electronic money far beyond anything bankers are talking about today. Still, it is technologically possible, and, governments being what they are, it's well within the realm of possibility.

One reason electronic money has come on so slowly is that bankers are as worried about security and privacy as anyone else. A more basic reason is that once you start talking about thousands and thousands of ATMs, and millions of remote banking terminals, and the vast computers, and the incredibly complex interconnections to tie them all together, you're talking about billions of dollars that no one is in a burning hurry to pay.

There are some complex legal issues involved. Is an electronic teller a bank branch and so bound by current banking laws, or is it something else not covered by law at all? If it isn't a branch, then current branching laws are dead because a big bank can put ATMs in every corner of the land, limited only by its willingness to pay the bill. Back in 1975, consumer advocate Ralph Nader warned the House Banking Committee that nationwide electronic banking "would result in the McDonaldization of the banking industry." In fact, with interest-rate ceilings on the way out and all financial institutions allowed to offer roughly the same kinds of accounts and the same kinds of services, the U.S. financial system is going to be "McDonaldized" come what may.

Ready or Not, Here It Comes

Indeed, all the objections and all the perils notwithstanding, money is going electronic, even if the process is taking longer than anyone expected. The potential cost saving is just too great—all the more so as technological advances bring down the cost of going electronic. Another thing is that, for all their resistance, once people are exposed to electronic banking, most find they like it. Citibank finds that 70 percent of all cash withdrawals from the bank are now made through a machine rather than through a human teller.

Bankers used to talk about the "cashless society," and it was never in the cards that we would give up cash. We pay cash only on small purchases, and any system that tried to handle those electronically would soon drown in blips as the present system is drowning in paper. What we're really heading toward is a checkless, less-cash society. Top priority for banks is to cut the cost of handling checks—especially since most checking accounts are being turned into interest-paying transaction accounts.

Do you know your banker wants to practice "truncation" on you, and you may not like it very much? Still, it's coming, and you might as well learn to enjoy it. When it does come, you'll no longer get your canceled checks back at the end of each month, and that will save the banks a bundle.

The clearing of checks is almost totally electronic now—by the bank for whoever cashed your check, by the Federal Reserve as it routes the check back to your bank, and by your bank as it charges your account. You can live in El Paso and cash a check in Portland, Maine, and those funny-looking code numbers at the bottom of your check will steer it unerringly back to your account.

And then all the electronics stop and someone must gather your checks together, stuff them into an envelope, and mail them back to you along with your monthly statement. With 40 billion checks a year, that's a lot of stuffing and mailing, and a lot of expense—which the banks would be spared if only you'd accept truncation. You'd still get a monthly statement listing all the checks you wrote, but the bank would hold the checks—available if you needed them.

Credit-card bills used to come with a copy of the receipt of each transaction. Now you merely get a statement on which each transaction is listed, but without those receipts. Banks that favor truncation fear the wrath of customers should they try it. Yet credit-card customers stopped getting receipts along with the bill without yelling too much, and soon the banks, too, will stop sending receipts.

Each ATM can replace a few human tellers and enough ATMs can permit the bank to open more installations without the cost of opening a branch (and, in time, without having to fret about restrictions on branching). An ATM can now handle about 90 percent of what people now come to a bank to do, and more advanced machines will do even more. Machines don't shut down at 3 P.M., and no machine has ever flipped a "next teller please" sign in the face of a customer who has been waiting in line for 30 minutes. A machine can go into airports or shopping centers or even onto city street corners, where the bank wouldn't want to open a full branch.

Electronic terminals in retail outlets—"electronic cash registers" that automatically charge your account and credit the merchant's account when you make a purchase—will be the last element of electronic money to come on line. The terminals themselves will be expensive and the connections from even one bank to all its merchant customers will be even more expensive. Ultimately, in the full flower of electronic money, all banks would have to be interconnected, and that will be more expensive still. And finally, consumers will resist the idea because it will mean giving up the float once and for all.

But merchants like the idea of instantaneous payment and in most towns the biggest retailers are the bank's biggest customers. And bit and pieces of the system are already falling into place. More banks have electronic check and credit verification devices out in stores and it will be easy enough to replace those devices with full-blown electronic cash registers.

Smart Cards and Smart Machines

But electronic technology is developing at such a pace that what appear to be serious drawbacks to electronic money may soon prove not to be drawbacks at all.

Each debit card features a magnetic stripe in which your personal identification number is hidden away. That's how the bank (and, in theory, no one else) knows it's you when you use an ATM. In France, however, they are now developing a "smart" bank card in which is embedded a tiny electronic circuit of the sort that has made possible the digital watch and the hand-held calculator. These chips are marvels to behold—each about the size of a dime and each containing the equivalent of thousands of transistors. Yet each costs a pittance to make, which is why the cost of digital watches and calculators has plummeted.

Each time you use a debit card, the transaction must be flashed to your bank's computer. With the French smart card, which is to be tested in 1982, each transaction will be recorded by the electronic chip within the card. A smart card could record more than 100 different transactions, adjusting your balance each time you used an ATM or an electronic cash register. The tiny chip will also contain more, and different, ways of letting the bank know it is indeed you making the transaction, providing for a lot more security than the magnetic stripe with its personal identification number. A smart card would have no trouble storing your fingerprint, and while a thief might tumble onto your PIN, he still couldn't duplicate your fingerprint.

It is precisely the revolution in electronic technology that will hasten the day of electronic money by providing such things as the smart card. The sorts of devices that can be made with these tiny electronic chips strain the imagination, while the cost of making the chips keeps falling.

There are already chips bearing the equivalent of 100,000 transistors, and these chips, in turn, can make some very smart machines. In time there will be chips with 1 million transistors and then we'll have supersmart machines.

For these supersmart machines, solving the riddles of electronic money will be child's play. The real challenge won't be to develop the machines, but to get us to live with them.

Would you feel more comfortable with a machine you can talk to ("Hello, machine. How are you today?")? Or would you rather work through a keyboard? Do you want a machine that is simply a machine, or would you like a few human touches ("Oh, Mr. Beasley, you've overdrawn your account again. Whatever are we going to do about you, you naughty man?")?

Clearly a technology that can fit 1 million transistors onto a chip the size of a dime can design a machine that can do about anything. And one of the things the machines will do, whether you're ready for it or not, is turn our money all the way into electronic money.

Chapter 15

How Drugs, Money Mules, and Numbered Bank Accounts Meet in the World of Hot Money

SAN YSIDRO is scarcely more than a dot on the map, a wide spot in the road on the California side of the Mexican border, just below San Diego—a noplace in the gazetteer of international money.

Still, it was there, in September 1976, that account 06–0036198 was opened at the San Ysidro branch of the Mexican-American Bank in the name of the "architect" Jaime Araujo, alias Pedro De La Cruz-Alvarez—setting in play one of the biggest drug, tax evasion, and money-washing schemes in U.S. history.

The profits from drugs can be staggering—on the order of $10 back for each $1 invested. At its peak, Araujo's operation was taking in $900,000 a month—tax-free, of course, since Araujo paid no taxes. The drugs came from Mexico in secret compartments in junk automobiles. The profits got washed through a maze of U.S. and Mexican banks, and while Araujo is in prison, most of the money is still in Mexico—out of sight and beyond the reach of U.S. authorities.

296

What makes the case so remarkable is not just its size but the marvelous profusion of detail the government was able to collect. When it comes to drugs and dirty money, most of the time there are merely myths and shadows. In the architect's case there are names and dates and times and places.

Buried deep within the world of money is the supersecret world of hot money—fortunes carried covertly across borders, out of sight of the police and the tax collector. It's the world of numbered bank accounts, of skilled couriers called "money mules" who carry money from country to country, of dictators hoarding wealth in some safe haven against the day a regime tumbles, of criminal money smuggled abroad so it can be washed and spent safely and openly back home.

Switzerland offers numbered accounts and bank secrecy, and it's still the capital of the world of hot money. But laws are changing and Switzerland isn't the safe haven for crooks it used to be. And it's far from the only country with bank secrecy and numbered bank accounts.

Robert J. Perry, the assistant U.S. Attorney in Los Angeles who sent Araujo to prison, calls the flow of hot money to the Cayman Islands "incredible." Indeed the Cayman Islands—and the Bahamas as well—have enough offices of foreign banks to handle the financial affairs of countries 100 times their size.

Hot money also goes to Panama, Singapore, Hong Kong, the Netherlands Antilles, and to various spots in the Middle East. All offer secret bank accounts, favorable tax laws, and a minimum of embarrassing questions where money is concerned. Liechtenstein is another matter—not a banking center but the home of "paper" companies, created to shield hot-money flows. Open a numbered bank account in Switzerland in the name of a Liechtenstein company and your secret is doubly safe. Have the Liechtenstein company owned, in turn, by a Panamanian holding company, and a brigade of Philadelphia lawyers couldn't trace your money.

Wherever you live and wherever you earn your money, if

you're a U.S. citizen you're liable for U.S. taxes. The Treasury worries a lot about tax evaders and it has acquired some powerful weapons in recent years to help ferret them out. If you carry more than $5,000 in cash out of the country, you must report that to the government. Every bank doing business in the U.S. must report cash deposits of $10,000 or more. If you have a foreign bank account, you must report that to the government, and 155,000 Americans did so in 1978. The Treasury knows there are unreported foreign bank accounts, but it doesn't think there are many. Most people, it reasons, may try to minimize the amount in the foreign account but will not deny its existence altogether.

Still, for every $1 of hot money that's spotted, $100 gets by. A lot of the money used to reelect Richard Nixon in 1972 was moved through foreign banks to mask the identity of the donor. Most of the U.S. corporations caught paying bribes to foreign officials used foreign bank accounts.

Organized crime throws off money by the ton, but the money can't be spent openly until some legitimate source for it has been established, which is why dirty money must be washed through foreign banks. Crooks all the way back to Al Capone have gone to jail because the government could prove they spent beyond any visible source of income. Gambling casinos bring in millions each year—all in cash—and some of that cash gets "skimmed." The casino earns $5 million, reports $4 million to the Internal Revenue Service, and the other $1 million is smuggled abroad to be washed. When the government indicted racketeer Meyer Lansky in 1970, it claimed that $36 million had been skimmed over a decade from just one Las Vegas casino.

But the biggest source of hot money these days is drugs —reckoned at a $50 billion-a-year business in the U.S. and at several times that worldwide.

There's what U.S. officials call the "Florida connection." Because we use more money each year, almost every Federal Reserve bank pays out more cash during the year than it takes in. The exception is in Florida, where the Fed is awash in cash, most of it tied to drugs. Colombia is now the biggest supplier of drugs to the U.S. and Florida is the port of entry.

So many dollars flow to Colombia that its central bank now makes direct cash deposits to the Federal Reserve branch in Miami and those deposits now run about $400 million a year. The Drug Enforcement Administration tells of a Florida bank that got one $950,000 cash deposit, most of it in $20 bills, and of another bank that accepted $20 million in cash in a month from known or suspected drug dealers. Once in a Florida bank, the money can be moved to banks anywhere in the world, since the $5,000 rule doesn't apply to transactions among banks. That Florida cash surplus ran to $5 billion in 1979 and $7 billion in 1980, and most of it was tied to drugs.

The Architect Exposed

Never, though, has the world of hot money been sliced open so cleanly as in the case of Jaime Araujo, alias the architect. His operation brought in nearly $33 million in three years, and when the authorities crashed in they found drugs worth at least another $10 million awaiting sale. U.S. Attorney Perry calls that the biggest drug bust in the western U.S.

The $13 million in federal taxes Araujo didn't pay makes him one of the biggest tax cheats in U.S. history. The Araujo indictment, handed down in March 1979, runs 53 pages and is so rich in detail it could serve as a how-to guide for the serious student of washing dirty money. Araujo pleaded guilty to tax evasion, failure to report the export of U.S. currency, and to having operated, as the law puts it, "a continuous criminal narcotics enterprise." He could have gotten life and did get 35 years in prison, the first 15 to be served without parole, and a $1.2 million fine. Most of the 22 members of his gang fled to Mexico.

The Mexican-American Bank, with $18 million in assets at the end of 1978, is a pygmy among U.S. banks. Its home office is in San Diego, and it does have that branch in San Ysidro. Government documents show that number 06–0036198 was opened on September 16, 1976, on behalf of Pedro De La Cruz-Alvarez, who was described as a "Tijuana architect." There were certain problems with the immigration people, it was explained, and De La Cruz-Alvarez couldn't appear at the bank. Couriers, it was explained, would handle everything. The initial deposit was $405,000—all in cash. Not on its busiest day had the bank seen a deposit one-tenth that big. And that was just the beginning.

The government says that couriers for the architect appeared in San Ysidro 39 times between September 16, 1976, and April 14, 1978, with deposits for account 06–0036198. Each deposit was in cash, mostly in small bills, and the money was always delivered in shopping bags or grocery cartons. The courier would dump the money on the counter and the bemused tellers would count it. The 39 deposits totaled $15,444,881—the smallest $99,500 on December 27, 1977, and the largest $860,000 on April 13, 1977.

Had bank officials looked more closely at their mysterious customer, they would have learned there was no architect named Pedro De La Cruz-Alvarez in Tijuana or anywhere else. They would have also learned that the architect's address was a phony and his telephone number that of a Tijuana used-car dealer.

The bank, says U.S. Attorney Perry, didn't exactly go out of its way to blow the whistle on the architect and his magic bank account. It did notify the Treasury of those cash deposits. Once at the Treasury, though, the reports were filed away and forgotten, and it was a U.S. Customs agent who tipped off Perry. By that time, says Perry, "millions of dollars had been deposited," and, in fact, the law was very close to nailing Araujo.

The delay, says the government, allowed Araujo to move

all but $9,000 out of the architect's account and into Mexico. Cash went into the architect's account. It was then withdrawn in the form of huge cashier's checks, which were smuggled across the border and put into accounts in two Tijuana banks—Banco de Comercio and Multibanco Comermex. The names on those accounts—Sanchez and Ibarra —were as phony as the De La Cruz-Alvarez name on the architect's account.

As long as the money stayed in the U.S., it was dirty money from the sale of drugs—wealth beyond anything Araujo could legitimately claim as income. Once in Mexico, in an account guarded by a phony name, the money could have come from anywhere—profits from a Mexican business, gifts from a relative—and it could return to the U.S. as clean money.

On March 16, 1978, for instance, a courier brought $675,790 to the Mexican-American bank in San Ysidro. He put $275,790 into the architect's account and used the rest to buy three cashier's checks, each made out to a different Mexican company. The checks were then carried into Mexico, one of them going to open the Ibarra account at Multibanco Comermex.

Obviously three cashier's checks are easier to smuggle than $675,790 in small bills. But the cash could also have been smuggled into Mexico without much trouble because, while the U.S. is curious about what comes into the country, it doesn't pay much attention to what leaves. In May 1978, according to government records, couriers for Araujo carried $439,000 in cash across the border into Mexico and put it into the Comermex account. Another $196,665 in cash was smuggled into Mexico on July 14, and $334,614 more on August 30. That cash, too, was carried in shopping bags and grocery cartons and not a cent of it was ever spotted at the border.

Even with all those bank accounts, Araujo still had a problem. The drug business was earning money faster than his couriers could deposit it. So Araujo bought a house in Bonita, California, where money could be stored until someone could take it to the bank. Typically, the house was paid for by withdrawing $63,000 from the Mexican-American Bank and buying a $60,000 cashier's check from the Banco de Comercio in Tijuana.

Once the money went into Mexico it could be openly invested back in the U.S. Jesus Araujo, Jaime's brother, used $143,000 from a Tijuana account to buy a home in Chatsworth, California. Another $100,000 went to buy land in Thousand Oaks, California—a very nice deal as it turned out, since the investment turned a $125,000 profit in seven months (the rich, even the crooked rich, get richer, etc.).

The most complicated wash scheme—all neatly laid out in those government documents—involved the purchase of a restaurant in Encino, California for $695,000. The money came from the architect's account, was laundered through two Mexican accounts, and finally passed through the very respectable Security Pacific National Bank, which had no idea it was part of a money wash.

On November 17, 1976, $200,000 from the San Ysidro account was used to buy four cashier's checks, which were deposited a day later in the Sanchez account in Tijuana. On November 20, another $300,000 came out of the San Ysidro account, bought three more cashier's checks, and went into the Sanchez account. On November 22, the San Ysidro account was tapped a third time—this time for $261,000, which went to buy still more cashier's checks. One, for $61,000 went into the Sanchez account, and two, for $200,000 in all, went into the Ibarra account. In five days $761,000 had been moved from San Ysidro into Mexico.

On November 23, the money—now clean—was ready to come back to the U.S. The Tijuana accounts were tapped for $700,000, which bought a bank draft payable to Security Pacific. Whatever suspicions it might have had, all Security Pacific knew for sure was that it had a draft for $700,000 from a legitimate Mexican bank. The $700,000 went to collateralize a loan from Security Pacific to an Araujo front to buy the restaurant and to open two checking accounts at the Century Plaza branch of Security Pacific.

Araujo was wily enough to stay ahead of the law for three years. Fearing his own phone might be tapped (it was), Araujo once drove more than 50 miles to Disneyland, paid his way into the park, made a single call from a pay phone, and drove home again. Still, the noose was tightening. There were taps on a dozen phone lines, and government photographers were recording each visit to the San Ysidro bank by an Araujo courier. In a tapped phone call on July 13, 1978, Araujo finally said what the authorities had been waiting to hear. "Is that you, architect?" asks a voice on the phone. "Yes, it's me," says Jaime Araujo. That established that Araujo was the mysterious architect, and it nailed down the link between Araujo and the architect's account in San Ysidro. And that link, in turn, finally nailed Araujo.

Behind the Swiss Bank Account

Araujo used Mexican banks, and that was a mistake. U.S. authorities were able to get complete records of all his Mexican transactions—though not before the money was pulled from the Tijuana accounts and sent elsewhere in Mexico. However, even Swiss bank accounts aren't quite as secret as they used to be. In 1977, the U.S. and Switzerland signed a legal assistance treaty, and once it's established that a depositor in a Swiss bank has committed a crime under Swiss law—no matter where the crime took place—the money in the account can be seized and the bank records turned over to the U.S. government. The Swiss regard as unlawful pretty much what we regard as unlawful and U.S. and Swiss authorities have now teamed up on a dozen investigations.

Still, Switzerland remains Number One in the world of hot money, and for good reason. It has some of the world's biggest banks, with outposts all over the world. Wherever you are, you aren't far from an office of one of the country's giant banks: Swiss Bank Corporation, Union Bank, and Swiss Credit Bank. Further, Swiss banks have a reputation for skilled money management. It doesn't make sense to smuggle money halfway around the world if the bank is going to lose that money through poor investments. Swiss banks may not deserve their reputation, but they have it, and in international finance image counts for a lot. Swiss banks manage $150 billion of other people's money, and, at a rough guess, 20 percent of that is hot money.

What the Swiss have that's choice is the Swiss franc, which is the world's most cherished currency. It has slipped lately, but between 1971 and 1980 its value against the dollar increased by about 140 percent. Had you smuggled dollars into Switzerland, converted them into Swiss francs, and buried the money in a hole in the ground, you still would have made a handsome profit over the years.

You can walk into any Swiss bank—and there are scores of them, from the Big Three down to some small but highly respected private banks—and open a numbered account without too many questions being asked. You'd do well not to walk in carrying a smoking revolver or boasting about your killing in cocaine, since robbery and dealing in drugs are crimes in Switzerland. You can't open the account anonymously. A few top officers will want to know who you are, and they may ask for references. You can't simply open a numbered account with the odd dollar; the bank will expect an initial deposit of $100,000 or more. But assuming you have the money, and unless the Swiss have good reason to believe you're a crook under Swiss law, you'll have little trouble opening a numbered account, the number of which will be known to very few people. Bankers, including Swiss bankers, don't get rich by turning away customers. Or you can open a regular account—still shielded by bank secrecy if not a number—for almost any amount.

And then there's this about Swiss law: There are a lot of things that violate Swiss law, but evading your U.S. income taxes isn't one of them. Evading taxes will bring down the wrath of the IRS, but it won't turn a hair on the head of a Swiss banker, because tax evasion isn't a criminal offense in Switzerland. Nor will the Swiss lift a finger to help U.S. authorities nail a tax cheat.

Swiss banks don't exactly advertise in the world of hot money, but neither do they make themselves hard to find. Lugano sits on the Italian border, and the Italian lira is one of the world's least popular currencies. And wealthy Italians are not very keen about paying taxes. Each weekend, hundreds of Italians carrying suitcases and satchels set out for a nice drive to Lugano. Happily enough, Lugano is crammed with banks that just happen to stay open on weekends. At least $1 billion in lire passes into Switzerland each year, and that's probably a very conservative estimate.

There have been some breaches in Swiss bank secrecy— that treaty with the U.S. being one. But U.S. officials would have to know you have a Swiss bank account, and they'd have to convince the Swiss you've committed what is a crime under Swiss law. Otherwise, secrecy remains as tight as ever, and to violate bank secrecy is to violate Article 47 of the Swiss bank law—the penalty for which is a fine of up to 50,000 francs (about $30,000) or a six-month prison term. Swiss bankers have been closemouthed by custom for years. Secrecy was written into law in 1934 when the Nazis demanded an accounting of wealth sent into hiding by German Jews.

Still, Switzerland is far from having a monopoly on hot money. Banks elsewhere offer the same features Swiss banks offer, and no other country has a legal assistance treaty with the U.S. If you're pressed for time you can find a friendly bank in Panama, the Bahamas, or the Cayman

Islands that will serve as well, and all three spots are regarded as major stopping-off points for money from the drug
trade.

There's considerable evidence that U.S. banks have gotten caught up wasting money—not the banks themselves,
but bank employees operating freelance. Once the money is
in a bank it can be moved anywhere, since the reporting
rules don't apply to interbank transfers. Chemical Bank in
New York—sixth biggest in the U.S.—pleaded guilty in
1977 to 445 misdemeanor counts of failing to file reports on
large cash deposits. The deposits in question came to $8½
million, and government prosecutors believe a lot of that was
drug money. The bank itself wasn't involved, but 25 bank
employees in various branches were fired for failing to file
the requisite reports, and the bank paid a fine of $222,500.

If your object is to launder money—as opposed to sending
it overseas for safekeeping—you don't even need a bank.
Say, purely for purposes of illustration, you've just moved a
kilo of cocaine, or skimmed a million from your Las Vegas
casino. You could smuggle the money into an offshore bank.
But you might also start a legitimate business—preferably
overseas and so beyond the reach of U.S. authorities. The
dirty money would go abroad as an investment in the company, and profits from the business would come back as
clean money. You can do it at so many removes that no one
will ever tumble onto you. William W. Nickerson, deputy
assistant secretary for enforcement at the Treasury in the
Carter Administration, tells of a case that involved a company formed in an African country, run through a Liechtenstein trust, that used one bank in Switzerland and another in
New York.

A fair number of otherwise legitimate companies around
the world will help you wash money for a fee. You make
what, for the record, is an investment in the company. The
company takes 10 percent or 15 percent as its cut and returns
the rest as a "profit" on your investment. You sent out dirty

money, got back clean money, and that, of course, is the name of the game.

A Tale Told to the Feds

The world is littered with dummy corporations that are part of someone's money-wash scheme, and dummy companies figure very large in one of the more bizarre cases the government ever cracked. The case involved Raymond A. Enstam and Harold E. Oldham, Jr., and the details come from papers filed at the federal court in Dallas. Oldham is identified as a drug dealer and Enstam as his attorney.

Their money wash involved a dummy finance company in Georgetown on Grand Cayman Island called Esmeraldas y Mariposas, Ltd., and a string of dummy corporations back in the U.S. Oldham and Enstam were kind enough to lay out details to two men who identified themselves as dealers in search of both drugs and a safe way of washing money. As luck would have it, the two were Paul Clayton and Herb House, undercover agents of the Drug Enforcement Administration.

Oldham, according to the government's complaint, explained that dirty money could be smuggled past U.S. customs and deposited in a Cayman Islands bank. The money could then be withdrawn in the form of a cashier's check and carried back home as a loan from Esmeraldas y Mariposas —E&M—to a dummy company in the U.S. "Hundreds of millions of dollars are 'washed' through the Cayman Islands annually to avoid taxes or to make legal dollars from illegal dollars," Enstam told the undercover agents. Oldham boasted he had recently laundered $300,000 in a morning with no problems. "What are all those banks doing on that little island if something wasn't going on?" Enstam asked. It was a fair enough question.

Oldham and Enstam told the agents they had a contact in

Georgetown who would handle the details. Once the "loan" was made, there would be monthly statements showing the "unpaid balance" and the "interest" paid on the loan. That, Enstam explained, was so the agents could deduct those "interest payments" on their income tax.

Oldham and Enstam not only explained their scheme but actually walked the agents through the process—thereby laundering $50,000 in government money. For their services, Enstam and Oldham collected a 6 percent fee.

Oldham assured the agents they needn't worry about smuggling money, since the Customs people never searched departing travelers. Nor, of course, did the Cayman Islands authorities care how much money travelers brought into their country. Once the money was in the Cayman Islands, Enstam explained, he would put it into the branch of a Canadian bank, since it would then be beyond the reach of the IRS. Had the agents been Canadian, he said, the money would go into a U.S. bank. "What the Internal Revenue Service doesn't know won't hurt them," said Enstam, who would shortly learn the IRS knew all.

The dummy company Oldham and Enstam created for the agents was called Grand-Vin Investments, and it would need lots of borrowed money since ostensibly it would be investing in vats of French wine, to be held for appreciation. Its office address was that of Enstam's Dallas law office. Grand-Vin got its own ledger book, also kept in Enstam's office, and its own U.S. bank account, opened with $1,000 in government money. Enstam even volunteered to handle Grand-Vin's tax work.

D Day was November 2, 1977—the day for the money wash. Enstam flew with the agents first from Dallas to Miami, and then on to Georgetown. In Miami, House opened his suitcase and pulled out a brown-paper bag with the $50,000 in government money. Enstam slipped the money into his briefcase. By mid-afternoon, all were in Georgetown and the money was in a safety-deposit box in the George-town branch of a Canadian bank.

Enstam then produced two letters—one supposedly written by agent Clayton as president of Grand-Vin, seeking a $47,000 loan from E&M, the other supposedly from E&M agreeing to make the loan at 9 percent interest.

By late afternoon the agents had a cashier's check for $46,720—the $50,000 less the 6 percent fee for Enstam and Oldham and less some taxes and other charges. All then flew back to Miami with agent Clayton carrying the check. As they passed through Customs in Miami, they saw signs warning travelers about the $5,000 rule. "When seeing these signs," says the government's complaint, "special agent Clayton turned to attorney Enstam and they both laughed."

Enstam, presumably, didn't laugh long. In 1979 he was found guilty of tax evasion and sentenced to five years in prison. Oldham was arraigned in Dallas and then fled to Australia. He was recaptured there in 1980 and in the summer of 1980 drew a ten-year sentence after pleading guilty to a drug charge. For both Enstam and Oldham, the world of hot money had suddenly turned bitter cold.

Chapter 16

Tax Havens, Tax Shelters, Tax Dodges, and Other Tales of the Very Rich

SAY, FOR purposes of illustration, fortune has indeed smiled upon you. After years of unremitting toil, you've finally perfected a process for turning peanut shells into gasoline and a major oil company has just paid you an obscenely large sum of money for your secret.

Alternatively, say that you're an overnight success; dear old Dad has just passed away in his sleep, leaving you the sole owner of the family business, which happens to net well into seven figures a year.

Either way you're now rich: not merely comfortable, not merely well off, but rich. All would be bliss were it not for the unwelcome attention of the most repressive law-enforcement body the world has known since the demise of the Gestapo: the Internal Revenue Service. It's out for blood—your blood—and unless you take care, a goodly share of your wealth will be carted off as the IRS has its way with you.

Happily for you, by becoming rich you have gained entry

into the world of trusts and tax-exempt foundations, of tax shelters and tax havens: the world of high-priced lawyers and accountants who themselves earn a pretty penny by keeping the IRS at bay and out of your pocket. Money won't buy happiness but it will buy a lot of useful advice about what to do with your money. The IRS has won some rounds lately, and foundations, tax havens, and most tax shelters aren't as tax-collector-proof as they used to be. Still, those lawyers and accountants are infinitely clever, and while the IRS is going to get some, a lot will be left over for you.

As long as you work for a living, the door to this world of big money is forever closed to you. Your salary will be taxed at rates that run to 50 percent, even after the 1981 tax cut, and there isn't a thing you can do but gnash your teeth and maybe cheat a little on your tax return.

Wealth means living off your capital, and the maximum tax rate on capital gains is 20 percent. If you have enough capital, you can invest and defer paying taxes on your gains for a good long while, piling up enough deductions to reduce your overall tax bill to the bone. If you have enough capital, you can give a lot of it to charity and take a fat deduction on that. You can then arrange to get your capital back at some future date, and even if the value of that capital has gone up 1,000 percent over the years, you won't pay a penny of tax on the gain.

Wealth begets wealth and you can augment your own capital by investing with borrowed money, and most of the interest on the loan will be a tax deduction. If you can take fat tax deductions now and defer paying taxes on your gain for a number of years, you obviously are going to do very well, which is what tax shelters are all about. They shelter your wealth from taxation.

Besides income taxes there are also stiff estate taxes and gift taxes to worry about—softened by the 1981 law, but still waiting to snare your wealth. Play your cards right, though, and you can avoid paying those taxes as well.

If you want a measure of power and visibility—even if the tax advantages aren't what they used to be—you can create your own tax-exempt foundation: the Ronald J. Beasley Foundation, if you will, with your name engraved in stone over the door. If you hanker after the limelight, you can buy a professional sports team, your players being depreciable assets just like a machine tool or a freight car, and depreciation a tax deduction.

In short, and if you didn't know it already, it pays to be rich—all the more so in this age of new money, when investments that outrun inflation aren't all that easy to find. If you don't have to share your profits with the tax collector, obviously your chances of outrunning inflation are better.

If you have just a little capital, you can buy a six-month savings certificate, or invest in a money-market mutual fund and get a return that before taxes will come close to matching the inflation rate. But then the IRS will take a fat share of that in return, and what you have left after taxes is a bare pittance. If you have lots of capital, you can get a return that outruns the inflation rate, and most of it will still be there after the IRS calls.

Introducing Mr. X

If you have just a little capital, you have to make your own decisions about your investments, and the higher the promised return, the greater the chance you've walked into someone's con game that will leave you poorer than when you started. If you are rich, says a man who shall be known as Mr. X, "you can buy enough expertise to find the best investment."

Mr. X should know, being both a tax lawyer and an accountant who has spent two decades helping the very rich stay very rich. If you want his advice (or his name), you'd best have $1 million or more in capital and be prepared to pay several hundred dollars an hour for his help. The best things in life aren't free.

The age of new money is Gold Strike Time in the Klondike for Mr. X and his fellows. It's harder to find investments that will outrun inflation when inflation is in double digits, and that won't collapse when the economy slumps. Further, the IRS—and Congress at the behest of the IRS—has slammed the door on a great many back alleys that people use to get around the tax code.

Seen from the perspective of those who aren't wealthy, there's a certain justice in this—in the rich being made to dance to the same tune the rest of us dance to. And indeed the world of tax shelters and tax havens and tax-free foundations was so rotten with abuses it cried out for punitive action.

Yet it's the investment of capital that keeps the economy growing, and it's the potential for a rich return on that capital that makes people want to invest. To penalize those with capital to invest is to guarantee there will be less capital invested in the future of the United States—which is precisely what happened. In 1981, of course, Congress rewrote the tax laws, and the bite on capital gains was reduced from 28 percent to its current 20 percent maximum, so that life has become just a little easier for the very rich.

And capital gains, and that nifty 20 percent capital gains rate, is the key to how the very rich manage their money. If you can cut your tax rate from 50 percent (now the maximum rate on all forms of income) to just 20 percent, you're obviously that much ahead of the game. If you can build your capital while putting off the payment of even the capital-gains tax for many years, you've hit what is the financial equivalent of a home run with the bases loaded.

One way to minimize your tax bill is to cheat—understating income, overstating deductions, or both. In time, however, the IRS computers will probably find you out and then you'll owe the IRS a ton of money in unpaid taxes, interest, and penalties, and you could go to jail.

Another way is to smuggle your money out of the country to one of those havens that offer numbered accounts and don't ask a lot of questions. That's the route you'd take if your wealth came from drugs or crime and you didn't dare reveal its source, or you might do it if you just didn't feel like paying taxes.

But let's assume that you're both wealthy and tolerably honest. You don't want to cheat the IRS—you just don't want to pay a penny more in taxes than you absolutely have to.

First you'd probably think about that traditional haven for the wealthy, the tax-exempt municipal bond. You're doing good by helping the cities and states of America raise needed capital, and you're doing well because not a penny of the interest you receive from a municipal bond is subject to federal income tax. Buy a bond from a municipality in your state and you probably won't have to pay state or local income taxes either.

The wealthy have always bought municipal bonds, and some of the wealthiest Americans pay very little tax because so much of their wealth is in municipal bonds. But if municipal bonds are for the wealthy, they aren't necessarily for the clever. One reason is that you can't stretch your capital by buying municipal bonds with borrowed money. That, in turn, means you can't pick up the tax deduction on the interest on borrowed money. You already get tax-free income from municipal bonds, and the IRS isn't about to give you two breaks on the same investment.

Another reason is that the municipal-bond market, in common with all markets in this age of new money, has turned wildly erratic. Prices plunged as interest rates soared in 1979 and early 1980. Prices soared as interest rates plunged in the spring of 1980. Prices plunged as interest rates soared from the summer of 1980 into 1981. If you sold out when prices were plunging, you wound up with a loss. If you sold out when prices were soaring you made a profit, but while the income from a municipal bond is tax-free, you do pay a tax on any capital gains you make.

Municipal-bond salesmen have lots of nifty charts showing that if you're in a high tax bracket, a bond with an 8 percent rate will provide the equivalent of a 16 percent rate, given the tax exemption. And that 16 percent would beat inflation most (but not all) of the time. But, again, you can't borrow to buy municipal bonds and you do face taxation on capital gains—two significant drawbacks that make municipal bonds less than ideal for the rich. Elderly widows and the timid among the wealthy buy municipal bonds. The rest buy tax shelters.

Seeking Shelter

As the name implies, the aim of any tax shelter is to shelter as much income from taxation as possible while postponing the realization of capital gains on your investment for some years. The shelter may invest in real estate, oil, cattle, box-cars, coal, movies, or a dozen other areas the tax-shelter industry has embraced in recent years. As fast as the IRS declares one area of tax-sheltered investment unfit for human consumption, another comes along. The basic element in all shelters is the same. You want something that will produce such massive tax deductions that those deductions will offset a lot of income from other sources, with the gain on your capital postponed into the future—if possible into the far distant future.

No one goes into a tax shelter expecting to lose money—although plenty of shelters do just that. The wealthy work very hard at preserving their capital, and nearly all the better shelters promise a juicy return on capital down the road;

taxable at that 20 percent maximum capital-gains rate. You go into a shelter to reduce your tax bite to the irreducible minimum with at least a fighting chance of getting your capital back.

Each shelter offers its own means of sheltering income, meaning its own particular array of deductions to offset income. In real estate it's the deduction for the depreciation of your property (now called the "recovery deduction" in the 1981 tax law)—the money that you, in theory at least, must set aside to replace your original capital asset as it wears out. In gas and oil it's the deduction for the cost of drilling and exploring. In cattle deals it's the expense of fattening your cattle for market. If the shelter involves buying equipment to be leased to someone else, you get the depreciation deduction and you get a 10 percent credit on your tax bill for having invested in productive equipment—the government's gift to you for investing in the future of the economy.

Finally, you don't buy into a shelter with your own money. You buy in mostly with borrowed money, and, within limits, the interest you pay on that borrowed money is a tax deduction.

Play your cards right and any income from your investment will be sheltered from taxation. Meanwhile the capital you have invested is growing and growing, and not until you cash in your investment will you pay taxes on your capital gain. Pick the right shelter and you emerge with deductions that far exceed the money you have invested in the deal. Those deductions can then be used to offset income from other sources.

It used to be you could invest a little, borrow the rest through what was called a loan but which you really weren't expected to repay, and so pick up a truly gigantic tax deduction no matter what sort of shelter you bought. Your share of the shelter might come to $1 million, of which you put up $50,000 of your own money and "borrowed" the rest through a "non-recourse" loan. In theory the lender would be repaid through having a share in the profits on the deal. In practice, most non-recourse loans were fictions, designed solely to increase the amount of tax deductions you could take. In any event, the interest on that "borrowed" money might easily come to $150,000 a year, and the other tax deductions from whatever the shelter invested in might easily come to another $150,000 a year. You have put up $50,000 in cash and you have bought $300,000 worth of tax deductions in a year. That would shelter any income from your investment from taxes, and it would shelter a lot more of your other income as well. You weren't really buying an investment, you were buying a tax deduction.

In 1976 Congress changed all that by adopting the "at-risk" rule. No longer can you take deductions beyond what you actually have at risk in the shelter: the cash you have invested and your liability on whatever money has been borrowed to make the deal work. That killed off a lot of the more bizarre sorts of shelters and it took away some of the allure from shelters generally. Two key exceptions are oil and gas deals, where the potential for gain if you strike something is so tremendous, and real estate deals, where the at-risk rule still doesn't apply.

Suppose that you and a few wealthy friends form a partnership in real estate. The property is a handsome apartment house that generates about $1 million a year in rent. The building costs $5 million, of which you and your friends put up $500,000 and borrow the rest at 15 percent interest. Under the 1981 law the building has a useful life of 15 years, after which time (in theory at least) wear and tear will have reduced it to a pile of rubble.

On one hand you have $1 million a year in rent, and since rents tend to be indexed to inflation, that rental will increase as inflation eats away at the value of the dollar. Expenses and paying off the principal of the loan will eat up about

$625,000 a year, leaving $375,000 in net profit per year. But along with that profit you get a handsome array of tax deductions.

First. you have the depreciation on the building. It has a useful life of 15 years, meaning that for each of those 15 years you deduct $333,333 (⅟₁₅th of $5 million) against the day the building simply collapses from old age and must be replaced. You have further borrowed $4,500,000 at 15 percent and your annual interest on that is $675,000. You have $375,000 a year in net income and approximately $1 million a year in deductions (depreciation and interest) to offset that and a lot of other income. Since you only put up $500,000 in cash to begin with, you plainly are doing very well.

Finally you approach the 15th year and, incredibly enough, the building is not a pile of rubble. It's still standing, and because you chose the property well and have kept it in tiptop shape, it's no longer worth the $5 million you paid for it, but $10 million. You've now run out of depreciation, meaning one big deduction gone. You've paid off the loan and another big deduction is gone. At that point you sell the building for $10 million to another band of seekers after shelter. Your profit on the deal is $5 million (actually $9½ million on the cash you put up) and the tax bite on that is 20 percent.

The illustration is hypothetical, and it also happens to be somewhat over-simplified—the rules on depreciation being very complex things, especially after the 1981 tax law. Times and neighborhoods change, and you might not find a ready buyer when you want to sell. In 15 years, modern construction methods being what they are, the building might truly be little more than a pile of rubble. Still, you have gotten some choice tax deductions through the years, and if you bought wisely you've probably come out the other end with a building that can be sold at a nice profit.

There are tax shelters available to the general public, put together by a brokerage house or some other packager of shelters, and most of them are even registered with the Securities and Exchange Commission just as an offering of stock or bonds is registered. You can buy in for a relatively modest amount—$5,000 or $10,000 in some cases. Still, it's someone else's deal, and you're absolutely at the mercy of whoever put it together—which isn't always so great, because when snake oil went out of fashion, many of those who sold it went into tax shelters instead. You may indeed hit oil, or the piece of real estate your shelter invests in could come up a winner. But the wrong kind of deal will produce neither the income nor the deductions promised, and it could produce a fat capital loss instead of a gain. Or the IRS may decide the whole deal stinks and force you to pay taxes on all that income you thought you had sheltered.

The rich do things differently. Their shelter deals are private, with the general investing public invited to stay the hell out. They will be put together with the help of Mr. X or some other lawyer or accountant who is a specialist in such things. The deductions will be as promised, the potential for ultimate gain will have been analyzed by a very knowing professional, and the shelter will be as IRS-proof as the mind of man can make it.

Actually, says Mr. X, the best shelter is none of the above, but a closely held business—meaning one in which only a few people, and maybe just a family, holds control. The kind of business is immaterial as long as the company can keep growing faster than the rate of inflation.

Because it is closely held, there are no nosy shareholders to report to and no lengthy documents to file with the SEC. Nor are there shareholders to balk if the owners want to reward their toil with handsome salaries and bonuses. The owners can pretty much shape their pension and profit-sharing plans to fit their whims, and they can take as many "lifestyle" perks as the IRS will allow: cars, homes, travel, club memberships, clothing, insurance, all paid for by the company and then counted as a tax-deductible expense.

All the time the company is building wealth, which ultimately can be cashed in. Until the age of new money happened along, the owners could figure on eventually cashing in by going public—selling off a chunk of the business to other investors for a lot of money. The public stock market hasn't been very receptive to such issues in recent years— an exception being various high-technology stocks that have been very warmly received. Still, the owners can sell out to someone else for cash, paying a maximum 20 percent rate on their gain, or they can sell out for stock in another company and pay no tax at all. The profits made by selling out can then be invested in tax-sheltered investments—and so it goes: the rich getting richer and the poor paying taxes.

How the Rich Give It Away

The laws offer the wealthy innumerable opportunities to do well by doing good. When United Way or the Red Cross comes calling, you or I hand over a check or some cash. To Mr. X, the wealthy person who contributes cash is stupid, there being so many better ways of doing it.

Say that years ago you bought Amalgamated Cough Drop stock at $5 per share. Successive strains of influenza have meant boom times in the cough-drop game, and each Amalgamated share now sells for $100. You can sell those shares and pay the capital-gains tax on the gain. Or you can donate the shares to your favorite charity, taking as a tax deduction the current value of the stock and not paying a penny of tax on the gain. You can similarly donate works of art, antiques, or almost anything else. The IRS may demand you get a professional appraisal on the worth of your donation. But if you can establish that the item is worth what you say it is, the IRS probably will allow the deduction.

Or thanks to such devices as the "charitable lead trust" and the "charitable remainder trust," you can do even better than that. With a charitable lead trust, you give your Amalgamated shares to the charity, taking the current value of those shares as a tax deduction and paying no tax on the gain. The charity holds those shares for a set number of years, after which the shares come back to you. The charity collects the dividends on the stock during those years, which is why it wanted the stock in the first place. Should the value of Amalgamated shares have climbed to $5,000 each during the years the trust held them, you still wouldn't pay a penny of tax on the gain when you get the shares back.

In the charitable remainder trust you get the deduction now, collect the dividends on the stock until you die, at which point ownership of the stock passes to the charity. Again, say you own Amalgamated Cough Drop shares, which currently yield about 6 percent a year. You create the trust and place your stock in the trust. As long as you live you keep earning the 6 percent a year from the stock, and when you die the charity becomes owner of the stock. And you get a hefty tax deduction in the year you created the trust.

Everyone has heard of tax havens—those charming places in foreign lands that don't collect taxes the way the IRS does, and that welcome dollars with open arms and no questions. Unfortunately the IRS has heard of them too, and tax havens aren't what they used to be. If you have income from U.S. sources, you owe the IRS taxes on it and if the IRS gets wind of someone trying to use a tax haven to avoid payment it will move heaven and earth to nail him. You can move assets to someplace friendly—Bermuda, say—and claim that all subsequent gains in the value of those assets are subject to the capital-gains tax of Bermuda (which is nil) and not to the 20 percent U.S. rate. The IRS, in turn, will claim the assets are still being managed from the U.S., and it will slap you with a tax bill.

Some well-known movie stars and artists and international sports figures have set themselves up in such low-tax countries as Monaco and Ireland and have escaped the tax rates of the U.S., or whatever country they came from. But that means renouncing your citizenship and becoming a citizen of Monaco or Ireland, and few of us, even the wealthiest, go that far.

International business has a somewhat easier time of it because it has more opportunities to outflank the IRS. Amalgamated Cough Drop, for instance, sells its cough drops in no fewer than 101 foreign lands. Amalgamated Cough Drop USA will sell its cough drops to Amalgamated Cough Drop Europe at the lowest prices it can get away with. That will diminish the profits—and the tax bill—of Amalgamated Cough Drop USA. Amalgamated Cough Drop Europe happens to be based in Ireland, which offers plenty of tax breaks to foreign companies that want to set up there. It will then sell the cough drops in Europe at higher prices, reap huge profits, and pay hardly any taxes.

An oil company operating abroad must make substantial payments to the host country whose oil it's pumping. If the payment is counted as a royalty, all the company gets on its U.S. tax bill is just another deduction. Since the U.S. corporate tax rate is 46 percent, each $1 of tax deduction cuts the oil company's tax bill by just 46 cents. If the payment to the host country can be counted as a tax payment, then the oil company gets a tax credit on its U.S. tax bill, and each $1 paid in foreign taxes will reduce its U.S. tax bill by $1. Not only do the rich get richer, but the very rich get very much richer.

The Algernon Larynx Foundation

In the good old days, about the best way for the wealthy to beat the tax collector was to create a foundation, which surely was one of the more marvelous creations of man.

Say that this is still 1960 and Amalgamated Cough Drop is still a closely held company just getting ready to sell shares to the public for the first time. The president still is that legendary freebooter, Algernon J. Larynx—a robber baron in the classic mold whose ruthless demolition of his rivals enabled Amalgamated to grow to vast size. But the federal income tax, which was a pittance when Algernon Larynx founded the company, has now become a considerable burden. So is the federal estate tax, which will bite heavily when Algernon Larynx dies and his wealth passes on to his son, Algernon, Jr. Further, Algernon, Sr., correctly perceives Junior to be a dolt who will surely lose control of the company just as soon as a large share of the stock passes into the public's hands.

So there—still back in 1960—is Algernon Larynx, faced with staggering income- and estate-tax burdens, fearful his son will lose control of the family business—and more than a little concerned about the eternal judgment that will be passed upon him when his hour at last comes. Eternal damnation is a high price to pay for starting a cough drop company.

The answer—still back in 1960—is to create the Algernon J. Larynx Foundation, whose principal asset is 51 percent of the stock of Amalgamated Cough Drop. There's first the juicy tax deduction to be taken on the donation of so much wealth to a not-for-profit, and hence tax-free, foundation. Nor, under the terms of the gift, can the foundation ever sell so much as a share of Amalgamated stock. Algernon Larynx, Sr., as director of the foundation, has an absolute lock on 51 percent of the company's stock, and even if all the public shareholders band together as one, they can't get control of the company. When Algernon, Sr., dies, his son becomes head of the foundation, and control of 51 percent of the stock passes to him without the payment of a penny in estate taxes. And since the foundation can't sell a share of stock, no matter how doltish Algernon, Jr., is, he can't ever have control of the company wrested away from him.

Finally, armed with the income from the Amalgamated

stock, the Larynx Foundation sets off on a course of good works, such that the image of Algernon Larynx the freebooter is quickly transformed into that of Algernon Larynx the philanthropist. Thanks to the foundation, there are now the Larynx School of Medicine and the Larynx Institute for the Thinking of Profound Thoughts, and there are countless artists and authors who owe their success to timely aid from the Larynx Foundation. The place of Algernon Larynx in heaven is assured.

And so it was in times gone by: great foundations, each bearing the name of a freebooter of old—Ford, Rockefeller, Duke, Carnegie, Mellon, Russell Sage. Those foundations and many more endure to this day, and some of them are repositories of great wealth. The Ford Foundation, the largest of them all, can boast of some $2½ billion in assets, and while it has given away billions since its birth in 1936, it also owns, through its investment portfolio, a fat share of American business. At the end of 1979, its common stock holdings amounted to $1½ billion, including $92 million of IBM and $89 million of Exxon.

And then there are the thousands of smaller foundations, some of them operating from a shoebox, created solely to shelter someone's wealth from taxation and to perpetuate someone's control over a company. The abuses of foundations would fill a book, and many a book on the subject has been written.

Grants by the biggest and best foundations are the result of careful and serious study. Grants by many of the smaller foundations (and a few of the bigger ones) used to be pretty much by whim. Some foundations (again including some very big ones) gave away almost nothing despite their wealth. In some cases a successful investment would be kept by the founding family while a failed one would be shuffled off to the foundation as a tax-deductible donation. The biggest payout at some foundations (and sometimes the only payout) was salaries and loans to the founders.

In 1969, Congress finally cracked down. It first banned self-dealing—meaning that foundation money could no longer be used for salaries and loans to the founders. Foundations were required to spend at least a certain share of their assets each year. If a foundation controlled a company before 1969, it had to whittle down its stake to 50 percent, and for anything since 1969 the limit is 20 percent. (Ford Foundation, which once owned 90 percent of Ford Motor Co., now owns not a single share.) Finally, the law set limits on the kinds of assets that might be given a foundation.

Far from being one of the best tax dodges around, the foundation has become one of the worst, and Mr. X calls it the "least preferred" method of sheltering income. You can still seek immortality and a choice seat on the Judgment Day by creating your own foundation, and there are still some tax breaks to be had. But all is not as it was, and when it comes to managing money, even the wealthiest suffer an occasional comeuppance.

Chapter 17

Planning Your Own Survival in the Age of New Money

WHAT ABOUT individual survival? What must you do to survive this age of new money?

You'll have to do it on your own. There's no oil company waiting to shower riches upon you, because you really don't know how to turn peanut shells into gasoline (but neither does anyone else). Unless you're one of the lucky one in a million, dear old Dad didn't leave you a family business that earns well into seven figures a year. The world is afloat in petrodollars but you won't see one of them, because you aren't an Arab oil sheik and you don't own one of the giant international banks where petrodollars go.

You can't borrow the way the Treasury does, and you can't coin money the way the Mint does, or print it as the Bureau of Engraving and Printing does. You can't expand money the way the banking system does, and you certainly can't create it the way the Federal Reserve does.

It's a terrible time in the world of money, and you must get by with what you earn and whatever capital you can accumulate. While the U.S. tax code is less inflationary than it used to be, you still must shelter from taxation any income you have in order to have any income left. And since no one knows when things will get better, you can't simply sit back and hope for a brighter tomorrow. The age of new money has been around for more than a decade, and it could be around a decade from now. If it isn't, something worse may have taken its place: hyperinflation or another Great Depression.

Inflation is so ingrained that no President, including Ronald Reagan, can eradicate it quickly without pushing the economy into deep and prolonged recession. The President can, by restoring stability and common sense to the managing of our economy, stop things from getting worse—which would be no small accomplishment. He can reduce government spending, which will reduce government borrowing, which will reduce the need for the Federal Reserve to create tons of new money. By cutting taxes—not merely in 1981 but again in 1982 and yet again in 1983—he can make the tax code less inflationary than it is, and less punitive, too.

If all works as the President hopes it will, then, slowly—very slowly—the inflationary pressures will ease and a measure of economic sanity will return to our lives.

But the danger is great that in the name of fighting inflation the government and the Federal Reserve will cast us into deep, dark, and prolonged recession. In 1932, the third year of the Great Depression, both the government and the Federal Reserve still thought they were combating the inflation of the 1920s, and they acted accordingly, the Fed keeping money tight and Congress raising taxes.

The danger is equally great that if there are substantial cuts in taxes without matching cuts in government spending and borrowing, we'll have still worse inflation. With salaries, interest rates, Social Security, and lots of other things, all indexed to inflation, the tendency for years to come will be for prices to go higher, not lower.

To survive in this age of new money, you must plan to endure continued inflation. Yet you also must plan to endure recessions that verge on depressions. You must invest to survive, but you'll have to do so in financial markets that will remain erratic. There will be new investment markets, but it won't be easy to determine if they are any less perilous than existing markets. You must prepare to see investments in some of America's greatest companies written off, and you must learn about new companies in new industries that are only now beginning to peek over the horizon.

Survival won't be easy, but you can survive. It will take scrimping and saving, a lot of common sense, and a strong sense of self-preservation. If you're willing to work at it, you'll get by, and if you get lucky you can even prosper no matter what the age of new money throws your way.

Living by the Rules

There are rules to live by in this age of new money, and Rule Number One is "Play it safe."

Capital, once lost, is harder to replace in the age of new money than it was when times were good. If you lost on one stock in the 1950s and 1960s, it didn't matter so much because most stocks were going up most of the time and you could be pretty sure of making it up another day. If you lost in the 1974–75 market break, it took five years and more to make it up, if you ever made it up at all. And because of inflation, you have to earn nearly $2 today to make up each dollar you lost in 1974. This isn't a time for playing long shots, unless you're playing with money you're absolutely sure you can afford to lose.

Rule Number Two is "Stay loose and stay liquid."

There was a concept on Wall Street a decade or so ago called the "one-decision" stock. The idea was that there were stocks of such extraordinary promise that your only decision was whether to buy them. Once you bought, you'd never want to sell. When the market collapsed in 1974–75, the one-decision stocks fared no better than the others, and many fared worse. For some investors, the one decision then became whether to file for bankruptcy.

Times change, circumstances change, markets change—and never more rapidly than in this age of new money. Early 1980 was a time to keep your money in a money-market mutual fund or a six-month savings certificate, because interest rates were going to the skies and the investment markets were tumbling. By the spring of 1980 it was time to shift to the stock market, where prices were shooting up as interest rates fell. In late 1980, and early 1981, with interest rates again shooting up, it was a time to return to money-market funds and savings certificates. Gold and silver were incredibly good investments late in 1979 and dismal investments thereafter.

Don't put your money into anything you can't get out of quickly, and without taking a bigger loss—should it come to that—than market conditions dictate. You can get out of a money-market fund or a stock quickly enough, but money in arts and antiques or in the wrong piece of real estate could be tied up for a long time, and when you're finally able to sell, it might be at a terrible loss.

Rule Number Three is "Before you even think about investing, put aside money against a rainy day, since rainy days are inevitable in this age of new money."

This is money to tide you through unemployment or major illness. The old rule was to put aside enough to live on for six months. If you can manage six months' worth of living expenses, fine and dandy. Most of us can't these days. On the other hand, there are unemployment benefits and disability coverage to help out if things really get bad. If you put aside enough to carry you for at least three months, you're taking a gamble, but not an outrageous gamble.

But you absolutely must have enough to get you through for three months, and if you aren't saving enough to do that, you must rejuggle your budget so that you do. At least five cents of every take-home dollar should go into your pool for saving and investing—saving first, and then, when you have your three-month cushion, investment. It would be better if you could save 10 percent of your take-home pay, but 5 percent is a rock-bottom minimum.

This is your hard-core saving—liquid and as safe as you can make it. But since you don't want to give anything away to inflation, your savings should also yield as much as you can get.

A standard savings account is liquid enough, but why settle for a 5¼ percent return (the current ceiling at commercial banks), or 5½ percent (the current ceiling at thrifts)? Six-month savings certificates yield a great deal more if you can come up with the $10,000 minimum deposit, and a savings certificate is insured by the federal government. Six months isn't an eternity, although it may have seemed like one if your money was locked into a savings certificate when the stock market rallied in 1980. You can buy a 30-month savings certificate for as little as $100, and it will yield much more than a conventional savings account. Unfortunately, the yield on a 30-month certificate usually is less than the yield on a six-month certificate, and 30 months can truly be an eternity in the age of new money. Even a day can be an eternity if you lose your job and need cash in a hurry. You pay a stiff penalty if you cash in one of these certificates before maturity.

A money-market fund tends to yield close to what a six-month certificate yields; you can buy into many funds for as little as $1,000 and you can get out by simply writing a check. Had you been in a fund in 1980, you could have gotten the high yields early in the year, shifted your money elsewhere when interest rates fell, and bought back when rates shot up late in 1980. Most of the outfits that sell money-market funds also sell funds that invest in stocks and bonds and other things, and you can usually shift from one type of fund to another simply by making a telephone call.

Still, money funds aren't insured by the federal government, while money in a savings certificate is, and that's a consideration. There is also a matter of timing on when you buy a certificate and when you buy a money fund. The rate for the week on new six-month savings certificates is set each Tuesday, based on what the Treasury paid when it sold six-month bills on Monday afternoon. Once set, the rate on a certificate won't change during its six-month life. The return on a money-market fund changes daily according to the return on the securities owned by the fund. It takes time until the total portfolio of the money fund catches up with higher rates, and the return on funds tends to lag behind what certificates are paying when interest rates are rising. When rates drop, the return on a savings certificate drops immediately, while the money funds continue to profit from the older, higher-yielding securities in their portfolios. Thus the funds tend to outperform certificates when interest rates are falling.

Unfortunately, the 1981 tax law takes away some goodies. Until 1981, the first $100 in dividend income ($200 for a couple) was excluded from taxation, but with nothing comparable for interest income (and both money funds and savings certificates pay interest). In 1981, that became $200 ($400 for couples) on both dividends *and* interest. In 1982 it goes back to $100 ($200), and on dividends only.

You can get $1,000 in interest-free income ($2,000 for a couple) on the new All-Savers Certificate—if you're content to have your money locked up for a full year.

The NOW account, which is a checking account that pays interest, is fast becoming the standard bank account, and you should keep all your working cash in such an account. Your money will earn 5¼ percent interest and it will continue earning that until the checks you write against the account clear. If you have money in a 5¼ percent savings account, combine it with money in your checking account, and you'll probably meet whatever minimum-balance rule the bank or thrift institution has on NOW accounts. This is working cash rather than savings, and you'll keep only enough in the account to handle the minimum balance. Still, 5¼ percent isn't much in the face of today's inflation, and anything beyond the required minimum balance must go into a savings certificate or a money fund.

The purveyors of gold have done a good job of convincing many people to buy a little gold against hard times, and in this age of new money it's a pretty easy sell.

Chances are you can't afford enough gold, at $500 an ounce or so, to make much difference if times really get hard. But the potential for really hard times in our economy is considerable and $500 worth of gold would have bought a good hunk of Germany back in 1923 when inflation turned hyper. The price of gold has more than doubled within two years and increased more than 10-fold in a decade and until the economic outlook brightens, the price probably won't go down very much, and it could go a lot higher. It couldn't hurt to buy a few ounces of gold and put them away in your safety-deposit box.

If you're buying for peace of mind, it obviously makes sense only to buy bullion. There are institutions that will buy small amounts of gold for you and issue you a certificate showing you own the gold, which is held for safekeeping in the institution's vaults. But since you're buying against the dread possibility that even a Citibank or a Merrill Lynch may not make it through the hard times, you might as well buy the real thing.

You wouldn't buy gold bars, of course, since the standard bar now goes for about $200,000. But you can buy South African Krugerrands (now available in both one-ounce and smaller sizes), Canadian Maple Leafs, Mexican 50-peso pieces, and so on. All are readily available and readily salable.

Do not, however, buy the new U.S. gold medallions. The government never did want to issue them and did so only because Congress ordered it to. Buying the medallions involves endless bureaucratic red tape, and selling them could prove a problem, since the government has neglected to stamp the fineness of the gold on the coin. It is very fine gold, but buyers still like to be reassured. Finally, to buy the U.S. medallions, you must provide the government with a lot of paperwork and it's likely that that paperwork will come to the attention of the Internal Revenue Service. The IRS will then peg you as the nasty sort who buys gold, and it may well audit your tax returns each year until you die, looking for other signs of mischief-making. In truth, most buyers of gold have no intention of letting the IRS find out. Gold coins are mostly bought for cash, put into a safety-deposit box, and sold for cash.

Why You Must Invest

Once you've built your hard-core savings, regard everything else as money to be invested. And that gets to Rule Number Four for survival in the age of new money, which is "You must invest. You must put your money where it can produce capital gains."

It isn't likely your salary has done more than keep up with inflation—if that. The average person saw his or her purchasing power reduced by about 7 percent in 1980, which is how much gains in prices outraced gains in after-tax income. And that was during a recession year when inflation should have slowed. It didn't, of course, and our portion in 1980 was stagflation—the numbing combination of economic stagnation and inflation. And that isn't the last we'll see of stagflation before the age of new money ends.

Salary alone won't carry you through whatever inflation lies ahead, and your salary can dwindle or disappear during whatever recessions lie ahead. Your savings can earn a return that pretty much matches the rate of inflation—before taxes. Your after-tax return isn't going to come close to matching inflation in most years.

To make it through the age of new money intact, you're going to have to invest in something that can appreciate in value—stocks, bonds, real estate, art and antiques, precious gems, whatever—because that's the only way your capital is going to grow. You don't want to gamble, because you don't want to let your capital fritter away. But unless you build capital, you're always going to be at the mercy of whatever economic winds are blowing at the moment, and you're always going to be a hostage to the tax laws.

Your stake in a pension fund and in Social Security offers some protection against an uncertain future. But it's far from total protection, and if you've been banking on either, or both, to get you through, think again.

Pension funds are now insured by the government, and there's less reason today to fear your pension fund won't be around when you retire than there was before Congress passed the Employee Retirement Insurance Security Act (ERISA) a few years back. But more than likely, when you do retire, you're going to get a fixed payment each month, based on what you earned when you were on the job. And inflation being what it is, that payment is going to be stretched thinner and thinner as time goes on. Retirement pay of $1,000 a month was pretty good back in 1970. Today it puts you just a hair above the poverty level. The government will rescue those pension funds that fail amid the coming economic turmoil, but in doing so it will have to print a lot more money, and that will simply add to inflation.

The Social Security system is fast approaching bankruptcy, just as its critics say it is. The elderly constitute a powerful voting bloc, and between that and whatever human decency you find in Congress (which isn't a great deal), Social Security payments have been indexed to inflation, making your contributions to the Social Security system the most inflationary element in our whole economy. The system is barely getting by now, and it will go into the tank when the relatively few children born in the 1960s and 1970s are asked to support the children of the postwar baby boom. It will be an inverted pyramid—the many living off the few—and inverted pyramids invariably topple.

The government won't let the system founder. Most likely it will do what it always does when it needs more money: It will print more money to support Social Security and the consequence of that will be still more inflation. You'll get your money, but each dollar will be worth less and less.

You're a little better off if you can take advantage of one of the plans available to those not covered by a pension plan: a Keogh Plan for the self-employed, and an Individual Retirement Account (IRA) for those who work at places that don't have pension plans, or who don't qualify for the pension fund where they work. You don't pay taxes on income contributed to a Keogh Plan or an IRA until you start taking money out, which will be years from now when you'll almost certainly be in a lower tax bracket. You can decide how you want the money invested, and with a little common sense you can probably do better than one of the giant banks that manage corporate pension-fund money.

Still, the amount you can contribute, tax-free, to a Keogh Plan or an IRA is limited, even after liberalization in the 1981 tax law, and that means the size of the retirement fund you can build up is limited. And that, in turn, means the amount you can start taking out of the fund when you retire is limited. By all means contribute to your corporate pension plan, and get into a Keogh Plan or an IRA if you can. But don't expect a corporate plan or a Keogh or an IRA to do it all for you. You'll need something else going for you.

Unless you're fast approaching retirement and want maximum current income, you must invest in hopes of capital gains. If you'd rather not, keep in mind that the government is literally ordering you to invest.

It doesn't take a very high income to put you in a fairly

high tax bracket, even under the new tax law. The actual cut in tax rates is 1¼ percent in 1981, 10 percent in 1982, 19 percent in 1983, and 23 percent in 1984, with the greatest tax relief reserved for those in the highest tax brackets. Until the new law was passed, for instance, the top tax rate on salary income was 50 percent, but on interest and dividends it was 70 percent. Granted, it took $215,400 a year in taxable income to get you into that 70 percent bracket. Still, this is America, the Land of Opportunity, and someday you might have made it.

Beyond cutting rates, the 1981 law dropped the top bracket from 70 percent to 50 percent, no matter what the source of income. Further, under the old law, you hit 50 percent when your taxable income hit $60,000, assuming you were married and filing a joint return. That 50 percent level is now about $61,000 and it climbs to $85,600 in 1982, $109,400 in 1983, and $162,400 in 1984.

If you aren't up in the top brackets, you get relief, but not the sort of relief the rich folks get, and you don't get the last particle of relief until 1984.

There is further the loss of the tax exclusion on interest income and the cut in the exclusion on dividend income from $200 ($400) to $100 ($200). Since money funds and savings certificates pay interest, you could actually lose money under the 1981 tax law. The law does contain a tax break on interest income—but it won't happen until 1985.

That's saving. Investing is something else because the new law cut the maximum tax rate on capital gains from 28 percent to 20 percent. Unless you're in the top bracket, you'll pay even less (10 percent if your taxable income is $20,000 and 15.6 percent if it's $45,000). Hang onto what you have invested in for a year and 20 percent (or less) is all you pay on any gains in your capital. All costs connected with your investment—including the interest on borrowed money—is deducted before the tax bites.

Further, if you should lose (heaven forbid), a consoling

government will share your loss. If the loss is on assets held for less than a year, you can deduct up to $3,000 of the lossfrom other income (from your salary, interest, and dividends) in that year. And if your loss exceeds $3,000, you can carry it over to the next year, and to the year after that if you really took a pasting. If the loss is on assets held for more than a year, you can deduct half the loss, up to $3,000 from other income. Again, if you lost more than $3,000, you can carry that over to the next year.

If you win, the government can't take more than 20 percent of your gain, and for most people the tax will be less than that. If you lose, the government will swallow part of that loss. You can't ask for better than that.

Getting Your Finances in Order

We'll get to where to invest in a moment. The first thing to do is get your own financial house in order. It's an exercise big corporations go through all the time, using staffs of accountants and great computers. You can do it yourself, with pencil, paper, and a pocket calculator.

First, to help you determine your own investment goals and also to help you plan your day-to-day spending, calculate your own personal inflation rate, which is probably different from any inflation rate the government publishes. The government offers inflation rates for consumer prices, wholesale prices, and for the whole economy. You want an inflation rate just for you so you know how much your investments have to return to beat inflation and where your spending is really getting away from you.

You're a consumer, so the consumer price index—the CPI —is the one most applicable to you. It measures the cost of a typical array of goods bought by a typical urban family. But you may not be part of a typical urban family, and what the government regards as a typical array of goods you may not regard as typical at all. If you live in a rented apartment in a big city, with children in college, and a fairly handsome lifestyle, your inflation rate is dramatically different from that of a retired couple living in their own home in rural North Dakota.

Since the government won't tell you what your personal inflation rate is, you'll have to do it yourself.

Make use of whatever you use to manage your finances: canceled checks, budget books, notes jotted on the backs of envelopes, whatever. Take two months this year and two months last year—a winter month and a summer month to cancel out seasonal differences—and compare what you're spending this year with what you spent last year.

How much more are you spending on food? On gasoline and other car expenses? How much more on mortgage payments, on utility bills, house upkeep? How much more are you paying for liquor? For dining out? How much more on medical expenses? Compare spending this year and last, item by item, and you'll see where inflation has hit you the hardest. Compare total spending this year with total spending last year, and you'll get your own personal rate of inflation: the SPI if your name is Smith, or the BPI if it's Beasley. Keep updating your list every six months so you can see how things are going.

Right away, you'll have a basis for sound budgeting because you'll see where inflation is doing the deepest damage and where you have to cut back. You might think you're a wise and careful food shopper, buying the best bargains available each week. Your own personal consumer price index will show you where you're holding the line and where you aren't.

Inflation is pernicious. A 15 percent rise in the price of food over a year is made up of a penny more on this item one week, and a dime more on that item the next week. Your favorite brand of canned goose-liver pâté costs $2.75 one week, and $2.79 the next, and $2.85 the next. The increases come so gradually you hardly notice, until suddenly the can of pâté that used to cost $2.75 now costs $3.75. Months ago you should have apologized to your taste buds and switched to pork pâté, which costs a lot less.

Years ago, when Jimmy Carter first became President, there was a lot of talk about "zero base budgeting." That meant the government would approach each year as though it had just been created—not taking past years' budgets and adding on, but starting from zero on a new budget each year. Obviously the idea never caught hold in government, but it's something you might think about.

As the name implies, you start from zero, as though you've never had a budget before. You begin by listing the absolutely essential, bedrock items: mortgage payments, food, clothing, and transportation. This is called your "minimum increment from zero," and you want to keep it as tight as you can—the absolute least you can get along on.

Then, on three-by-five cards, list all expenses beyond this bare-bones minimum, being as specific as you can. List the amount you spend dining out on one card, the cost of lawn care on another, and the cost of keeping a second car on another. As you do each card, think about ways of doing each thing for less than you now spend. If you spent $200 on liquor, maybe your liquor store has house brands that sell for less. Say you spent $300 on lawn care. Had you tended your own lawn, you'd still have that $300, and $300 added to your money-market fund would have brought in another $40 or so over the year.

Finally, list all you'd like to spend on—or save for—beyond current expenses: a nifty vacation, college for the kids, a new car. Each of those items also goes on its own three-by-five card.

Now arrange the cards by priority, and total everything up —that minimum increment, current expenses, and those things you'd like to spend on. If the grand total is $30,000 and you earn $25,000, you've got some cutting to do. You can drop out the lowest-priority items, or you can opt for some of the cheaper alternatives to how you're doing things now. Because you're looking at your spending in a new way, you should be able to find cheaper ways of doing things instead of automatically adding on more each year to cover inflation—which is what most of us do. Whatever you save can go into your basic savings pool, and once you have your savings pool set, you can think about investing.

And that's what you're going to do next—think about investing. What are you investing for? Are you older and saving for retirement, or are you trying to build a nest egg to send kids to college? What sort of person are you? Do you have nerves of steel or will you lie awake fretting at night over every dollar you have at risk? And your investment money *is* at risk, since no investment is absolutely risk-free. How much do you have to invest, and is there any portion of it you could afford to lose without having to file under the bankruptcy laws?

The World of Exotic Investments

And that gets to Rule Number Five for survival in the age of new money: "Stick with what you know, or what you can learn in the time you're willing to commit to the subject."

For instance, understand right from the start that the world of exotic investments—art, antiques, gems, collectibles of all sorts—isn't for you unless you're a serious student of the subject or are willing to become one.

Prices of most worthwhile objects have been bid out of sight by investors a lot more knowledgeable than you. Works of art that cost a pittance a decade ago cost fortunes now. High-quality gems cost five times and more what they cost a few years ago. What's available today at prices the average person can afford is mostly junk that has been passed over by others. If you are an expert on antiques, you might find a choice piece tucked away in a hayloft somewhere. If you're not, you'll probably wind up with just another thing to clutter the attic.

When you buy into any of these exotic investments, you're at the mercy of the seller. Should you want to get out, you're at the mercy of the buyer. Fads and fashions change from time to time and today's superstar could very well be tomorrow's has-been; and if we do tumble into deep, prolonged recession, prices on most of these things will fall as fast as they went up.

Shun absolutely those well-advertised offers where someone else does the picking for you: sets of coins or medals from the private mints, and the like. Almost never will you get out what you paid, as they are not the sort of thing serious collectors collect.

Plenty of small investors have gone into art and photographic prints because there's a lot available for relatively little money, and because prices on some art and photo prints have done rather nicely over the years. But you're still playing by someone else's rules and you're paying whatever the seller feels like charging with no certainty you'll ever find a buyer. Further, because so many investors have been drawn in, the market has been flooded with garbage, and even for this, prices have been bid fairly high. True, you won't pay all that much and you'll get something to decorate your walls, but you won't make much most of the time, either. If you buy art or photographic prints, do it because you like them, with the possibility of a profit a secondary consideration.

Indeed, that's a good rule for any of the exotic markets: Buy it because you like it, and if you ultimately make a profit, that's frosting on the cake.

And before you enter any of the exotic markets, learn all you can about the subject. Read books, visit art galleries, take whatever courses on the subject are available. Talk to dealers and collectors until you honestly feel you know what the sellers are talking about. If you aren't willing to make that commitment, and if you want to buy in hopes of a profit instead of just having something pretty to look at, stay out.

Finally, if you must try the markets in exotica, you'll do best if you stick with such collectibles as coins and stamps, where each item is cataloged, with a published "list" price. That way you'll know what it costs to buy in and how much to expect when you sell out.

Are There Futures in Your Future?

The futures markets have grown enormously in this age of new money, and you can't read a newspaper or listen to the radio without one commodities house or another screaming that these are the markets for you. And indeed, if you get lucky, you can make profits in futures that will more than offset any inflation we've had or are likely to have.

Of course, if you get unlucky, you'll see your capital disappear before you've memorized your broker's telephone number. The futures markets are for plungers with ice water in their veins and enough capital in the bank so the inevitable losses (frequently on nine of every ten trades) won't send them to the poorhouse. What these plungers play for is the occasional gain so big it more than offsets all the losses—in silver and gold early in 1980, and in sugar later in the year. Given the eccentricities of the markets in this age of new money, there's a real risk of losing on ten out of ten trades, and there goes your capital right out the window. There are 33 commodities traded on U.S. exchanges, and on one day early in 1981, prices of all 33 of those commodities went right through the floor. The loss to players in commodities that day was in the billions.

You can hedge your bets by buying into one of the funds that pool your money with that of a lot of other investors, and then hedges its own bets by trading in a lot of different commodities at one time. These professionally managed commodity funds advertise widely, and you shouldn't have any trouble finding one. Buying into one of these pools will minimize your risk, but it won't eliminate it, and just because a pool has done well in the past is no guarantee it will do well in the future.

Beware of Bonds

Bonds—corporate, municipal, and government—are mostly for institutions, not individuals. They represent a long-term commitment at a time you want to stay as flexible as possible. The income on bonds is pretty good these days and the capital gains can be impressive when the interest rates fall and bonds shoot up. More often in recent years, interest rates have gone up, bond prices have gone down, and the carnage among investors has been terrible.

The age of new money has bred some bonds that might do better for you. There are bonds whose interest rate floats up as current interest rates float up. There are "put" bonds where the company must buy the bond back if you aren't happy with the interest rate. But most bonds still are the old-fashioned, fixed-return sort, and those hybrids are mostly for skilled investors. Unless you're willing to work very hard at it, figure that bonds aren't for you.

To invest in bonds, your timing must be impeccable. You must buy on the eve of a recession, when rates are at a peak and bond prices have no place to go but up. You can get capital gains as rates fall and bond prices do go up. Or you can nail down those high yields for years to come—provided the company whose bonds you bought survives the recession and earns enough to avoid defaulting on the interest payments. If you do buy, never go below an A rating, and AA or even AAA would be better. Some of the choicest corporate names of only a couple of years ago are in deep financial trouble today. Should you guess wrong, of course—buying only to see rates go higher and prices lower—you're in trouble.

Municipal bonds start to make sense when your taxable income goes above $35,000, at which point you're in the 43 percent tax bracket. The return on money in a six-month certificate or a money-market fund is cut nearly in half by taxes, while the income from a municipal bond is exempt from federal taxes. If you buy municipal bonds issued locally, the income is probably exempt from state and local taxes as well.

You could buy municipal bonds outright, paying a pretty penny, since most sell for $5,000 apiece. Or you can invest in a mutual fund or a unit trust (the difference between the two is rather technical), in which a professional picks the bonds. The entry fee in a municipal-bond fund can be just a few dollars per share.

There's the chance for capital gains with municipal bonds as with any bond, although the past few years have mostly brought capital losses. Here you are investing primarily for yield because if you're in a high enough tax bracket the yield can outrun inflation. One drawback to municipal bonds is that you can't buy them with borrowed money and still take the interest on the loan as a tax deduction, so you lose the ability to borrow to make your investing dollars go farther. Whether the average investor should borrow to make his or her investing dollars go farther (except in real estate) is another matter.

And a final note on fixed-income investing: If you have $10,000 to buy a savings certificate, you could also use the money to buy a Treasury bill—a government security maturing in less than a year. You can buy a three-month bill or a six-month bill, and new issues of Treasury bills appear every week. In most cases, a savings certificate will yield a little more than a Treasury bill and you can get a certificate by walking into the nearest bank or thrift. If you buy a bill through your bank or broker, you'll pay a fee. But the interest on a Treasury bill is exempt from state and local taxes, while the interest on a savings certificate is taxable, and that could make a difference if you live in a high tax area. And you can avoid the middleman by buying a Treasury bill (or any other Treasury issue) directly from the government and paying no fee at all. You simply put in your bid in person or by mail at the nearest Federal Reserve bank, up to lunchtime on the day the security goes on sale.

Whether you are interested in government securities or you just want the best available forecasts on where interest rates are heading, most big banks and brokerage houses have economists who specialize in following the cost of money and the meanderings of the Federal Reserve. David Jones of Aubrey Lanston and Company, a government-bond house in New York, is widely quoted in the financial press. You'll see the name of Albert Wojnilower of First Boston Corporation quoted less frequently, but when you do see it, pay heed. He has one of the best forecasting records around, especially when it comes to spotting longer-range trends. First Boston, incidentally, is a banking house based not in Boston but in New York.

Henry Kaufman, managing partner and chief economist for Salomon Brothers, another New York banking house, is in a class by himself these days—the most widely followed financial economist of today. Years ago he correctly predicted the sort of economic and financial turmoil we'd be in today, and he was almost alone in predicting that inflation and interest rates would go higher in 1979, when virtually all economists were forecasting a recession they thought would send inflation and interest rates lower. These days, Kaufman's forecasts have the quality of self-fulfilling prophecies. If he forecasts higher interest rates, nervous investors will duly push them higher. Kaufman is the only economist whose predictions can turn entire markets around—the stock market as well as the bond market. It's not surprising that he's the most widely quoted financial economist these days.

Sticking with Stocks

If bonds aren't for you (and they very likely aren't), at
least consider the stock market—wild, woolly, wicked, and
not all that hospitable to most people most of the time. Most
of the blue chips of old—Ford, U.S. Steel, Sears Roebuck,
International Harvester—look pretty ragged now. And most
of the favorite growth stocks of old—IBM, Polaroid, Citicorp—now sell at ratios of price to earnings that would have
been unthinkable ten years ago. The big winners in the stock
market lately have been stocks you wouldn't, and probably
shouldn't, touch with a ten-foot pole: small oil companies,
miners of precious metals, and anything that smacks, however remotely, of high technology.

And yet, all caveats about investing in stocks in inflationary times notwithstanding, you simply can't ignore the stock
market. Its advantages are legion. You can buy or sell in an
instant and at prices that are posted after every trade. You
know in advance how much commission you'll pay on each
trade. You deal in markets that are generally well regulated.
You can study in detail every company you might want to
invest in, and there are so many stocks available that there's
always something for every taste and for every price range.

Finally, the stock market has had its moments in the past
couple of years and may well have them again, simply because people (and institutions) with money to invest have
found all the other markets so dicey that they're buying
stocks somewhat as a last resort. After years in which stock-
prices moved very little, the past couple of years have seen
fairly dramatic price swings, and it's out of such swings that
capital gains are made.

Because so many investors have shunned stocks in this
age of new money, there still are many stocks selling at
price-earnings ratios last seen during the early 1950s when
the long postwar bull market was just getting under way.

Only time will tell whether these really are bargains. If the economy tumbles into a new depression, or if inflation turns hyper, they won't be. At the moment, to many people they look like bargains. So approach the stock market cautiously, ready to turn tail at the slightest sign of trouble. But approach it.

You certainly won't want for advice on playing the stock market; the number of books on the subject would fill the Grand Canyon. Avoid the books that promise to show you how to make big killings in the market. You aren't after big killings, which are seldom made by small investors anyway. What you're looking for is the best potential for capital gain with the smallest amount of risk.

What you want first is plenty of background knowledge about the workings of the stock market, and how developments in the economy influence the stock market. As a rule, stock prices rally in the later stages of a recession, when interest rates are still relatively low and there's a hint of the coming recovery that will fatten company earnings. Rallies end in the later stages of a recovery when interest rates are high and investors are looking toward the recession which must surely lie ahead.

In going from the general to the specific—to what stocks to buy—every brokerage house will cheerfully flood you with investment advice. Such publications as *Forbes* and *Barrons* offer considerable investment advice in each issue. There are various investment advisory services, and for plenty of generally sound, well-reasoned advice—including specific buy and sell recommendations—you can do a lot worse than studying the publications of Standard & Poor's Corporation. There are market letters and tip sheets beyond counting, from great, glossy jobs that cost a mint to flimsy flyers from fly-by-night operators. Most simply aren't worth the cost.

Or, if you want to take a fatalistic view, there's the "random walk" theory, which holds that no one can successfully pick winning stocks over the longer run, and a portfolio randomly put together—flicking ink blots at a page of stock listings from *The Wall Street Journal*—will do as well as one put together by the keenest minds on Wall Street. That was true enough in the 1950s and 1960s when stock prices generally were going up. It has been true intermittently since. Almost all stocks rallied after the market collapse of 1974–75, and most stocks went up through most of 1980. But there were long periods in the 1970s when most stocks went down, and there are so many sick companies around today that you can't even be sure which companies will be around in a year or two. It's best to leave the random-walking to others and to put some thought into what you buy.

And so you might take what capital you have, after meeting your hard-core savings goals, and put some of it—but absolutely no more than 50 percent—into stocks.

By learning about the economy, you've developed some sense of how the economy influences the stock market. By study, you've developed some feel for how the stock market works. By further study, by consulting with brokers and reading widely, you have some feel for the kinds of stocks you'd like to invest in. Any time you invest in the stock market you're gambling. You're taking the gamble because you need capital gains and because there are relatively few sources of capital gains open to the average investor today.

If a stock is cheap, make sure you understand why it's cheap. Ford was cheap in 1980 because most investors thought it would be a good, long while before the company solved its financial problems. What you really want are stocks that offer considerable potential for growth in the years ahead, even if you have to pay a little more to buy into that potential growth. You want to steer clear of out-and-out speculations—this means you should leave most of the fledgling high-technology companies to someone else. Some of these new companies will make it, but most won't. The dividend the stock pays should be a secondary consideration (again, unless you're approaching retirement and want income most of all). If all you want is yield, you'll be better off with your money in a savings certificate. What you want from stocks are capital gains.

The domestic oil and natural gas companies probably fit your bill. So do most of the better-managed computer and electronics giants, since we're heading into a new industrial revolution based on dramatic advances in electronics. Many of the drug companies look promising because we're also heading toward a revolution in medical technology. It's a tense time in world affairs, and Ronald Reagan has promised to spend more on defense, so the defense contractors should do well for at least the next few years. Ultimately the biggest and best-managed commercial banks and thrift institutions, especially the ones that are strong throughout a region, are going to dominate our financial system, and they should do pretty well.

You can hedge your bets by taking part—or maybe all— of the capital you've set aside for stocks and putting it into a mutual fund that invests in stocks. You're buying someone else's expertise, and while that's no guarantee of success, most stock funds have done better than the overall market the past couple of years. The track records of all mutual funds are published, as are their investment objectives. (Your library should have a copy of the Wiesenberger Investment Companies Service, which lists all the funds.) Some funds specialize in growth stocks, some in income stocks, some in foreign stocks, some in stocks tied to gold. Since you want growth, pick a fund that invests in growth stocks. Further, pick a fund from a management company that also offers a money-market fund so you can move out of stocks the instant you think things are turning against you, or when the return on the money fund becomes irresistible.

If you choose to invest directly in the market, keep these rules of safe-conduct in mind:

1. Find a stockbroker you instinctively feel you can trust, and who feels he or she can live with your investment goals. Brokers make money from commissions, which come when you buy or sell a stock, and there's a temptation to get you

to buy and sell stocks frequently simply to generate more commissions. Make sure the broker knows how much you have to invest and how much trading you want to do. The giant brokerage houses—Merrill Lynch et al—are fine as far as they go. You're probably better off going to a smaller, local firm that might work harder to make you a satisfied customer.

2. Keep your time horizons short. Buy every stock with the intention of selling it as soon as you have made a reasonable gain—or as soon as you have sound reason to conclude you shouldn't have bought it in the first place. Take the gain when you have it because tomorrow it might be gone.

3. Buy on margin as your conscience dictates. You're doubling your pool of investment funds—the rules require you to put up only 50 percent in cash—and you get a tax deduction on the interest on the borrowed 50 percent of the price. On the other hand, the interest on margin buying can eat you alive these days, and if your stock falls, you must commit more of your capital to protect your investment.

4. Never go short on a stock—meaning don't sell borrowed shares in hopes of buying them back at a cheaper price. You'll pay a hefty interest on the borrowed stock, and markets move so rapidly in this age of new money that you might find the price going higher and higher instead of lower. You, of course, must buy back the shares, no matter how much they cost.

5. Spread your bets. Instead of buying a single stock, buy smaller amounts of several stocks, each in a different part of the market. You'll increase your chances for a gain and reduce your chances for a loss.

Puts and Calls for Fun and Profit

Then there's the market in stock options to consider—in which you don't buy the stock itself but purchase an option to buy (if it's a call option) or sell (if it's a put option) 100 shares of a stock at a predetermined price before the expiration date of the option. Your broker can buy options for you, and if you've picked your broker wisely, he can explain the various option strategies.

Say you buy the July 60 option in Cosmic Running Shoe, which means that between now and next July you have the option of buying 100 Cosmic shares at $60 a share no matter what Cosmic shares are bringing in the market on the day you exercise the option. You bought the option at a premium (your cost) of $1 a share or $100 for the 100-share option. Should Cosmic soar to $100 a share in the market before next July, the person you contracted with must still sell you 100 Cosmic shares at $60. You paid a $100 premium for the option, $6,000 for the 100 Cosmic shares when you exercised the option, plus some commissions. You have stock you can sell in the market for $10,000—a profit of close to $4,000 on a cash investment of $100. Or, as Cosmic stock moved up, you might have sold the option itself to someone else for more than you paid for it. Had Cosmic shares not soared in the market, you wouldn't have exercised the option, and you'd have lost your $100. But you knew the moment you bought the option that the most you could lose was $100. And you've put up only $100 of your money, which is obviously much less than the cost of 100 Cosmic shares bought in the market. You could buy options on thousands of Cosmic shares for what it would cost to buy a 100-share block of Cosmic stock.

And that's the obvious appeal of options—the potential for large gains on a small investment and the comfort of knowing the most you can lose the day you enter the market. It's still a chancy market, and most players lose on most plays. Yet it's a way to play for capital gains with a minimum cash investment, and it can work for the small investor who's willing to spend the time learning the market.

The knowledge you gained in understanding the stock market can serve you well in options. You're still investing in stocks, and the better you are at picking winning stocks, the better you'll do in playing the options market, since you can make money on the option only if the underlying stock moves up. If it goes down or doesn't move at all, you lose.

Since options run for no more than nine months, you'll want stocks that are likely to move fairly quickly. Once the option expires, it's worthless. The longer an option has to run before expiration, the more it will cost, because there's more time for the underlying stock to move as you want it to. Because there's more time in which you can turn a profit, it pays to buy an option that will expire later rather than one that will expire sooner, even if it does cost more.

Once you get good enough at options, there are other tricks you can try. You can sell a call option against stock you own, pocketing the premium on the sale of the option. If the stock falls or stays steady, the option won't be exercised and the premium is yours to keep. If the stock goes up, and the option is exercised, you must sell the shares. But you still keep the premium and you still sell the shares at a profit —just not as big a profit as if you could sell them directly in the market. If you own shares and fear the price might go down, you can buy a put option, in which someone must buy the stock from you at the option price no matter at what the stock itself is selling. You keep the premium, and if the stock does fall, you have someone who must buy the shares from you at a price higher than the current market price of the stock.

Greed is the killer in the options market—the desire to stay in for the last dollar. The advice of all professionals in this market is to take small profits as they appear—exercising, or selling, the option. If you hang on in hopes of a fatter profit, you risk losing it all. The other side is to get out quickly when the market starts to run against you, rather than hanging on in hopes of a turnaround. When the market price of the option falls to half what you paid for it, sell the option and put your money elsewhere.

It isn't a market for the faint of heart, and you'll have to watch an option much closer than you would a stock, since your chance for a profit can come and go in a twinkling. You might try a few "paper" option plays—pretend betting—to see how you do. If you do fairly well, you might shift some of the capital you've earmarked for stocks into stock options. Once you get the hang of it, and if you're willing to spend the time watching the market, it may prove the best way for a small investor to play the stock market.

Next, there's real estate—all the way from gigantic office towers and mammoth shopping malls to small apartment buildings and small centers. And then—last but certainly not least—there's your own home, which is probably your best investment of all.

A House Is Not Merely a Home

If you catch it right in real estate, you get it all: impressive capital gains and fat tax deductions. And while the market has had its bad times, when high interest rates and tight money made it difficult to buy or sell anything, lots of people have caught it right in recent years.

Obviously gigantic office buildings and mammoth shopping malls aren't for the small investor. That still leaves small apartment buildings, small shopping centers, vacation property, undeveloped land, cooperative and condominium apartments, and private homes. All can be bought with very little of your own money, and a lot of money borrowed from a bank or thrift institution or from an insurance company.

Small apartment houses and small shopping centers are usually bought by small groups of investors in search of both capital appreciation and tax-sheltered income. You get depreciation on the property and the tax deduction on your borrowed money, and those deductions can shelter some other income from taxation. If you've picked wisely, you'll eventually get a capital gain. Picking wisely is the key to it all, of course. You'll want help from an expert on local real estate conditions and help from a lawyer or an accountant to structure the deal. Certainly you'll want to stick to geo-graphic areas you know best. Because we're talking small, the actual cash you'll need might be $20,000 or $30,000, with the rest borrowed. You're putting together a tax shelter just the way the rich folks do, but on a much smaller scale.

Again, if this sort of thing appeals to you, there are books by the score available at any library or in any bookstore. If you have that kind of capital to invest, you probably also have an accountant, a lawyer, and a banker. If they can't help you, they can certainly put you in touch with someone who can.

Obviously there are risks. Neighborhoods that were choice a generation ago are slums today. Neighborhoods that are choice today will be slums a generation from now. A shopping center isn't much fun if all the tenants have failed and gone away. Prices for just about all real estate are very high now and a prolonged slump in the economy could send them toppling. Mortgage rates are also incredibly high. Still, people have to live someplace and they have to shop some-place, and if you're careful, there's a pretty good chance your investment will pay off. Further, the tax breaks in real estate are sufficient to turn some marginal deals into lucra-tive deals. On the other hand, if you can't get the right terms when you borrow, the deal may not work at all. In fact, if you can't get the right terms when you borrow it probably doesn't pay to do the deal at all.

Vacation property covers everything from a piece of raw land in the country to a condominium in a resort area. The raw land can be speculation—betting someone will want to buy it at a profit before the taxes eat away your profit. This was the red-hot play of a couple of years ago. Now, with the high cost of energy, people are doing less driving to the more remote places, and land that is now undeveloped may stay undeveloped.

It makes more sense to think of a vacation home—a cot-tage somewhere or a resort condominium. Handled correctly, it gives you someplace to go for vacation, generates income, and gives you some nice tax breaks as well. As long as you don't stay in the place for more than 14 days a year, you can treat it as income-producing property—renting it out to others and taking all the appropriate tax breaks, including depreciation. You still get some tax breaks, though not as many, if you occupy it part of the year and rent it out the rest of the time.

The trick, again, is to pick your property wisely. Can people get there other than by car? Or is it close enough to urban centers so that people will still drive there? Properties that were marginal once—because the location was wrong or because there was just too much of what you were trying to rent available—became more promising when the airlines began offering all those cut-rate promotional fares to resort areas. Again, you'll want to talk to your lawyer, accountant, banker, or whoever, before you do anything. If you can swing it, a piece of income-producing property is probably the best all-around investment in this age of new money.

In fact, when it comes to real estate, everyone should own something. If you rent, buy a house or an apartment. If you own, think about a second home or apartment. If you have enough capital, think about income-producing property. For just about everyone, nothing matches the tax advantages and the ability to invest with someone else's money that real estate offers.

Unless your house stands next to a slaughterhouse or a bustling freeway, you probably made a very smart move buying it. For years, house prices have been going up by 10 percent and more a year, and with the postwar baby-boom kids now into their peak home-buying years, nothing short of a full-blown depression is going to sink the market for any length of time. The interest on your mortgage payments is deductible, as are your tax payments. You can sell the house at a profit and pay no tax on the gain if you move immediately into a more expensive house. If you hold on until you're fifty-five or older, you can now take up to a $125,000 gain tax-free.

So your house was probably a pretty good investment, and it's not a bad tax shelter, either. And if your mortgage is pretty well paid down and your house has indeed appreciated through the years, the equity you've built up represents a pool of money you can use for other investments (maybe a second house) or for paying college bills.

You can borrow on the house by taking out a second mortgage. But second mortgages don't make much sense most of the time, and with high interest rates, they don't make any sense at all. Since the equity you've built up in the house isn't doing you a particle of good just sitting there, think about pulling some of it out by refinancing—taking on a brand-new mortgage.

You'll pay no tax on the money you take out, and you'll get a pot of money to pay big bills or to invest elsewhere. Your new mortgage will be bigger, which is where all the cash comes from. But if inflation in the 1980s is anything close to what it was in the 1970s, you'll probably make up the cost with further appreciation of your property before you finally sell. You'll be paying today's sky-high mortgage rates instead of those of a decade or two ago. But, depending on your tax bracket, up to 50 percent of the interest payment will be a deduction.

You can enhance the value of your investment by making sensible improvements to your home. If they have to do with saving energy, the government will give you a 15 percent tax credit on those improvements, and a tax credit is at least twice as good as a tax deduction. A deduction reduces the taxable income from which your tax bill is computed. A tax credit reduces, dollar for dollar, the taxes you owe. If you plan your improvements wisely, you should get your money back, and more, when you sell, as long as the value of the house stays in line with others in your neighborhood. Spending $50,000 on home improvements won't give you a $150,000 house if all others in the neighborhood go for

$100,000. Talk it over with the bank that holds your mortgage and with your realtor before you take on costly improvements. They can tell you what will add to the value of your house and what won't.

If you're in the market for a house (or a cooperative or condominium apartment), think big. The old rule of thumb was that you could afford a house costing twice your annual salary, and monthly payments equal to 25 percent of your take-home pay. Rules of thumb have pretty much gone out the window, and you'll be lucky to get monthly payments equal to one-third your pay. Put as little money down as you can and borrow as much as the lender will provide, as long as the monthly payments won't bankrupt you. The gamble, of course, is that inflation will push up the value of your house and validate whatever you spent on it. That remains a pretty fair gamble.

If you can get a straight, fixed-rate mortgage, take it. More and more mortgages now are variable-rate mortgages, meaning that the rate moves up or down according to what interest rates in the market are doing. Since interest rates could easily go higher in coming years, a variable-rate mortgage could prove costly. A new wrinkle is the equity mortgage in which the lender gives you a lower rate now in return for a slice of the profits when you ultimately sell the house. It isn't widely available now, but if you can find one, it's worth exploring.

Other things being equal, a condominium makes more financial sense than a cooperative apartment. With a condo, you own a piece of property—your apartment—and you can mortgage it. With a co-op, you own shares in the corporation that owns the building (including your apartment), and you'll have to settle for a bank loan to buy the co-op since you can't mortgage shares of stock. Generally co-op loan rates are higher than mortgage rates, and in most cases you'll have to put up more of your own money. The trick of getting by in the age of new money is to make maximum use of other people's money.

Why Light Bulbs May Be Your Best Investment

Or you may want to invest some of your money another way—in the tangible, day-to-day necessities. Your invest-ment objective there is to buy things at current prices be-cause tomorrow's prices are going to be higher.

My hardware store some months ago had a sale on light bulbs and I laid away a year's supply—saving about $50 by doing so. I also bought a year's supply of plastic garbage bags, also on sale, and there I saved about $10. Since my total investment was about $125, I got what amounted to a 50 percent return on my money, tax-free. And since I charged everything with a credit card, I paid off the $125 over a period of months, with inflation reducing the value of the dollars I was paying by a little each month.

A few months ago I saw a pair of shoes I liked on sale—reduced from $100 to $60. I didn't need another pair of shoes just then, but I would in a year or so. I bought them anyway, figuring that in a year a comparable pair of shoes would cost $120. Again I paid with a credit card, letting inflation help me pay off the loan, and with a portion of the interest on the loan a tax deduction. I further paid my credit-card bill with a check from an interest-bearing NOW account.

Some people buy cases of food on sale. I read somewhere about a man who years ago bought five Volkswagen Beetles back when they cost about $2,000 each. He used one and mothballed the others. Every five years or so he sells off a used Beetle and unwraps another one for his own use. Car prices being what they are, he profits each time he sells off a used Beetle and he gets a new car for $2,000 at a time when there isn't a car on the road for under $6,000.

The point is, buy it now, because the price is probably going to be higher tomorrow and, given our inflation, a penny saved today is about a penny and a half earned.

Bargain-hunt as you have never bargain-hunted before.

Before you buy, check garage sales to see if someone isn't selling what you want. Flea markets are mostly pretty commercial nowadays and you won't find many bargains, but garage sales can yield some wonders, and you won't pay tax on what you've bought, which is a nice saving right there. More and more barter services are springing up. For a small fee they help you swap something you have for something you want, and again you pay no taxes on the transaction. Think about banding together your friends and neighbors into a food cooperative that can buy in bulk and save money for all of you by paying wholesale prices.

Whatever you buy, don't pay a penny more cash than you can help, and don't be afraid to borrow. Within reason, borrowing to buy, as well as borrowing to invest, is among your strongest weapons today. Even if you intend to pay within your credit card's regular 30-day billing period, still charge a purchase instead of paying cash. At current inflation rates, you'll get goods worth $1 and you'll be paying back with dollars worth about 99 cents. If you buy at the end of one billing period, you won't be billed for another month, and you'll have another month after that before you have to pay. You get the use of the money for two full months and the store gets dollars cheapened by two months of inflation.

There are limits on how much debt you can take on. If debt repayment, not counting mortgage debt, is taking 15 percent or more of your disposable (after-tax) income, you're bumping against the ceiling. If you're up to 20 percent, you're in over your head. Up to that limit, however, it makes sense to borrow. You'll pay dearly for the borrowed money, but interest is a tax deduction and the government will cover up to half your interest payments. Inflation will further reduce the cost of borrowing by cheapening each month the value of the dollars you use to pay down the loan. You can keep the money in a transaction account or a money fund and earn interest until the moment your payment check clears. Finally, you've gotten something at today's high price instead of tomorrow's still higher price.

If you're borrowing to buy something big, first look into tapping the cash value of your life insurance, where the interest rate can be as low as 5 percent. Next, try a credit union, or your bank. Avoid finance and small loan companies, where rates are the highest of all.

Most towns of any size have stores that buy job lots of distress merchandise and sell for less. Most of what they sell is junk, but occasionally you'll find some real gems. The electric typewriter I use in my office came from just such a store—a $1,000 typewriter that sold for $375 because the manufacturer had discontinued that model and because the store was willing to buy up a lot of its inventory. If possible, wait and buy only at sales. It costs stores so much to finance inventories that they will often cut prices drastically just to clean out their inventories. If prices are higher than ever, price cuts during sales are bigger than ever.

Wringing the Most Out of Your Dollars

The other side of the coin is what you can do to supplement your income.

There are the obvious things—taking a second job—and the not-so-obvious ones. Do you have some skill or talent that people might pay money for? I know one woman who bakes fancy pastries and another who caters parties—each turning a skill into a profit. Both have comfortable incomes, but the little extra helps.

If you have the usual amount of clutter in the house, turn it into cash by having a garage sale of your own. Or donate things still usable or repairable to the Salvation Army or to Goodwill, or some other charity. Most will allow you to do your own valuation for tax purposes, and as long as the valuation sounds reasonable, the IRS probably won't challenge it and you'll wind up with a nice tax deduction.

For really serious inflation-proofing, you'll want to talk to a tax lawyer or an accountant. There are any number of things you can do, if you have capital enough to make them worthwhile.

Since the income tax is still among the most inflationary things around, it makes sense to get the best-quality help you can afford on your income taxes. You'll pay for that help, but you'll probably save enough on your tax bill to more than pay your accountant's bill. And money spent on tax preparation is itself a tax deduction.

A tax lawyer or an accountant can help you with other things, too. If you'll be sending children to college in ten years or more, you can put income-producing property into a short-term trust. The trust must run at least ten years, and during those years all income from the assets in the trust goes onto your kids' tax bill, not yours. The income each year from the trust can then be invested—in a savings certificate or a money-market fund—giving you a nice return with no tax bite. At the end of ten years the assets revert to you. The rich create trusts that hold millions in assets. You can create a trust with just a few thousand in assets, and it's neither complicated nor expensive to create one.

You and your spouse can each give $10,000 a year to each of your children, free of any gift tax. That money can be put into a custodial account at a bank or in a money fund, and the income will then be taxable to your children—who presumably won't earn enough to pay any taxes—and not to you. You can shift the money from one investment to another, as long as you observe the standards of prudence.

The money is given under the Uniform Gift to Minors Act of your state, and you don't need a lawyer's help to give it. And there are plenty of other things you yourself can do.

Check with the employee-benefits people at your office to make sure you understand how all your benefits work, and that you've structured the benefits package—and your pension—to your best advantage.

Check your homeowner's insurance to make sure it's been brought into line with inflation. You'll want to get a new appraisal on your house because the replacement cost of the house has almost certainly gone through the roof, inflation hitting construction costs very hard. Unless your home is insured for 80 percent of its replacement value (not the market value but what it would cost to rebuild your house, which probably is a lot more than the market value), you're going to get less than a full reimbursement if there's any damage to the house.

Most policies insure the contents of a house up to 50 percent of the coverage on the house itself. But on some items the coverage is wildly inadequate. You usually get a total of only $500 on all furs and jewelry stolen in a burglary, with even more stringent limits on cash, securities, stamp and coin collections, and precious metals.

The first thing to do is survey your house for things that inflation has made more valuable. With gold at $500 an ounce, mere baubles can now be worth big money. The value of antiques has gone through the roof. Jewelry, furs, expensive cameras, expensive guns, stamp and coin collections, golf equipment, silverware, and musical instruments should be covered by a separate floater policy. Most insurance companies will accept appraisals done by local jewelers, camera stores, or coin and stamp dealers.

And so the list goes, on and on and on. Mostly what you should do are common-sense things requiring only a little effort and a little diligence. Think of it as a war—the age of new money pressing at the gates and you doing what you must to defend yourself against the invader. And it is war of a sort—the age of new money tearing at our lives and our country—threatening to overwhelm us with inflation or devastating recession or both. What no foreign invader has ever been able to do the age of new money may yet do—unless we are very, very careful and more than a little lucky.

Index

363

Monaco, as tax haven, 321–22
Monetarists, 50–51
  and floating vs. fixed rates, 278–279
  vs. Keynesians, 39–45
Money, 48–49
  buying, 150–53
  changes in, 74–76
  cost vs. supply, 39–45
  creation of, 122–23
  definition of, 32–38
  gold or silver backing, 38–39
  high-powered vs. real, 117, 122–23
  lexicon of, 56
  photographing, 83
  purchasing power of, 21
  short-term, 151–52
  size and color of, 73
  stability of, 50–51
  substitutes for, 63
  unneeded, 207
  velocity of, 34, 41, 51, 86
  worn-out, 81
  see also Electronic money;
    Funny money; Hot money;
    New money; New new
    money; Old money; Paper
    money
Money-market mutual funds, 35,
    186, 204, 205, 312, 329, 330–331, 336, 344, 349
Money supply, 44–45
  and Federal Reserve, 39, 41–42,
    46–47, 48, 50, 51, 69, 95–97,
    107–8, 122–23, 139, 276
  and inflation, 49
  and silver, 67–68
Mongol conquerors, 39
Moody's Investor Service, 213
Morgan, J. P., and Company, 158
Morgan Stanley and Company,
    158
Mortgage bonds, 211
Mortgage loans, 165, 183, 184
  interest rates on, 28, 184, 219,
    355–56

and thrift institutions, 173, 174,
    176–78, 182
  types of, 357
  see also Real estate loans
Mortgage pools, 220
Mortgages, 28
  fixed-rate, 177
  variable-rate, 177
Mulberry bark, as money, 61
Multibanco Comermex (Tijuana,
    Mexico), 301
Multiple expansion, 116, 117–20,
    123
Municipal-bond fund, 344
Municipal bonds, tax-exempt,
    120, 165–66, 208, 209, 216,
    217, 314–15, 344
Mutual funds, 189
  and commodity futures, 235
  and gold, 252
  money-market, 35, 186, 204,
    205, 312, 329, 330–31, 336,
    344, 349

Nader, Ralph, quoted, 291
National Bank Act of 1863, 66, 75,
    165
National bank notes, 66, 75
National banks, 69, 154, 155, 156,
    165
  vs. state banks, 66
National Credit Union
    Administration, 180
National debt, 132, 133, 214, 215
  interest on, 22, 125
Natural gas companies stock,
    349
Navy Federal Credit Union, 180
Near-banks, 174, 178
Negotiability, and certificates of
    deposit, 148
New banking, 143–53, 161–63
New Deal, 134
New England, thrift institutions
    of, 161
New Jersey dollar, 253, 254